Gallivan's Gang

Gallivan's Gang

by
Don Riley

Cartoons by Jerry Fearing

Nodin Press

ISBN: 0-931714-81-8

Library of Congress Card Number: 99-068124

First Edition: November 1999

Nodin Press, a division of Micawber's, Inc.
525 North Third Street
Minneapolis, MN 55401

Dedicated to the women and children who stood behind Gallivan's Longshots—and even a salute to those who ran. Special thanks to D and the SS girls.

Special thanks to award-winning cartoonist Jerry Fearing for his clever work on cover and contents.

Table of Contents

Foreword

No Hollywood screenwriter could begin to conjure the characters and action in this story of dreams, laughs, depression, and utter chaos. You will meet the local buffoons, characters, and national celebrities. Only a few names have been changed to protect the innocent. These pages document magnificent obsessions and myopic vision; bravado instincts, cool-hearted courage and spine-cracking emotional downfalls.

But you have to laugh.

Not even association with the famous like Bronko Nagurski, Lassie, Michael Landon, Joe Louis, Pat O'Brien, Jack Hurley, Peggy Lee, Craig Breedlove, Rocky Marciano, Robert Goulet, Norm Van Brocklin, George Mikan, Red Foley, Bernie Bierman, Jackie Vernon, Jack Dempsey, Margaret Mitchell, Willie Pep, Gene Mauch, John Denver, Bob Short, Frank Leahy or George Foreman could change the destinies of Gallivan's gang of Longshots.

And that's to name only a segment of influential people who rubbed elbows or influenced this hilarious and unpredictable coalition of would-be entrepreneurs.

And along the way you will be introduced to chow cones, moonburgers, super seed-sucking machines and the rent-a-relative business.

All of this to the accompaniment of soft, sweet piano and organ strains from a young and lovely blonde woman performing in various St. Paul dinner clubs. She seemed to know the favorite songs of every character who patronized her places of employment. Then she was known as Joan Smith. Later you will learn of her planet-shaking accomplishments.

In the sixties, when flower children were sprinkling their love/joy in the pastures of the world, you could either revere or despise St. Paul. It didn't require much passion to wing it either way. One thing: you couldn't ignore it.

For years, this river town, with all the hills, narrow streets, and amazingly varied bars, was known as the Boston of the East. That's the period when F. Scott Fitzgerald's mother moved from mansion to mansion on shady and stately Summit Avenue, preparing him to conquer the world of literature. He eventually fled to the ivy of New England's eastern seaboard culture.

Since objective perusal was one of his gifts, Scott probably ascertained at an early age that St. Paul was composed of stodgy old wealth, whose fires of ambition had long since cooled, and a bewildering surplus of self-destructive dreamers and lovable losers.

This is a condition which legendary humorist Irvin S. Cobb might have pointed out, "Ain't all bad."

For instance, St. Paul chose in its earliest days to host the state capitol rather than the University of Minnesota, which Minneapolis landed just a few miles upstream on the meandering Mississippi. So St. Paul wound up with a few hundred laconic and chiseling politicians and the Mill City became home to 40,000 enthusiastic and creative students.

But then again didn't St. Paul spawn the strange fat fellow who built a mini mansion, replete with all white carpet and picture windows, in the middle of a Jackson Street junkyard? He explained, "Some day, people will realize how exquisite aging chunks of rusting metal really are and there will be a stampede for this real estate!"

And what about the practical embalmer who designed and built a curved coal slide on which to deposit his chilly corpses in his mortuary basement, saving time and energy for a few more drinks at the Gopher Grill? Creative huh?

And didn't the inventor who first put handles on mattresses come from St. Paul?

While the Midwest was chasing the likes of desperadoes John Dillinger, Baby Face Nelson, Homer Van Meter, and the Ma Barker thugs, St. Paul's offbeat but highly enterprising philosophy and unique moral code enabled the city to become a happy sanctuary to this collection of human waste. So, in the turbulent thirties, St. Paul named by the F.B.I. the "sin-spot of the U.S.A." gunmen were able to stay safely insulated from capture as long as they kept their shooting sprees and robberies outside the city limits.

Eventually, emboldened by the hospitality, the zealous hoods overstepped the city's congeniality and kidnapped a local brewery president and also a banker. Naturally, this brought in the Feds. But it was a laugher while it lasted. This period is still referred to by seniors as the "good old days." And still, when visitors come to town many are shown the bullet holes in the Lexington apartments from where Dillinger shot his way out. That's even before they inspect the magnificent cathedral, the gilded capitol, or the famed Ordway Music Theatre.

But that ain't all bad.

While Minneapolis was growing taller and noisier and richer by the year, St. Paul held on determinedly to its theory that small is better. At least, more comfortable. As a West St. Paul merchant once noted while Minneapolis was adding a building that encroached on the airlines' holding patterns, "Who the hell wants our streets cluttered with a bunch of pushy salesmen from Chicago and New York?" Good point.

And talk about characters. Let's just concentrate on those irrational sixties and early seventies. You can even forget the dudes with pins in their noses, weed on their lips, and water lilies embedded in their hairy skulls. This town had odd-balls in spades and the street scene was far more exciting than the days when Dillinger sat with his back to the wall in the Green Lantern.

Walk through the Minneapolis Athletic Club and all you heard was conversation about the vast riches of the wheat fields and the milling industries and the major league sports franchises in the offing. Then stop at Napoleon's Bar on University Avenue in St. Paul where a collection of splashy car salesmen would try to entice you into a near-perfect machine, even if it didn't have a transmission. "This is a hilly town and mostly down hill," they reasoned.

Or, as my wife learned, when we first visited the G&M Saloon across from the bus depot, anything not tethered was for sale. Like the batch of hot undies she was offered at a bargain price from a grocery bag.

Cities can live and die with their street characters. And St. Paul's share made Damon Runyon's Times Square collection look like a Boy Scout brigade. Nobody could visit "Tone the Phone" on his death bed in St. Joseph's Hospital because no one knew this veteran bookie's family name.

Bartender George Cook used to post pari-mutuel odds on cockroach racing at his dingy watering hole. Another joint walled in a small telephone port with its last drunken client crumbled on the floor, unseen by the workmen. Nearly a day later, low moans called attention to his plight. His first words on being extracted from the tomb were, "Glory-be-to-God! It's the Resurrection—and I'm the first one out!"

St. Paul was a town where John Denver, early in his career, once sang before only a handful of admirers at The Flamingo Club. Just forty feet away in the same establishment, you had to know somebody to squeeze in among the masses to catch a glimpse of the two hundred pound Turkish belly dancer.

And didn't Bobby Dylan use egg cartons to deaden echos while getting his career started at the Red Onion on Snelling and Minnehaha avenues?

While Minneapolis was engaging in spirited conversation about who might become the Junior Chamber's man of the year, St. Paul insiders were chuckling about living in the only city on the planet with a professional hockey club president who was known as the town's leading bookie. Not until a scrupulously clean one-eyed goalie punched him in the nose for suggesting he might, for a few bucks, see fit to play with less zeal now and then, did the situation become clear to the owners.

While Minneapolis thought it would be noble to bring in a snow leopard for a sportsman's exhibition, the owner of an East Side eatery in St. Paul let his pet 180-pound mountain lion roam unimpeached over the roof of his establishment. It wasn't until the beast leapt to the pavement and caused six minor auto accidents while prowling Payne Avenue that authorities intervened.

Mill Citians always complained about getting lost in the Saintly confines, prompting locals to inquire why they'd ever want to find their way back to the Mill town. When sports promoter Joe Duffy explored St. Paul to raise funds for a new Bloomington stadium, he naturally lost his car. He explained later, "I didn't raise a buck but I never had so much fun getting turned down."

A Minneapolis writer lost more than his auto at a St. Paul St. Patrick's Day celebration, managing to lose his family, home, and job in a bitter divorce case—all because he met and wooed a cute Irish-looking waitress who was really a Swede!

But that ain't all bad.

And while visitors to Minneapolis most likely would be shown the Museum of Arts by enthusiastic hosts, St. Paulites took more delight in pointing out Nina Clifford's world-class house of ill repute. That's the place where Babe Ruth stole Nina's beloved parrot following a New York Yankee exhibition game and sent it back from Chicago two days later.

Oh, you could always hear the big concerts in Minneapolis. But the big floating craps games were usually in St. Paul.

This was a city the Irish politicked and patrolled. Jews and Bohemians seemed to have a lock on all the choice real estate that the Archdiocese didn't own. Long before they became nationally popular,

Mexican eateries on the Flats packed them in for bulging jowls and steaming eyeballs.

On the East Side, Italians and Swedes produced gorgeous children with hair the color of Thor's or the pitch black of Naples leather. The city had its own French connection, which owned pieces of a dozen successful bars. And strict German mothers on Rice Street explained the profusion of Catholic churches with the wisdom, "We bring up our kids to go straight and pray a lot."

Throw in the few aristocrats who managed to get diplomas from Brown, Harvard or Yale, along with a few ex-jocks from Notre Dame, Marquette, St. Thomas College and the University of Minnesota and you had a cauldron that simmered and served up many lovable dreamers and irrepressible cons.

And when did Minneapolis ever open a professional basketball season where the tipsy mayor's own ceremonial jump ball came down and landed on his head? Minneapolis had the Lakers and St. Paul had its Fakers. The two St. Paul pro teams, the Lights and the Saints, went out of business shortly after inaugurating their seasons when their leagues collapsed from lack of fan support. Sports pages pointed out that St. Paul is a fight and hockey town.

Maybe it all happened this way because St. Paul's founder was a thief named Pig's Eye, who holed up in the caves along the river, where a gal named Klondike Kate was once a bartender. On the other hand, Minneapolis was built on the solid rock of missionaries' discoveries.

St. Paul loved hockey, boxing, baseball and auto racing, along with boozing, pompous balls, uniforms, ice sculptures, and odd celebrations like the Winter Carnival—that's where silly believers freeze their fingers and toes while professing their love of nature.

Even today, they'd consider hocking the city's treasury to build an ice palace and watch it melt into oblivion three weeks later. The city still draws record minor league baseball crowds while Minneapolis entertains the World Series, Super Bowls and national collegiate basketball tournaments.

You photograph Minnepolis with sophisticated lenses and strobes. You paint St. Paul in oils.

Don't you get it? Smaller is better.

This is all territory where only nine miles and ten minutes of driving separates the two loops and takes a wise man to recognize physical borders. More to the point, a mountain of philosophical and social passions have always split the two. St. Paul still says, "We don't know what we want to be—but it isn't Minneapolis." Minneapolis merely smiles and says, "How quaint!"

But that ain't all bad.

This is the factual story of a small group of St. Paul men in the '60s and '70s, who personified the eccentricities and heart of St. Paul. We shall call them "Gallivan's Longshots." "With this one, we retire!" was their battle cry.

They each dreamed of millions. They each pursued reckless hopes of grandeur while walking the shaky edge of financial extinction. But wasn't headlining heavyweight contender George Foreman in St. Paul a coup for their town? Didn't a publicly owned Indy race car bring St. Paul prestige?

They gambled and gamboled with a rare, almost diabolical courage. Wouldn't a personal appearance by Lassie bring smiles to thousands of children and also make a tidy profit?

Being an entrepreneur was worth the sweat and the risk. They'd proclaim, "With this one we franchise all over the world!" Kibitzers said, "They don't need investors, they need keepers!"

It was a wizened old bartender who, after observing Gallivan's gang flounder and flounce, rage and reverberate for nearly two decades said, "There isn't an ounce of dog in them. But the vultures are always circling."

They laughed and cried a lot.

But, Jeez, that ain't all bad.

Prologue

Meet the Longshots

The large round table in the deeper recesses of Gallivan's tavern on Wabasha Street was pretty much isolated from prying eyes and inquisitive ears. That's where the Longshots generally congregated during late mornings.

They liked to beat the lunch hour rush and slip quietly into the tavern's shadows around 11:30 a.m. The mahogany beams, long bar and cardinal carpet of the restaurant, located in the heart of the St. Paul loop, was an oasis for the proven and untested. Those who had made it bought rounds for those still trying.

Spare ribs, potatoes and rolls, with a choice of salad or soup was a basic $3.95 meal. Add a quarter for a steak sandwich. Martinis were a gift from the gods at 90¢. The double for 50¢ more was like a steal.

Unseen benefactors were always sending a round over to the Longshots. Nobody knew who, but most of them suspected owner, Bob Gallivan, as the righteous one. The Longshots generated an undercurrent of excitement. Most side glances elicited the question, "What are they up to now?"

The politicos held sway on a raised section, where they could be seen easily by the patrons and slip casually into the masses on hand-shaking missions.

The young gray and blue clad attorneys huddled at small tables on another side of the establishment. The loud sports talkers permeated the bar. This arrangement left the front of the place open to shoppers, newcomers and the downtown workforce. You could always sprinkle in a few chasers on the early prowl.

The waitresses were old and weary but Gallivan lived by tradition. He rebelled at change and perpetuated the idea that Gallivan's had stood firm since he arrived on the arc. Nobody pried into Gallivan's business connections but everyone presumed he had made impressive earnings in the stock market.

Gallivan was obviously in good financial shape since he spent two months each winter following the ponies at Florida's Gulfstream Park and a month in the fall hunting the big birds in Ontario. Throw in two months each summer fishing at his lake cabin and it often appeared that running the bar was more recreation than business.

One thing everyone knew: Gallivan could get tickets for anything from the Kentucky Derby to title fights in Las Vegas. He nurtured friends from coast to coast with his repeated assertion: "I may surprise you, but I'll never disappoint you!"

It was common for sports celebrities as diverse as boxing great Jack Sharkey and Ollie Matson of football fame and Sammy Snead of the links to show up when they were in town.

Meet Jesse Rogers, he of the immaculate suits, shadowed, hooded eyes of the black Irishman and always well-groomed hair—a mixture of dark and early gray. Here was a man who could manage to look sad even if he'd just won a fortune at roulette. His was a sardonic grin. Jesse parceled out smiles as if they were on a budget.

He was usually first on the scene since his business was located only a half block away. His was the oldest family-owned insurance company in the city. His father died of a heart attack at the age of forty after partying during the holidays. A graduate in business from Notre Dame, Jesse was perpetually groping for happiness. "Saddest looking guy I ever saw," Gallivan observed. "Always looks like he was just at a wake."

It might have had something to do with his home life. Rogers indulged four pampered children who thrived on lavish birthday parties at the White Bear Yacht Club. He built his family a swimming pool and splurged on vacation trips interspersed with heavy spending weekend sprees for himself back to his campus for football and hockey games.

Or perhaps he was driven to depression by his wife, the heiress to a small brewery fortune. She drove a red Cadillac convertible and often wore her white ermine coat while volunteering for the Welcome Wagon. She also drank right along with Jesse all the while insulting him unmercifully in public.

Then again, maybe her vitriolic nature was molded by Jesse's inexplicable disappearances for days at a time—a big game in Texas, a trip to the Grand Prix in France or to a boxing match in New York. He was no pearl as a family man. And he admitted it.

It was almost expected that the rare times she accompanied him to social events he would be exposed to her glares and ridicule. Jesse wordlessly accepted her string of insults. Never did Jesse respond other than to give a faint smile of resignation. Asked why he didn't dump her, he responded, "Hey, I'm Catholic." That explained everything in '60s St. Paul.

The first inkling Race Regan got that Jesse wasn't the rock he presumed him to be came on a visit to his inner-sanctum office, the one he guarded with a knight's devotion. You got in only if you were a trusted friend.

This particular space was a near shambles. Premiums, business letters and claims were in dozens of piles, each like a sprawling white mushroom of disorganization on the brown carpet.

"Christ, how do you know what's what?" a friend asked incredulously.

"I know. I know. The third row from that wall are claims. The next pile is full of incoming mail. That pile by the desk is personal stuff. Hey, it's okay! I really do know what's in every pile. But it's driving my secretary nuts. She thinks I'm freaking out." The wan smile. His only one for another hour or so.

Nearing 40, Jesse at times looked 10 years older. His drooping eyes fell into the pools of their dark circles as if he were wearing a Mardi Gras mask; the face of a man surviving, not really living. It was only when he focused on a new venture with the Longshots that his leaden lids seemed to open a little wider and disclose faint animation.

Oh, yes. He loved hockey and had become a scout for the Montreal Canadiens. "It's not the pay. But I love to show my card. They're a class act."

Race Regan was usually the second man to arrive at the table. Regan was a feisty, almost intimidating, sports columnist with the St. Paul paper. He managed to make a decent living by insulting fans, players and coaches. Almost single-handedly he created a two-state feud between the once-idolized Green Bay Packers and the Minnesota Vikings. He called the Packers "Green Bushers" and their coach, the legendary Vince Lombardi, the "Dictator with the growl, three plays and 22 robots."

A friend said caustically, "Regan, at times I think you're the best damn sports writer in the country. But when you profess to know more about Wall Street than the Rockefellers you presume crap."

Without a quaver, Regan snapped back, "If I tried to peddle you for half of what you think you're worth, I'd have to find change for fifty cents." His nasty rebuttals were the prime reason so few of the Longshots exchanged needles with him.

It was amazing to Gallivan's Gang that Regan could write so well at 6:30 a.m. after consuming so many straight gins during the preceding day. It was equally astounding to them that he could rush to an evening talk show on WLOL, which he hosted for years, always making it just three or four minutes before air time. Then he'd proceed to regale listeners with so much information on so many subjects and insult so many callers that his show wound up with a giant slice of the market, clobbering even powerful WCCO.

It wasn't just sports that commanded his interest. After slicing up Muhammad Ali and the Black Muslims one night, a few fractured members of the group tied up his six phone lines, threatening to storm the station and do him serious bodily harm. At the same time, a group of Regan's old Hell's Outcasts motorcycle pals, who had made him an honorary lifetime member, heard the threats. They stopped long enough to call the station manager to tell him they'd be arriving in full leather and for Regan not to panic.

Of course the crusty scribe loved this type of action and met them with a gleam in his eye. The Outcasts arrived, cycles barking, snakes and chains bouncing around necks and shoulders, while station employees shook in terror. A few Muslims were presumed to be in the big black car at the end of the block. But when they saw the commotion and got a glimpse of the cycle ruffians they quickly sped off. Regan raged on the microphone asking, "Where are you phonies? We want a showdown! The Outcasts rule the streets and the airwaves!" Nobody was sure if the troubles would resurface but one station announcer purchased a pistol the next day.

Regan had an insatiable need for more than just the boundaries of his column and radio shows. Oh, he loved the football trips, the six-day stints before championship fights in Las Vegas and New York and annual trips to the Indianapolis 500. But he also wanted to write "more serious" things. He sold the publishers at Prentice Hall on a sales motivation book on the "give and get technique" that he was ghostwriting for Bob Gallivan, Jr., the son of the saloon owner.

The book sold over 70,000 copies and brought them a slice of fame on promotional tours and got Gallivan a spot on several radio shows. The book even wound up in the window of Jack Dempsey's New York restaurant. It also earned them $300 an hour from a

Chicago cemetery that hired them to inspire the sales force peddling mausoleums.

Beneath the hard exterior of a proficient journalist, Regan harbored the soul of a circus huckster. He married a beautiful former high fashion model and professional singer named Dots. She was the soprano stunner singing with the Sheiks Sextet in Minneapolis. Regan enjoyed complete support from her and their two daughters, who agreed he was the most exciting thing since swimsuits for Barbie dolls.

Dot's philosophy summed it up: "Race's adventures are fun as long as they don't cost us the house." At the University of Minnesota, she had been Kappa Delta sorority's White Rose. She was well traveled and introduced Race to ballet, opera and musical comedies. Naturally he became an expert on these arty entertainments.

Regan never knew why he misplaced things—like his car a half-dozen times, even his wife, whom he left behind in a service station far from home while returning from a trip. But more about that later.

It was Regan to whom the Longshots came for advice and solace before their adventures and after their defeats. Regan himself adhered to one iron fast rule when it came to publicity: "Don't ever ask for any ink in my column. I'm not plugging any of your crap unless it's sports and then it better be legit."

He never mentioned to anyone that he once did stringer work for the infamous New York Inquirer or that he used as many as seven nom de plumes while writing and editing the Pro Football Weekly for two years. In this role, he was editorial writer Jack Stroud, western scout Dick Ridgeway, southern scout Mel Tipenski, eastern scout Chet York and northern scout Peter Donworthy, along with special assignment writers Tuck Wheeler and Armen Drackowski. Each week he'd have a consensus prediction for his fall forecast for the NFL and he'd become all of them at once.

"It's driving me nuts," he'd complain to the pair of zany businessmen who owned the football paper. The owners advised him, "Give it time Regan, it's expanding your brain. You can become the world's most sportsworthy split personality." The weekly collapsed after two seasons when both owners ignored tax notices. They eventually disappeared, cashing in two 50-year-old wives for two young sales clerks.

Once Green Bay became the Minnesota Vikings' prime rival, Regan antagonized the large Wisconsin following of his column with a steady stream of degrading critiques. So much so that Green Bay officials tried to get his bosses at the St. Paul paper to silence him, only to have publisher Bernie Ridder back him to the limit.

This could be attributed to the fact that Ridder owned a share of the Vikings and everyone knew that Regan sold more game tickets than Paul Hornung running off tackle for 50 yards while carrying a 700 pound hangover.

To teach him a lesson, Regan was once banned from the Green Bay press box and forced to sit in a blanket of snow in the last row of the stadium. Which prompted the unshakable Race to lead off his next column with the line, "They held a beauty contest Sunday in Green Bay and nobody won."

It was Regan who pointed out that, upon climbing into bed with Mrs. Lombardi, the famed coach was chastised by his wife, "God, your feet are cold!" To which the omnipotent leader replied, "You may still call me 'Vince,' dear."

It was easy to understand why Regan became shock-proof. During the Green Bay feud he had to change his unlisted home phone number four times to get away from enterprising fans and weird calls at all hours. His typewriter was filled with glue, apparently by a Green Bush writer, and angry fans threatened to storm a radio station near Green Bay, where he was being interviewed on a pre-game show.

When covering Green Bay games in Wisconsin, Race stayed 20 miles out of town under an assumed name. Once, having vowed he'd push a peanut to Appleton with his nose if the Vikes lost to the

Pack, Regan received over 4,000 letters from 30 states and 5 foreign countries after the Vikes were upset.

This outpouring of insulting mail was the result of the Appleton newspaper's front-page color cartoon showing Regan with his nose to the pavement. Regan shrugged off their pettiness by explaining that Green Bay fans' consumption of straight brandy on frigid days eventually cost them control of their minds; while living in a burg whose only claim to fame was being the world's largest manufacturer of toilet paper.

Regan's ideas for immortality, great fame and a profit for the Longshots tumbled out of him like a cascade. So much so that at one meeting of the Longshots, one kibitzer asked why, if they searched people for weapons, Regan wasn't relieved of his ideas when he came in the door. Obviously, that sorehead had gambled and lost on one of Regan's hot tips in the market.

At 20, Race played golf at a charity tourney with Minneapolis mayor Marvin Kline. At 22, he was broadcasting wrestling and boxing matches from the Minneapolis Auditorium. At 23 he engineered a hot rod race at the fairgrounds track which drew 24,000 fans. At 25 he spent his own money to cover the legendary Notre Dame-SMU football contest in Dallas and won an award for proficient writing. By 26, he began covering the legendary five world's title drives of George Mikan and the Minneapolis Lakers pro kingpins.

In sad moments of reflection, he also admitted that for his youthful ill behavior his mother whacked him with the 10-inch crucifix that hung over the closet door. That is, he explained, until she developed a tennis elbow.

Race got in the business of journalism when he became the first student in 10 years to drop out of Roosevelt High School in Minneapolis to replace the eventually famous media whiz Harry Reasoner as a copy boy on the Minneapolis Times newspaper.

He called himself the world's fastest shaver and once made the front page of the St. Paul paper when a bevy of clockers timed him in 16.2 seconds!

It was natural for Regan and Rogers to gravitate toward each other. Jesse was a cloudy shadow. Regan was a bolt of lightening. Race said he admired Jesse because he was the only person Race knew whose eyes could fill with tears at a Notre Dame hockey game.

On the other hand, Rogers liked to tell the story of his first adventure with Regan, who called him from the Royal York Hotel in Toronto at 1 a.m.

"Now, I didn't know much about Regan, but his story was very interesting. He had just met an old Irish priest in the bar who was drinking scotch and milk. This priest said he had discovered many great young hockey players and had six of his protégés now playing in the National League, including Dave Keon and Frank Mahovlich.

"Regan was traveling to the All Star game with sweet little Jewish junkyard owner, Lou Kaplan, who also was an investor in the St. Paul Fighting Saints hockey team. Anyway, Regan and Kaplan invited this priest, Father Flanagan, to bring his junior team from St. Michael's Prep to play in St. Paul. Kaplan gave the priest a blank check to ensure he'd put together the trip and Regan wanted me to find some local hockey players to play Flanagan's team. I got the Cretin and St. Agnes teams to play them.

"So we draw about 5,000 people for the game and, of course, we lose a few hundred. But, as Regan pointed out, 'Look at it like it's charity.' Regan's always got another plan so there's never a dull moment. I'm sure he's going to wind up promoting a deal to lift the Titanic. It won't float, but it'll be fun while it's here."

Regan was also established permanently in the Make-a-Could-a-Would-a Foundation when he turned down the chance to grab the second McDonald's franchise in Minnesota. A friend opened the first one on Snelling Avenue, but Regan concluded, "Who in hell wants to spend $50,000 on a hamburger stand that nobody's ever heard of?

Just hamburgers and malts? The fickle public will be sick of it in six months."

The youthful looking Regan, with a big black, wavy pompadour piled on his head, loved Irish blazers, particularly the one in dark gray with purple stripes from the Tipperary Woolen Mills. He had a jutting jaw and a crooked smile. It was his energetic small stature, aggressive manner and unending supply of ideas that made him an irrepressible combination of inspiration and intimidation for the Longshots. That and a proudly worn ability to laugh at himself.

If Regan and Rogers gave the Longshots a touch of color, 50-year-old Chuck Van Avery brought an eccentricity that made any realistic approach to the game at hand seem too simple. Van was infatuated with the irrelevant and obscure. He not only read between the lines but over them and under them. He often saw in Regan's columns many meanings wholly unintended, imagining content for which there was no actual basis. He plucked innuendoes like migrant workers picking oranges. He brought strange but fresh viewpoints to the table.

All Van's idiosyncrasies may have been a reflection of the double thinking and double talking required of him as a youth. To understand Van, you had to know that his father was the foremost promoter of cock fights in the state. As a teen, Van parked cars at his father's farm on the shores of White Bear Lake for notorious gangsters such as Baby Face Floyd, the Ma Barker gang and John Dillinger.

The midnight fights on Saturday drew members of the sheriff's force and the tony Manitou Island crowd wearing tuxedos and silks. So Van had to learn to deal with them all at the scene of an illegal event, although these were strictly major league chickens from Texas, Cuba and Georgia in the barn.

Between bouts, you could buy copies of cock fighting magazines from Van and he often proclaimed that, while training his dad's chickens, he gave them nothing but the finest rum nips after their road work. "They really perk up with a shot. But too much could turn them into alkies. In the cock ring a hangover can be a real killer."

No question, these digs had an enormous effect on Van's life. At middle age he vividly remembered talking to Dillinger and running errands for Pat Riley, a mob chauffeur. He got autographs from Babe Ruth and most of the Yankees during their exhibition trips to St. Paul.

Van swore that one evening at the stroke of midnight, among those in the crowd watching the beastly birds gouge and claw, were a senator, a mayor, two bona fide gangsters, boxing great Harry Greb and a priest from Winona. Not to mention the notorious lady in red —Nina Clifford—two bank presidents, a brewery king and a railroad tycoon. All were a part of the raucous chorus of traveling men, socialites and con artists protected, of course, by the county sheriff.

At times, Van waxed sentimental over the old days and his little "gritty ones."

"Those chicks were courageous down to the last feather," he'd explain. "Jack Dempsey didn't have more guts than one little guy named Ivan the Terrible. He'd look me right in the eye before a fight and I swear he'd wink at me if he liked his chances."

In the early '50s, Van moved on to human fighters. But, as he said, "They don't have the discipline, intelligence, or courage of the chickens." Then he became a car salesman, a position for which he was born.

One Saturday morning, as he conned and cajoled visiting farmers from Pine City, Worthington and Fulda, he managed to get himself fired eight times. He'd offer the buyer an unbelievable deal and then come out of the manager's office dejected, with his head down and shoulders slumping like a hod carrier at the dinner table.

"Sorry. That offer got me canned, but it's not your fault. I'll get another job." Only one in ten saw through his chicanery. The rest paid the full price and left feeling downright good within themselves for having saved his position.

As an auto hustler, Van learned how to dress in bright plaid blazers and to wear matching tie and handkerchief sets. His shoes were always polished like mirrors, he would pass out steady compliments to the wives of car buyers and drink just enough to whet his appetite for a free meal. A quake could do nothing to shake his composure.

In fact, he was most proud of the fact that fiery baseball manager Gene Mauch, while still in the minor leagues, stormed into the stands one day, flailing away at Van for heckling him and a relative he had playing at shortstop for the Minneapolis Millers. It was said that Van never so much as budged from his box seat position and that neither his nor Gene's fists provoked as much as a dent in his always jaunty tweed hat. Minutes after, he gently chastised Mauch, who was being led away by ushers, for being, "A very naughty boy."

Later, Van went to bat, so to speak, for Mauch when he faced a heavy suspension. Eventually, Van took him to dinner, after which the diamond leader told Regan, "That Van certainly knows baseball. I couldn't have swung at a better student of the game."

In fact, the only time anyone ever saw Van lose his poise or become seriously irritated was the time he loaned Regan and welterweight boxing contender Del Flanagan a new Ford, fresh off the showroom. They were to drive to Chicago for the second Joe Walcott-Rocky Marciano fight. Van drove with them to the Windy City and then met other friends for a three-day whirl at the racetrack.

Regan and Flanagan were then to drive the car back after the fight and Van would fly back. However, after two hours of gin and deliberation at the Sherman Hotel bar, Regan and Flanagan became indignant at the thought of such a tedious journey home. They removed their bags from the Ford, drove it to a no parking zone and grabbed a cab to the railroad station for a noon trip back to St. Paul on the Four Hundred Express.

Naturally, Van returned to find no car, necessitating another flight back to Chicago and a day-long search for the machine, plus $200 in fines. What really burned Van was the apparent fact that, "These guys didn't think they did anything wrong." He stayed bitter for all of 48 hours, until Flanagan got him six ringside for his next fight. Van thought they were a gift. That was before he got a bill from the fighter after the bout.

Van had a charitable streak a yard wide. He would volunteer for most anything, including reading a burial service for a friend's dog. He spoke glowingly of his wife and two daughters but rarely did anyone see him with his family. A Van family sighting was a rare as an ostrich egg in Duluth.

You wondered, as the ceiling light's shadows bounced off Billy "Swede" Larsen's balding scalp, how he could keep it so brilliantly shined. It made the nine ball look like a crusted muffin. The uninitiated always marveled, too, how Swede could keep the Camel dangling from his lips like a frosty leaf caught in a back draft. You kept wanting to reach out and catch it before its inevitable decline; at least flick away the long ash that always seemed to hang teasingly at its terminal.

The Swede was a work of art. He marched to a far-off drum. He was soft spoken with the tired, gentle voice of a parish priest giving absolution at the death bed. It was said that Larsen never made a quick move until he closed the door on the safe of his Mohawk bowling alley and bar property after the last line on a Sunday morning.

Naturally, he would then move quickly, since the Saturday night late bar crowd contained a volatile mixture of young and sometimes angry Mexicans, loud Lebanese and poor Jews off the Flats. Surprisingly, a large percentage of these customers would become college students and eventually successful businessmen. But in their teens and early twenties, they made up a rather threatening bowling crowd.

"Good people," the Swede would say. "But dammit, the politicians hired some stupid urban renewal guys in this town and they're wiping out the Flats." Never raising his voice above a hoarse whisper, he went on to maintain that, "They'll run out all my customers. In five years, they'll be living another seven or eight miles out and going to damn super-bowling alleys. You know the ones, with sixteen, twenty, maybe thirty lanes. I've got eight alleys and no room to expand unless they let me set up pins in the middle of Robert Street."

There was a reason that Larsen liked to get involved with the Longshots. First, he was always hoping that he might run into somebody who would help him buy a top quality race car. He had owned junkers and hot rods and street cars but never a really good sprinter. Then there was a chance to just get away from the joint. "Sometimes I get so tired hearing those same late-night tough-luck stories that I want to cut my throat."

Swede followed the auto racing action like an addict tracking an illegal shipment of weed. He knew every five and dime dirt track bullring in Indiana. He even married the Indiana widow of a young and promising rookie driver who went over the Winchester wall in the dust. Marie was thin, sweet and pretty. Even after her personal tragedy, she enjoyed the cold chicken wings and potato salad that was standard fare in the Hoosier infields.

Larsen and Regan really understood the emotions of race followers. They staged a yearly Race Night party at the Prom ballroom and invited a leading driver to speak and celebrate with them and hundreds of speed fans. However, this joyous event took on some frightening dimensions, beginning when their first guest, Pat O'Conner, went to a flaming death at the Indianapolis track three months after attending their function. He was killed on the first lap of the 500.

The next year they proudly paraded ageless racing wonder Tony Bettenhausen on Gallivan's premises and heard him forecast that he'd been involved in over a dozen 500-mile races and was destined to win the next one. Like O'Conner, their second guest crashed to his death just before the next 500 when an ill-fated Novi machine hammered into the wall during a test run. A 25¢ piece of equipment was blamed for the disaster.

At this stage, Swede wanted to call off the party, pointing out that they might be putting deadly jinxes on race drivers. Race argued successfully that it was better to honor their memories and to have enjoyed their spirit for a night, and that good luck was bound to follow bad. Swede finally agreed, while wiggling his drooping Camel to the other side of his mouth and saying softly to himself, "But damn, I hate to see good men die."

The Longshots were rewarded when the next guest, Jim Hurtubise, escaped the classic race unharmed. However, he did lose three fingers and burned half the skin on his body the following week in a horrifying crash at Milwaukee. "But we beat the Indy jinx," Regan was quick to point out.

Another member of the Longshots was a quick read right out of Horatio Alger. Chunky, short-legged Vern (Frenchy) Landreville, he of the curly black hair and perpetually surprised brown eyes, originated from the whistle stop of Argyle. Don't look for it on a map, Vern always advised it consisted only of a filling station with a cafe tacked on, a grocery, three walls of a long forsaken Catholic church and exactly 133 citizens living in a handful of small houses and scattered farms.

Frenchy's mother died when he was a tyke, leaving seven brothers and sisters to survive along with their father, Gabe. Compassion abounded in this area of small farms and relentlessly working French Canadians. So the youngsters were raised by a father, cousins, uncles, aunts and friends.

Frenchy grew up with one particularly annoying characteristic, at least to his closest companions: the art of incessantly asking ques-

31

tions of the mundane. He would eventually graduate to queries on more involved subjects. "He used to keep asking why they painted barns red and why dogs bark," father Gabe mused.

It was this insatiable curiosity that gave Landreville an education on a vast multitude of subjects ranging from sports to business to the arts. It was said that you could learn more with Frenchy on the streets in a month than you could by attending Harvard for a year.

In the Army infantry he learned quickly that athletes eat and live better. So he bought a book on boxing techniques and became his company's—and eventually his camp's—light heavyweight champion. He racked up 27 straight victories and earned the right to fight in a European military tournament. However, the war ended and Vern retired from the ring.

On returning to this country he ran the filling station and handled the chef's duties at the Argyle Cafe. It was not unusual for him to slap a hamburger and onions on the greasy grill, take the customer's gas order and then dash out the back door around to the pumps to fill 'er up. He would then race back around to the kitchen once more, serve the food and race through the back door to the front of the station to wash the windshield and then his hands. Then, of course, back again to collect the food bill.

"Some days I would actually come close to driving myself nuts. You see, I didn't want them to think I was so hard up that I had to do two jobs at once. But Jeeze, I learned speed and coordination. I also learned to stop for a second and rinse off my hands after gassing because you could smell the fuel when I served the sandwiches. Turned off a lot of ladies."

Frenchy could dead-pan a disaster like nobody else. Moving to St. Paul after a grasshopper infestation in Argyle, he quickly learned that a young body in reasonably good physical condition could live in a car and subsist on three Baby Ruth candy bars a day, liquids and a change of underwear. He lived like that while running a dingy bar in Frogtown. He also was promptly raided for selling illegal football cards. "I thought it was like Bingo."

By shrewdly investing in small restaurants and bars and then by putting his wife and relatives in the kitchen and tending bar himself, he became an owner of multiple properties. He continued to ask volumes of questions and gained a varied insight into the dealings of liquor companies, food vendors and union officials and inspectors. He also became a master of shrewd real estate deals.

In other words, he'd take a rundown business and hire ex-convicts, who would work behind locked doors and drawn windows, to refurbish the place. He'd open it with sidewalk hoopla, then work like a slave, pester businessmen for special parties and finally develop a profit-making following.

Invariably he'd show a marked rise in profits over a two- or three-year span and then sell, usually at twice what he put into the venture. This with the help, would you believe, of a small East Side bank president who once lived 20 miles outside Argyle! So, at the age of 35 years, Vern was a success story and somewhat of a ripening legend among bar owners.

He became a close friend of Regan's after a near ill-fated Super Bowl trip they arranged to New Orleans. With nearly 150 passengers aboard for the hotel stay in Biloxi, the plane got as far as St. Louis when Vern asked Race to dole out the game tickets along with the apples and champagne.

Regan replied, "No, you dole them out. I don't have them." Vern rushed to the cockpit, shouting to the pilots, "Turn this damn plane around! We don't have the tickets!" Of course, the pilots refused, but did agree to get on the phone and call Vern's wife. She remembered he put them in a safe in one of his three establishments. But with only 24 hours before kick-off, how would they get the tickets delivered in time?

Race pointed out that another Super Bowl special was due to take off four hours later than theirs and Vern's wife made contact with the St. Paul airport. She managed to get the ducats aboard five minutes before take-off.

Nobody knew as they went to bed in Biloxi if the tickets would arrive because the other chartered plane failed to land by midnight because it had encountered engine problems over Rochester and was eventually forced to land in Kansas City. After repairs, it staggered as far as Fort Smith, Arkansas, where wrestling promoter Eddie Williams had a heart attack and another emergency landing took place.

The captain of the plane did not deliver the tickets until five a.m. the morning of the game. It wasn't until breakfast when tickets were placed in the hands of the fans, none of whom were aware of the near catastrophe. The story made the pages in several papers around the country.

Returning to the hotel by bus after watching Kansas City demolish the Minnesota Vikings, Race turned to Frenchy and explained, "If the tickets hadn't arrived they would have torn us limb from limb." An enduring and understanding relationship was developed when Frenchy grinned and replied, "The publicity we got in the Twin Cities papers has to help my business for six months."

Needless to say, Frenchy was not difficult to lure into the games the Longshots played. He even suggested that a special trip to a big fight or the Kentucky Derby might be a worthwhile financial gain. At the mention of such a venture, Jesse, with understandable concern, was prone to ask, "Who will bring the tickets?"

But no bond joining Frenchy and Race was as great as the six hours they spent together getting lost in the Algiers Casbah, maybe the most dangerous four square miles on earth.

Just how they got to Algiers is a story in itself but suffice to say fire chief Steve Conroy ran 10-day ski trips to the French mountain ranges for $300 per person. This time, a motor accident put four participants in the hospital and their non-refundable full-pay deposits were forfeited.

Naturally, Race, Frenchy and Gabe, his 68-year-old father, picked them up. They also invited the shadowy but entertaining Jeff Mikko, of import and light-fingered fame, along for chuckles. Race atoned for the trip by sending Dots, the girls and his mother-in-law to Bermuda for 10 days, a fair trade-off in any counselor's eyes.

France, the foursome agreed, was too cold when they got a glimpse of the chilling fog over the Vasges mountains. So they headed for Paris and on a busy Saturday evening managed to get chased down a boulevard by a waiter for not paying the bill after taking hard-boiled eggs from a center service. Frenchy figured "They have to be free...like an introduction." Yeah, free for five bucks.

Anyway, they began heading south. First to Marseilles. Too chilly. How about sunny Spain? Splendid idea. The train let them off in Barcelona at midnight. Then it was five days on the Ramblas, the street of eccentrics, flower baskets and street bands. Why not a quick trip to Majorca island? Within 24 hours, Frenchy heard that it's a mere three-hour plane ride to Africa.

"Oh, you rascals!" Landreville shouted, "I always wanted to see the lions and tigers of Africa!"

"But it would be north Africa, where it's mostly Arabs and terrorists and a variety of guys in black hats," Jeff warned. Frenchy retorted, "Then there'll be lots for you, too, Jeff."

Algiers was all that and even more intimidating; the harbor for every terrorist and lost soul who has been thrown out of his native land. You could feel the undercurrents of plots and assassinations in the hot, still air.

Anyway, from the top of the Casbah it didn't look that dire. Too much walking for Gabe and Jeff was off looking for goat skins. But Frenchy and Race accepted the challenge. "All we have to do is walk downhill to the sea," Frenchy observed to Race. "An idiot could find his way down. Let's see what all the talk is about."

Within ten minutes they had their shoes stolen after taking them off for a visit inside a mosque. The narrow streets suddenly all seemed to level out, bordered by hundreds of shacks and small stores, with raw meat aging under waves of flies and mobs of begging urchins; children at your side, under your feet, shouting, laughing, pleading alms...their large brown eyes so beauteous, beacons of hope in scrubby stained blocks of poverty the likes of which Frenchy or Race could not even imagine.

Their bare feet steaming from the brick pavement, their first stop was a tiny shop for moccasins. Then a quick beer. Then instructions from jabbering citizens who had no idea what they were asking. It was all too bewildering to attempt to go back so they gave themselves up to the frightening yet fascinating aspects of their situation: missing persons who knew where they were but couldn't get out. Everyone and everything looked sinister. Even the obsessive milling of the children.

Frenchy wanted a "muzzle" for his wife, Cindy, but Regan was sure it was a veil she'd prefer.

With no view to see over the tops of the buildings and with the narrow, body-packed alleys closing in, Race and Frenchy decided to only follow paths in this tangled maze which had steps—be they one, two, or three—leading down. The sun was setting when they spotted the Mediterranean. They must have back-tracked a thousand steps.

Regan turned to Frenchy and suggested, "Now you know why the movie actor Charles Boyer always wanted to take his cuties to the Casbah; no how were they ever getting away."

And imagine Dot's surprise when Race called her in Bermuda and she asked him how the skiing was. "In Africa?" he explained, while she howled in disbelief.

From that day on, Frenchy and Race shared an appetite for the unexpected.

And when it came to cementing friendships, Race loved to tell the story of golf's worst ball disaster, which he shared with Frenchy, Cadillac dealer Dick Long and fellow scribe Mark Tierney. Regan had a gratis gift membership at the new Dellwood Country Club which, in its infancy, could have been a damp, messy spawning ground for alligators and exotic snakes.

On this particularly misty day, Regan demanded the professional supply him with a ball-watching guide. Despite the young man's reputed sharp eyesight, Long lost 16 balls, Regan had 13 disappear, Frenchy was short by 10 and Tierney was missing 9 in the muck and mire. The total of four dozen lost balls by a foursome is to this day considered a world's record!

After Regan suggested in his column that the course change its name to Dellslop, a move among the course's board of directors to drop his membership was stymied only by the vigorous defense of fellow Longshot, Pat Egan, who was a highly involved course founder.

Egan's creative defense: "An insult in Regan's column brought more notoriety and notice than a front page puff. They'll be lining up to break his lost-ball record." The bamboozled listeners finally agreed with Pat. Critical words are better than no words for a new country club scratching for members.

You might call these the hard-core of the Longshots. Founding fathers perhaps. Among Rogers, Regan, Van, Swede and Frenchy there was enough electricity to light up a small Dakota town. Others would come and disappear over varying periods of time, but they, too, made lasting impressions.

Aging sharks would swim in at times, trying desperately for a score and then drift out at the first loss. Drifters would have an idea, perhaps even a brilliant scheme, but could not take the pressure of the actual event. Some would offer their initial shares in an idea for little or nothing but wanted nothing of the tensions of implementation.

The mortician, Digger O'Halloran, was vague but trustworthy and owned a photogenic mind. Thunder Klunder was a former motorcycle racer and repairman who had trouble deciding whether he wanted to be a participant or run the show. Fred Macalus, a maturing grease jockey with a high wire mind, owned a growing tire replacement center. His macho physical presence dominated any production in which he was a part. He was the former street-fighting king of Rice Street. Super salesman Dayle Maloney was willing to give up his role as the leading leisure vehicle dealer to pursue almost any risk for recognition.

And elegant Pat Egan was the president of the Fighting Saints hockey club, a non-profit group which he vowed to keep penniless, even if it meant inviting 500 people to a victory bash planned for 50. Tall, handsome and glib, Pat was called "The Governor" by his friends. His business connections could be murky albeit brilliant at times. "A new world man," Race would call him.

It was an eclectic collection of bedfellows. They shared an enviable passion for living. They had visions of milk and honey and earth shattering overnight success. True Longshots. Trying to outrun themselves.

During this period, tornadoes and floods ravaged the Twin Cities at intermittent periods and St. Paul became the only city in the state to accept daylight saving time. So it was duly noted around the Midwest that St. Paul had no roofs on its homes, there was three feet of water in the basements, nobody knew what time it was and the state bird was a loon.

The Longshots fit perfectly into this environment. Their ideas blew in on the wind. They were always getting their feet wet and nobody looked at their watches for fear a loan department was closing in. If they were loons, they were laughable ones. But nobody ever flew the coop.

And that definitely ain't all bad!

Chapter One

Hot Horns and Cold Feet

On one gray, chilly November morning at Gallivan's, the leaders of the Longshots seemed to arrive almost simultaneously. There was an aura of urgency and excitement about them. Race wasn't even into his first of five morning cups of black coffee when he nudged Rogers with his elbow, "We've got three big ones to talk about men. All of these have hot potential. Some bigger than others—but all of them very, very good."

Nobody responded except Van, who smiled, wrung his cold hands together, pushed back his stylish cashmere hat and exclaimed, "Love you, Regan boy! You're going to make my day. I can feel it in my heart." With that, he slapped Regan on the shoulder and commanded, "Talk pretty!"

"Thanks for the early support, Van. You know, I've been doing some checking on that Wakota arena in South St. Paul, the new ice rink. Well, we can rent it on Lincoln's birthday for $500. I talked to Tom Warner, the football coach out at Cretin High School, who had this fabulous idea. He can line up a hot little rock band or two for maybe $500 more.

"But here's the beautiful thing, we can actually get the old basketball floor from the auditorium and transport the pieces over to Wakota for a measly rental price. Then we fit them together on top of the ice and form the best damn giant dance floor in the state.

"And the really wondrous part: we don't have to melt the ice and face all the big charges of resurfacing the thing. That means we don't spend a buck on all that high-powered mechanical crap. So, we save a big bundle there. Then Warner says he'll be the security guy and get a couple of Cretin kids to watch out for the hooligans.

"But, Jeeze, guys, the best is the date. Lincoln's birthday. Over 20,000 high school students with nothing to do! They've got time on their hands and they all love this new rock and roll crap."

Regan was almost out of breath. Fat Alice brought the coffee and rolls. Swede said politely, "Sounds great." The wily Landreville always wanted to hear the figures up front. "How much and how'll we advertise?"

"On target, Vern. It pays to have a French hard head in the group," Regan grinned. "Well, we paper all the schools, you know the bulletin boards, the walls, whatever. We can get on some cheap air shows for maybe fifty spots at twenty bucks each. And these damn kids today, I'll tell yeah, they get the word around by mouth. And they go all over. South St. Paul is nothing for the kids from Minneapolis. We could have a turn-away. And Frenchy, we figure we can do this for less than five grand!"

"How many does the place hold?" Jesse asked quietly.

"Maybe we squeeze in 3,000 at three bucks a head. Plus we got the concessions—you know, pop, popcorn, maybe even some burgers and dogs. But I think we can do maybe nine-ten grand. Come to think of it, Frenchy, I think we could chop the expenses down to three Gs. When I said big, I didn't mean enormous, but you get the implications, right?"

"Right!" answered Vern breezily. "Next year we hold it in seven or eight places and then maybe franchise the idea. Gosh, there's arenas all over the Twin Cities. Then maybe a gigantic one in the auditorium and we bring in Dick Clark . . ."

"Dammit, Van, hold on. This is just kind of a test run to feel out the situation," Race cautioned. None of us know a helluva lot about bands and dances and this stuff, but you like the potential?"

"Oh, potentiallll . . . oh, potentiallll, crooned Frenchy with his simulated French accent. " I'm putting in dance floors in two of my joints next year. I've got a guy whose got access to some very cheap tile. And, I've got three ex-cons who can lay it blindfolded."

Race winced. "Back to business. Who wants in on this one?"

Rogers could hardly wait to interject, "I'm in. But it's not big enough for more than a couple. Regan's in, it's his baby. Van? I hear you're running a little light after your last visit to Arlington."

Self-consciously, Van tipped back in his chair, "Yeah, I'm running light, just a little. I like the idea but it's probably too small for more than just a couple of us. And next year you guys can talk of expansion. Then I'll borrow a ton to get in. Ever tell ya my uncle was a band leader who used to play the sax before our chicken fights?"

He was cut short by Race, "Well, we'll work out the details and if this thing flies we'll talk big next time around. Now, about this kid from the University football team, Irish Paul Burke. Remember me telling you guys about him? I mean he's the most handsome muscle-man on the campus. Maybe All Big Ten, the way he's playing. His profile makes Tyrone Power look like a bum.

"This guy goes about six-one, two hundred and ten pounds and looks like he was chiseled in a granite quarry. But the beautiful thing, he can fight! They tell me he hits a lot harder with his fists than with his football gear!"

"Now you're talking my language," enthused Van. Race edged his chair closer to the table. His jaw muscles tightened.

"I've been fooling around with the boxing game for over 20 years. I've been searching for a heavy. The White Hope. God, how we need one. The problem as I see it is what Jack Dempsey said when I asked him what made great white heavyweights. Jack said, 'A depression.'

"Trouble is, times have been too damn good. Even the guys in the ghettoes are eating and growing like whales, getting to be seven feet tall and three hundred pounds. But if Burke can take the hammering he gets in football and still wants to fight, just maybe we got that rare bird."

"That's my kind of promotion, too," chimed Frenchy. "You know when I was fighting, I learned it's all in the heart. I fought some big tall black guys in the Army, I swear they had arms like grapevines. But when I got under them and banged to the ribs and kidneys and solarium, they faded like an orchid in Iceland."

Van wanted to know "Where'd you hit them? What's that solarium you said? Sol. . . ? Don't you mean solar plexus? Just above the belt on the right side?"

"That's what I said," Frenchy fired back, just a little anger in his voice. "The solar—the solar plebis. Oh, crap, you know what I mean. The one that makes the guy look like he's frozen. I won a lot with that punch. Best place to land a left hook."

Regan's irritation began to show only slightly. "Hell, I don't care if he hits you in your solar system or on your fanny, he can hurt big time. I talked to him and we really get along. He wants to try the pro ring. He's from Wisconsin, but he won an amateur title down in Nashville. That's a little mysterious, but I guess he spends a lot of time with some relatives in the south. Anyway, I took him over to Spike McCarthy's gym and had old-time boxer My Sullivan look at him.

"Now listen, peons, Sullivan, who had a great left hand, says Burke's the sweetest lookin' heavy he's seen since Joe Louis. I know that sounds ludicrous. I mean a white, handsome kid with brains and a potential pro football career wanting to fight and make us millions. But anyway, that's what he says.

"I've talked to Jack Raleigh . . . you know, the boxing promoter. He'll put him on the next Del Flanagan card. Raleigh has promised me he'll find some guy who's just waiting to be tipped over. Burke'll get a couple of rounds of work. He'll win big and then move on to better paydays. Raleigh'll probably give him $300 for his first shot but somebody's got to pick up the tab for the equipment. That means sparring partners, shoes, gym time and all the little details.

"Details can be rather large with Burke since he likes those 16 ounce sirloins and chomps them down like a hungry shepherd. Raleigh wants thirty percent. The kid gets fifty percent and the rest we split up."

Finally, the patient Larsen asked innocently, "Isn't that a little, I mean for the kid?"

"Good question," Regan answered without a trace of agitation." I once asked the same thing of Jack Hurley when he owned and trained Harry "The Kid" Matthews. Know what the greatest boxing mind of them all answered? Hurley explained to me that he needed $100,000 a year to live on and that meant that The Kid would have to earn $200,000. That was twenty times what The Kid ever got for a fight before he met Hurley.

"You see, Swede, fifty percent of $500,000 is huge. Believe me, Irish Paul won't complain. Just so there'll be no mistake, I'll be watching the papers drawn up over at Uncle Joe's."

"Joe Dudley?" Swede wanted to know.

"Yea, best damn attorney this side of Boston," Frenchy exclaimed. "But what's he doin' in boxing? Mostly he does those big deals like that casino deal in Vegas."

"Hey, he's pure gold," Race responded. "This guy never quits learning. He even handled my book contracts because he just wanted to learn. At 50 years, he's learning every day. He asks more questions than you do, Frenchy. And he likes to have a little fun because most of his work is heavy litigation. He just enjoys our deals. Hell, know something else? He never charged me a cent that time I got him into the hockey deal."

"What hockey deal?" Jesse wanted to know.

"I guess the word 'hockey' wakes you up, huh Jesse?" grinned Regan. "It was our International Hockey League playoffs in Minneapolis three years ago. I got the Saints ruffian, John Bailey, to scream that he'd like to bury the Minneapolis coach in the ice with his shiv in his ear. Then I called the Minneapolis coach and got his story of retaliation. He blasted Bailey as a goon who should be locked up in the Como zoo. A hot headline, eh?

"Then I went to Joe and asked him if he didn't think we should have Bailey sue their coach for defamation of character to the tune of $100,000. Joe said that figure was a little light for the damage which had obviously been done to Bailey's psyche. We raised the ante to $300,000 and had the papers delivered to their coach about ten minutes before the game at the old Dupont arena.

"The coach was so upset, he spent the night throwing up in the toilet. St. Paul won 4-2 and the Millers never recovered. Joe loves a little action. Sports is about all he has for a laugh."

Van was trimming his nails. "Okay, so we follow the Burke case and see what develops. Now what's the big third item we tackle today? Damn, my feet are getting cold, any heat back here, Alice?"

"I'll turn this one over to Mr. Rogers," Regan answered. "Jesse, let's hear about your super plan."

"Well, I can't go into too much detail at this moment," Rogers explained, while delicately cutting a small breakfast steak into tiny pieces. "But there is something very large in the distance, gentlemen."

"You're going to ask us to buy a racehorse?" Van queried.

"No, something much faster and better because it doesn't gulp twenty bucks worth of groceries every day," Jesse taunted. "It's called a race car. Not any car, but the fastest damn thing you have ever seen. You know the television show, "The Fugitive"? Well, on the intro they've got that mysterious looking speeding machine that's zapping the desert, chasing David Janssen!

"It's the fastest car in the world—something like 600 miles an hour across the salt. God, just imagine! You could be in Chicago from here in less than an hour if there were no friggin' speed cops.

Anyway, I'm working on a deal. Maybe the biggest any of us has seen. Sometime in the future, I think I can get the car. It's called the Spirit of America and it might cost a ton. But how'd you guys like to be a piece of something like that? Swede's got the details. He told me all about it."

An incredulous Frenchy wanted to know, "Who'd we race it against?"

A small ripple of laughter went through the Longshots. Swede, the expert on fast cars, who had raced three of his own at the State fair, tried to explain to Vern what this machine was all about.

"You see, Frenchy, you don't race this race car against others. It just runs against the clock by itself. You would bring it up here and maybe put it at a spot in the State fair and the customers shell out 75¢ or a buck just to look at it."

Jesse showed rare enthusiasm for this project. He almost opened both eyes beyond their usual slit.

"I really have to believe that at least 200,000 Fair fans will want to see the Spirit. It's not like it's on every street corner. You could spotlight this baby and they'd be coming in to see it from Des Moines.

"Yeah, but the cost'll kill. I mean if it's on TV," Frenchy warned.

"Maybe not," explained Jesse. "Swede says maybe five grand or so. I've got my secretary making all kinds of calls to track this one down. If we get it, I'd want it for at least a month. Not for just our fair, but how about the other big ones. Swede mentioned Wisconsin or Texas. Location is everything at the Fair. So we've got to go out and play footsie with the guys running the big show. Right, Regan?"

"You tell 'em, Jesse. Most of you guys recall that five or six years ago Mr. Gallivan, our gracious host, and I put together a new and exotic sandwich.

"Moonburgers!" the gang chorused.

"Yeah, right, guys. Moonburgers. We even tried to trademark the name. We got the first really big micro-oven so we could make em in thirty seconds. And listen, this was a helluva idea," Regan enthused, moving his chair close to the table. His eyes lit up as he talked about the venture.

"Bob and I put about six or seven kinds of special exotic juices with our own rounded, pre-baked meatballs into a specially constructed bun. It was a real moon-looking roll. Then we had little ray guns made of plastic and filled with ketchup and mustard so kids would have fun squirting condiments into their sandwiches.

"You fellows may have forgotten our master move, when we got located right next to the moon show exhibit on the Fair's Machinery Hill. All those crazy state fair people came to look at pictures of the moon and they would hear a loud pitch about our Moonburgers.

"We told those suckers they were only available at our stand or on the moon. We got good write-ups in the papers and the food was pretty good. But we hadn't counted on one serious blunder; we had seriously over-estimated the value of our location.

"No people?" Van asked.

"No, there were enough people. But the damn auto racetrack was located only about 300 feet away across the street. Right by the east turn. And the wind always seemed to be blowing toward us. The dirt and the dust and the clumps of mud almost made a cloud for four or five hours every afternoon.

"All this crap blew right over our Moonburgers. By the time the people got them into their mouths, they must've tasted like dirty sand—real sand-wiches. You should have seen the grime. It looked like half the track wound up on our equipment. We couldn't wipe it off fast enough. You might call it a distasteful situation.

"But," and Regan's eyes again sparkled like two Christmas decorations, "we really had some fun the last couple of days. We injected gin into the sandwiches and sold them for two bits to the Fair's ranger patrol."

"Next thing we knew, we got a letter from some attorney in Texas who claimed a guy in Texarkansas had registered the name Moonburger ahead of us. The name was everything. We even had the Peters Meat Company interested in making metal molds to produce the sandwiches. Gallivan thought he'd make enough money to

buy one of those silly horses he's always betting on. I would have settled for braces on my kids' teeth."

Regan decided to belt a gin before leaving. Jesse and Swede apparently agreed they'd work on the Spirit of America project. Regan
pledged to confer with Joe, the attorney, over Irish Paul Burke's boxing pact. Van wanted to know if anyone would want to whisk out and
inspect a $3,000 Ford Crown Victoria house car, "Like it was made
yesterday."

"Damn Moonburgers," Regan could be heard muttering as he
smacked his lips over the gin. "Damn dust."

Oh, yes, before the Longshots broke up, it was decided that the
dance show in South St. Paul should belong only to Race and his pal
Tom Warner. They seemed to have the most interest. And what
could happen to their two or three thousand investment? No way
they could get stung.

Chapter Two

Revenge of the Ice Age

Lincoln's holiday dawned brisk and dampish, with just a trace of fog in patches over the old South St. Paul stockyards. Traffic on Concord Street was sparse with the absence of school buses. Regan and his football coaching cohort, Tom Warner, were meeting at the Loop Diner to arrange final details on their prep rock bash at the Wakota Arena.

Regan was in an expansive mood since it was his day off and he could devote his entire energy to the promotion at hand.

"Great day for our matinee dance," Race enthused happily. "The kids won't feel like messing around downtown when they can be indoors and whooping it up in comfort, right Tom?"

"Bet your sweet fanny," the square-jawed, balding coach agreed. He was a profane, hard-bitten coach with a near genius capacity to organize and inspire his prep footballers. He ate up life like it were a ham sandwich and he was a starving lumberjack.

"Hey, I've had my prep kids out papering the town. We've got flyers up the mayor's rump. Last night we moved the basketball floor from the auditorium and I swear the lumber had to be in 50 pieces. You told me that was my job and I rented three trucks and got about 20 of my kids to put it on the arena ice sheet.

"Now Race, before you get your hair up on end over the cost, I've got these tons of high school kids working for me for just a couple bucks an hour. Most of them are my football players. Hell, I tell them it's good exercise. They all want to make my team so nobody complains about the work. They're cheap but damn, they're strong."

Regan nodded knowingly. "Really, you had a helluvan idea, Tom. I've never heard of a big dance on ice—in the afternoon. Really, a dance on a floor on the ice . . . jeez. You know, Tom, I was a little disappointed when we didn't get anybody else in on the idea. Like a no-confidence vote."

"Hell, Race, that's the best thing that ever happened. We've got maybe three grand in the whole thing. I got the Hot Rocks for $300 and the Kowambies for $250. They charge $500 to work at night. The kids are cheap, the security's cheap and our ticket sellers and takers are all A-students. I've loaded up five hun in change from the stockyard's bank, because I'm figuring we do real big at the gate.

"Race, we could sell maybe a thousand dogs, too. And I made a good deal on all the food and pop. We could be counting a solid five or six grand by tonight. I might even quit coaching next year. We could put on seven or eight of these."

Tom smiled and squeezed Race around the shoulders.

"Frankly, we've got a good combination. Glad nobody else is in it."

After two strong cups of coffee and a chocolate donut, Tom drove up the hill to Wakota. The building sat like a miniature airplane hangar on a crest overlooking South St. Paul. The sky was beginning to clear and Tom approached the building with a feeling of euphoria, not unlike the night his team rolled up its record twenty second straight football victory and he had a glorious feeling in his bones all the way to the game.

Inside the chilly arena, Tom could hear the laughs of his student workers and sharp noises of timber landing on ice and hammers rapping a steady tattoo. The last few pieces of the huge wooden jigsaw puzzle fell into a tight embrace. Just think, this was the floor the Minneapolis Lakers had used when they mopped it with the bodies of the Harlem Globetrotters before a record crowd last year.

The temperature suddenly became a factor after Tom had taken off his heavy stormcoat and began to direct his help in the final phases. "God, it's freezin' in here," he complained to one of the maintenance men. "Can't you put the heat up a little? Jeeze, I'm freezin' my rump off."

"Hey, it's about 45 outside and it's about 10 degrees warmer in the entry," came the reply from a grumpy janitor. "You can't get the heat up in the building much more or the ice melts. The ice melts and you've got one serious problem, like a floating dance floor."

Tom had never entertained even the most remote doubts about any of the project's technicalities. "Oh well, they'll just keep warm dancing," he mused, not really convincing himself. It was the coach's first attack of self-doubt.

By noon, the floor was ready and gleaming. The gates were scheduled to open at two p.m. Everything appeared to be in place. The bands were due to show up an hour early to check out the sound system. The possibility of a rush at the gate gnawed at the coach's mind and he finally decided to open three ticket windows rather than two. What's a few extra bucks when he'd already kept the shoestring budget below three thousand? A few minutes later, Race showed up with a couple of cups of coffee and they sat in his car going over the final details.

"I checked all the rock stations and heard two more of our plugs about an hour ago," Race told Tom. "I think we'll have another three or four shots before the dance. You know, Tom, they claim the teens listen to these stations all the time. I figure maybe 20,000 of them could hear our shots just today. If fifteen percent of them decide to come, we've got an overflow. You gotta believe all the kids from around this area'll show up. This could be the springboard for something so big neither one of us can even visualize it."

Warner was a little less optimistic, not over the numbers, but the physical aspects the project was developing. "Nothing to get excited about, Race, but we've got one little problem."

"What problem?"

"The temperature. We can't put it above 45 degrees in the building or the ice melts and our dance floor washes away."

Regan's eyes widened. "Washes away? Like in a flood or what?"

"Well, the maintenance guys say you can't heat up the temp to make it comfortable without the ice melting. Can you see the St. Paul auditorium's basketball floor floating down the embankment six blocks into town and coming to rest on Concord Street during rush hour? Or maybe ending up in Red Wing, 30 miles downstream?"

"Oh, my God!" Regan seemed petrified at the thought. "But what the hell, how do they make this thing work at the auditorium?"

"Special controls. They've got a half-million dollar thermostat system, but sometimes they even have trouble. I remember seeing Bob Cousy of the Celtics slip on his fanny and skid ten feet under the basket one night."

"How the devil could we miss on something like that?" Regan demanded to know. "Maybe that's why the other Longshots weren't so hot on this project. Maybe they didn't want to mention that they were frightened by the thought that you can't dance on ice no how."

"Don't lose your friggin' wheels" Tom cautioned. "It isn't like we've been robbed. I figure the kids'll be jamming away so hard they'll work up sweats if it's zero degrees. Hey, I know kids. I don't really see them complaining. They go to football games at 20 above in shirt sleeves."

"I suppose you're right. But I'd hate to have to eat this baby just because of the temperature. But like you say, what's temperature to teens? If the band's instruments don't freeze up we shouldn't even worry about it."

They walked briskly back to the arena entrance. Race ordered a Coke as they set up the concession stands. Tom went to greet the bands, which were scheduled to alternate every hour. Race eventually found a phone where he made a call to Jesse, just to inform him of the proceedings. Although he had no financial involvement in this promotion, Jesse could feel abused if the others in the group didn't report to him on their own events. He needed to know the latest information for whoever he encountered at lunch.

"Weather great and you can see the lines starting to form," Regan teased Jesse.

"Really? Hey, maybe I should have got in at the last minute."

"Well, relax, Jesse. It's too early to tell. We've got one problem. It's very cold inside."

"Ah, nuts, kids don't mind the cold, just so your music's hot."

"Right, Jesse. I feel good about the whole thing. Heard any of our commercials?"

"Yeah, I believe I did. 'LOL pumped it pretty good a few times. That Ricketts is a good announcer. I mean he talks the kids' jargon. He gave it a real blast about six this morning."

"Six? God, I wonder if anyone was up. I'd rather hear it at noon. You know, Jesse, they say kids make up their minds where to go on the spur. I had a dream last night. What if 30,000 kids wound up at the last minute and said, 'Let's go to the dance at Wakota!' My God, there'd be a traffic jam down in Rochester."

"Could happen. I'd be happy for you. But I'd be sick I wasn't in on it. Call me about three. By then you'll know if it's a biggie. By the way, how much did it wind up costing?"

"Oh, Tom's optimistic, but he doesn't realize expenses are always 20 percent more than you figure. I guess the break-even's about 1,200 kids and in my heart I think we'll do maybe twice that. I think we could shoehorn in maybe even another 200 over that. One nice thing, down here you don't worry much about safety inspectors. The only inspectors they seem to worry about down here are the ones in the stockyards checking on the pigs and steers. See ya, Jesse."

The first teens began arriving about 20 minutes before the gates opened. Regan, standing in the lobby, had his initial sense of elation. In tune-ups, the Hot Rocks sounded loud and brash. Although some of the notes seemed to get lost high in the cold steel girders. The Kowambie's played a sound unfamiliar to the ears of Tom and Race. However, a student workman told Warner, "They're weird but good." After all, three steel guitars, two alto sax and a piano have to produce something eerily way out.

Within a half hour over 300 youngsters had clogged the entry, piling jackets and coats in heaps and seemingly all knowing each other. Regan decided to ask a few of them where they'd come from. The response sent him into a near ecstasy of emotion.

"South Minneapolis" . . . "White Bear" . . . "St. Paul" . . . "Cottage Grove" . . .

They were indeed coming from all over. He walked nervously to the doors and peered into the parking lot. An almost steady stream of cars seemed to be slowly filing up the hill and onto the huge snow-thatched parking lot.

Regan could hardly wait to find Warner, who was now busily helping to get a greasy range started up for hamburgers and onion slices.

"Tom, baby! Can you see those little turkeys coming in?" Race almost shouted.

"I know, I know," grinned Tom. "Like I said, it's the beginning of a huge adventure."

At that moment, Race could no longer contain himself. He grabbed Tom by the arm, pulled him into a corner and began shouting out the notes to the "One O'clock Jump." "Dat-da-da, ta-da-da, ta-da . . . dada dah daaaa." He spun Tom in a Lindy step while Tom, in no particular tune, chimed in with "Doo-do-do . . . da-do-do-do da, hee hee . . ." They held on to each other like two children on the playground, embracing and dancing at the sheer thrill of having created something the world would long remember.

A half hour after the Hot Rocks began their shrill and then booming ode to reality rock, the crowds were still coming in. Regan and Warner had grabbed a couple of greasers from the hamburger range and were standing in the far corner of the lobby. Warner's scrubbed, high-cheeked face was flushed with elation, his usually cool green eyes almost ablaze.

"Just checked and we've got nearly 1,500 kids in here and if I know kids they'll keep coming for another hour or more. We've got a bonanza, Race! In fact, I know we've got our nut made and from now on it's pure gravy. Pure, unadulterated, first class gravy. Jeeze, this is better than a touchdown for a win on the last play."

Trying to sound like an experienced entrepreneur who had seen it all, Race answered, "Potential, potential, potential."

As they walked the concourse back to the arena dance floor, Tom noticed a teenage girl sitting on a bench, one shoe off and massaging her ankle. Pain was etched in her young frown.

"What happened, sweetie?"

"Fell, fell on the floor. Twisted my ankle. God, Mister, that floor's getting slippery or wet or something!"

Tom looked at Race. "Better check this out. We don't want any lawsuits."

Both of them moved into the dance area just in time to see a hulking Cretin footballer hit the deck. Then, toward the other end, they saw a group of four or five dancers surrounding another girl who had fallen.

The hundreds still dancing were doing it cautiously, almost preferring to walk rather than twist. Then, almost in front of them, a girl and her partner went down. Virtually at the same time, Lanny, the Hot Rocks leader, approached breathlessly.

"Hey, men, you gotta shut down the music! These kids are falling like jugs off a shelf. If you mowed them down with a repeater you couldn't drop them any faster!"

It wasn't exactly pandemonium, but it was leading to a first class catastrophe. By now, at least a dozen couples had toppled into what looked like pools of water. The girls were shrieking and the boys were trying to wipe themselves off. One kid pranced by on tiptoes and grinned, "Let's find some girls to fall on top of!"

The young security guards and two off-duty police officers working the gig arrived on the floor almost simultaneously.

Just as another eight or ten dancers hit the deck with frightening thuds, one police officer warned the promoters, "You guys better call a halt and wipe the floor. Somehow the damn condensation is building up from the ice and the warm bodies and they'll be breaking legs any minute!"

By the time Race rushed to the bandstand and Tom hurried to help up another falling teen, the Kowambies notes had leveled another two score dancers. Now more than five hundred rock fans were either tottering, sliding, or landing with a splash. Moonbeam, leader of the Kowambies, was already calling a halt to the music and issuing a warning over the speakers, "Keep your cool and walk off the floor as best you can. Here's one of your hosts, Mr. Regan."

"Okay, kids. We're sorry this happened." Before Race could utter another word, a couple of angry teens near the bandstand wanted to know, "When are we going to get our money back?"

And then the chant rose like the sound of 2,000 Canadian geese taking off from a swamp. "We want our money back! We want our money back! We want our money back!"

Thoroughly flustered, Tom and Race held a brief conference.

"We'd better do it, Race," Tom said in a hoarse whisper. "If they start breaking ankles and legs we're in for big trouble. How the hell could this happen?"

In an instant flashback, Warner again saw the scene of Cousy crashing on the same floor in an NBA playoff game. He had taken a horrendous spill but it didn't prevent him from scoring 20 points. Still, the scene had frightful implications. He always wondered if Cousy had suffered a serious injury would it have ruined his glorious career.

It was a tortuous two hours later before each of the students, including many who had just arrived, would receive back their $3 in ticket money. By now, the crushed Regan was ready for a gin. The rugged Warner was silent but shaking like a frozen leaf in a Superior gale.

That evening at the Stockmen's Inn, Tom was talking to himself. He kept muttering, "How could this happen?" He contemplated the task of telling his wife that he'd lost $1,500 in the venture and that they'd probably have to postpone their Easter vacation.

Regan, hardened to promotional disasters, tried to offer Tom solace. "You had a good one, Tom. Man, don't hit yerself over the head with a hammer. Did I ever tell you the story about my picture-button promotion at the state fair three years ago?"

"What the hell is a picture-button?"

"Well, I met this guy who could take your picture and put it on a big button or maybe your girlfriend's. Neat, eh? And it seems he never blew a picture. But when I get the creep and set him up for a grand he must have taken an average of 10 pictures to get one you could recognize. Those nine fuzzy ones cost us about a buck. Get this: we're charging a buck fifty. With the cost of the help and rent, we were actually losing money ever time he aimed the damned camera.

"I was so upset at the idiot I threatened to throw his friggin' camera equipment into the river. The stone head just said, 'Look at it as a learning experience.'"

Tom looked at Race and they both began to laugh.

Race, rarely one to wallow in regret, tried to buoy his friend by telling him, "Next time we let those teen tadpoles dance on ice it'll be with skates. So, let's just forget it, Tom. Let's talk football. How's Cretin going to be next fall?"

Tom couldn't believe his ears. He could only mumble, "Are you completely nuts or what?"

Chapter Three

They Forgot to Fix the "Fix"

The Wakota splash party had absolutely no effect on the Longshots' enthusiasm for the hunt. Within days after Race's ill-fated rock bash, Jesse and Frenchy had penciled in a meeting at Napoleon's. This was the University Avenue restaurant whose combination of chic fixtures, schmaltzy characters and unfathomable six-page menu would have made it the ideal watering hole for a Hollywood enclave.

"I can always tell whose drinking martinis at the bar when I stand behind them," claimed little Herb Napoleon. He was only five feet tall and co-owner, along with older brother, Jimmy, of the establishment.

"The gin seems to get into the blood real fast. After one martini, they're shrugging their shoulders and waving their hands a little. After two belts, they're really getting active and seem to be gabbing away in two conversations with the drinkers on each side of them. After three drinks, they become dangerous to themselves and others. We have to put in a three-martini watch because we've had a few of them take nine counts after falling off the bar stool."

It was from Herb that St. Paul first heard this admonition about martinis: "One is a wondrous experience, the second is a blessing from the Gods and the third is a serious mistake."

Herb's gentle, indulging manner made the bespectacled little host the ideal front man. Jimmy, his brother, tended to the food and used to claim, "We throw out better garbage than most other restaurants serve." Rumor had it that Napoleon's was up for sale because it threw out too much un-ordered food.

Napoleon, the name, conjured up French specialties. But in all honesty, the place blended Italian, American and French dishes in an exquisite goulash of delicacies which had won the brothers numerous local awards. Crab legs were fit for a king and the Pope would consider indulging in the garlic sauce on the linguini a serious sin.

This was the place where Jesse liked to meet members of the Longshots when, as he profanely explained, "you don't want all the cold-noses assin' around, like you get from the public at Gallivan's."

No mention was made of the dance debacle as Race, Jesse and Frenchy were ushered to the deep-cushioned semi-circular booth in the far corner.

Jesse and Race ordered double martinis with three light drops of vermouth. Frenchy asked for a beer and a chaser, not exactly the most subtle belt served in an establishment. Napoleon's was noted for its large exotic drinks, which at times resembled a salad set to brandy.

"Race, I did some checking on that boxer . . . what's his name? Oh, Irish Paul Burke. You know, you might just have something," Jesse enthused. "I watched him work out at Spike McCarthy's place over on Hennepin in Minneapolis the other night. He ripped the big bag pretty good. The kid can fight and lord, he's better looking than Clark Gable!"

It was an appraisal not without reasonable knowledge. Jesse's distant relative, Tommy Gibbons, was one of the great heavyweight boxers of all time. He had stayed the limit with Jack Dempsey in the infamous Shelby bout that bankrupted the Montana town. In the '20s he was credited with delivering the boxing rank's best left hook to the liver.

"And I went over the next night and liked what I saw," Landreville said enthusiastically, his eyes opening to the size of small saucers. "Holy Moses, he can hit! Only thing, he looks like a choir boy. I mean the guy is really cute. If I was a girl, I'd throw myself at him."

"If you were a girl, you'd be known as fat and ugly," Regan interjected.

The chubby Frenchman insisted, "He moved around like he knows what he's doing. Where'd he learn those moves?"

"From a priest at the Christian Brothers Academy in Nashville. And like I said before, don't ask me how he got there," Regan answered impatiently.

"Well," Frenchy continued, "I went up to him after his workout and introduced myself and told him I knew you, Race, and told him how great he looked. He kept calling me 'Mister.' I dunno. Is that good or bad? You know, when I was fighting in the Army, I wasn't too polite. All I wanted to know was: 'Where's the son-of-a-gun I fight?'"

"No question, he's prep school nice," Race agreed. "But so was Gene Tunney and look what he did to Dempsey. And Joe Louis was no snarling animal. This Burke is a special breed, but I'll tell you this, the Gopher footballers I talk to say he tackles like a wild man. And two of them told me they saw him in a street fight last year and he really messed up some big, rough hooligan.

"And he trains. I was over to his campus apartment and the refrigerator was filled with vegetables and lean meat cuts. Some of the crap I didn't even recognize. He's a nut on the right foods. Oh, yes, he had a shelf full of vitamins that would make Walgreen's jealous."

"Mean pills, I hope," Jesse interrupted. "You still have to have the killer instinct. Gibbons used to tell me that you had to have hunger in the belly and fire in the eyes to fight. You really have to think destruction. If you've got an ounce of compassion it's really a weakness.

"Remember, and this is another one from Gibbons, pro boxing's the only sport in the world where you step out of your corner intent on hurting the other guy. Same goes for the guy across the ring."

Regan agreed. "Good point, Jesse. But I once saw a fighter who didn't think that way. He was the greatest, the one and only Willie Pep. I saw him win a round in a bout I covered where he didn't throw a punch. Just box. Would ya believe he got a ten-nine edge on every score sheet? Nobody but Willie could have done that. And the guy he fought was our own Austin Atom, Jackie Graves, the number four feather in the world and a killer puncher."

"Yeah, but there was only one Pep," Jesse agreed.

"Amen. Now bow your heads you heathen blasphemers," Race joked.

"Pep was the deity. In a class by himself. But Burke has some of his traits. Like the good left hand. A real spear."

All of them concurred: Irish Paul Burke was an investment not to be taken lightly.

"Know what big-timers in the heavies get these days?" Race queried. "Well, Rocky Marciano over the past few years has been getting around $700,000. And you know they're dicing him fifty-fifty.

"What's this going to cost us?" Frenchy wanted to know, his chunky body almost vibrating in anticipation of a lifetime score.

"Well, like I said," Race explained deliberately, "Jack Raleigh, the promoter, has got to have a piece of the action. That's only right. He's giving us the showcase and he's agreed to pay the cost of Burke's equipment. That includes a Kelly-green silk robe with a big red Irish rose on the back. We've agreed to play "My Wild Irish Rose" when Paul comes joggin' down the aisle.

"Now contracts are a big thing. Like I said, we've got a helluva attorney to handle them in Dudley. He could find a loop hole in an English treaty. But we'll be fair to Burke. He'll get a solid fifty percent and the Longshots, whoever's in it, and Raleigh split the rest after we foot the bills."

"How soon? How soon?" the impatient Frenchman wanted to know.

"Slow down, Frenchy, you'll have spasms," Jesse cautioned.

Jesse began to talk. "In five weeks Jack Raleigh has a card at the Auditorium with Del Flanagan headlining against some Canadian punk. He's going to put Burke on the semi-windup in a sixer that should really go about six seconds."

"That's pretty big for a first fight, isn't it?" Frenchy interrupted. "Six rounds. Hey, Rascals, I know polar bears who can't go six rounds."

"Keep your ex-girlfriends out of it," Jesse demanded. Everyone chuckled. But Frenchy insisted a semi-windup was too much heat for a newcomer.

"Okay. Back to square one for Frenchy," a surprisingly patient Race said softly. "If I told Frenchy 'this is a boxing glove,' he'd say, 'not so fast.'"

The little group laughed, ordered lunch and then got back to business. Regan picked up the plan.

"Jack's called Smiley Crackers in Milwaukee and ordered a load of slag. That means a bum. A stiff. A guy wearing Esther Williams' swim trunks. Like starter fodder. A guy who goes around the country letting hometown prospects beat him without looking too bad. Simply a business fighter who wants to make two hundred bucks the easy way—taking a small dive and a long swim on the Auditorium boxing mat.

"No, Frenchy, we don't call it a 'fix.' It's a training fight. This means that the load of slag moves just enough to teach our guy a few new tricks. He'll help Paul's timing and improve his confidence. Nothing really is said on this situation. The load gets the message when he gets the bus ticket. He's all pro. He's done the same thing in probably 40 other cities. Forty other first-timers."

"But the Commissioner's office," Frenchy almost shouted, "will they give this guy the approval? You know the stamp, the okay?"

"Cinch," answered Regan. "They will because they like the promoter. He's been steady and since he owns that supper club in Wisconsin they get free meals and a chance to look like big shots. Jack puts on good cards and some great main events. But he knows you have to nurture young fighters. So the semi-rigged fight. Got it?

"Now, to the guy Burke is going to fight. From what I gather, he's just been released from a sanitarium for some type of non-threatening lung condition. But he's got nothing contagious. Paul should nail him in at least two or three rounds and maybe less. But we want Paul to have enough time to move around a little to impress the fans.

"And, oh, yes, Raleigh is going to invite the whole Minnesota football team and coach Murray Warmath to watch the show for free. Jesse says he's got some kids who'll hang up over 400 big green posters of Irish Paul in every barber shop within 50 miles. We're going to make him the hero of the barber shoppers. Over 100,000 guys get haircuts around the Twin Cities every month. If ten percent show up for the fight, it's a sell out."

The usually laconic Jesse beamed.

"I've even got some young guys with cars and Raleigh knows how to cover western Wisconsin with the same posters but we've only got five weeks and that isn't much time. By the way, we need about three hun for the posters. Raleigh is also going to send out notices about Burke's debut in his monthly newsletter."

Regan brought up something that could provide a tad of agitation for himself, namely his feelings about writing factual columns on Burke without crossing the line of hucksterism and taking advantage of his own media situation. Integrity was the hitch.

"I think I'll write one solid column about Burke's potential and the interesting aspects of having a grid star try a new sport. I don't think anybody really cares about who he fights in this first match. Raleigh plans to invest double his usual budget for advertising, which means the paper does very well on the ads. But I'm not going to hoopla this guy from Milwaukee like he's the second coming. Same goes for Burke. Just a factual story and let the fans decide if they want to see a comer."

"Good idea," agreed Jesse. "You're in a tough spot but don't forget, Race, you've been the number one boxing supporter and writer on the paper for a damn long time. It's nobody's business who really owns the fighter.

"You can also look at it another way, Race. Your paper plans on owning a big chunk of the Minnesota Vikings. I'm sure nobody's asking them to cut down on the publicity because of their financial interest in the team."

As usual, Frenchy broached the subject which interested him most, "What's Burke going to make?"

"Raleigh decided on $500, which is a whale of a piece for a first-time fight. I'm guessing the most in Twin Cities history," Race answered and made a suggestion:

"Let's run out to White Bear Lake tonight if you guys are open. The old heavyweight, Freddy Lenhart, is going to give Paul the once over on the heavy bag in the basement under his saloon. My old welterweight hero, My Sullivan, is going to be there, too. He's a little off-line but he still knows boxing. But we may have to listen to him preach about the values of Socialism first. He's really into politics." Regan rolled his eyes.

That night, about two dozen White Bear Lake boxing fans were on hand to watch Burke hammer the heavy bag, shadow box and skip rope for 45 minutes. Lenhart couldn't have been more appreciative. "He moves as well as any big man I've seen around these parts. It's easy to see how he played football so well. Good balance. I like his jab and his hook off the jab."

Sullivan was even more enthusiastic. "Reminds me of myself the way he moves and then sets himself to unload. I like his half-steps and yes, that left hook off the jab could stop a mule. All the weapons. But has anyone measured his heart?"

Burke overheard My's observation.

"Hey, Mr. Sullivan, you don't tackle a 210 pound low fanny fullback without some heart. I've hit a lot of them."

Everyone was grinning now. Van Avery, who had heard about the workout, even loosened his tie, marring his usual sartorial splendor.

"Too late to get in?" he asked of nobody in particular. "This kid moves as well as Jim Delaney who was the prettiest big man who ever slipped a toe into a pair of ring shoes. I like Burke's size, his bulk, his agility. Can the right hand hurt?"

"Hurt?" Jesse repeated. "You saw him nearly tear off the big bag. I doubt he knows how to hold back. The Milwaukee slag may not be around for number two."

Raleigh rarely saw a boxing figure he could completely trust. Unsavory managers would hold him hostage for more money minutes before a fight. He was known as a soft touch to most of the eastern crowd who looked at the Twin Cities as a cradle of naiveté. His Auditorium ticket takers were known to let in as many as three and four hundred friends to his major fights.

Raleigh was also a notorious card player. He'd been known to lose a night's fight profits three hours before the bouts playing gin rummy with self-proclaimed friends in the old St. Francis Hotel. He was a good card player, but always managed to find three or four better ones with whom to deal and duel.

It was rumored that Raleigh put too much trust in those who had been known to team up against him in high stakes games. Still, he always bounced back and nobody really knew how many boxing tickets he sold to guys who were supposed to be dealing him bad cards. Maybe he was the sharp one.

Raleigh ran an enormous supper club on the shores of the Apple River in Wisconsin, just 45 miles from the Twin Cities. Nationally, he was known as the man who inaugurated river floating on inner tubes and just five years before he entertained a crew from Life magazine. His place was immortalized with a cover shot and three pages of action photos.

He claimed the boxing business brought untold numbers of customers to his Rivers Edge restaurant. His wife, Alice and six children had their doubts. For the past year, his suppliers had demanded that his club pay its bills on delivery. Still, he always came up with his

$300 for the boxing license fee and also the advances for the entourage of boxers and trainers he brought in from all over the country. These included headliners like Joey Giardello, Kid Gavilan, Joey Maxim and Harry (Kid) Matthews. Dapper Del Flanagan was his mainstay; a dancing darling who was capable enough to derail the great Sandy Saddler in Detroit.

The fact that Raleigh used to wrestle all takers in carnivals around the midwest supplied the answer to how he lived; he was a born juggler. He juggled his boxing and food businesses along with his gaming escapades while still managing to gobble record sized triple dip ice cream cones and see three or four movies in a week.

His bookkeeper could not fathom his dealings, let alone find him. It was said that an observer from the Internal Revenue Service had once spent three days going over Jack's books, only to throw his hands up in exasperation. Bewildered, the Fed claimed the books would confuse the comptroller for the Rockefellers.

Raleigh could be cunning and assume a layer of vulnerability almost at the same time.

He could whittle down fighters' guarantees by pleading a deplorably unsteady economic situation. And then he'd hire the old cronies to man the turnstiles, the same shameless lot who had let in every acquaintance they had ever made. One night the deplorable situation was exposed when the Auditorium freight elevator got hung up between floors to reveal 33 gate crashers.

Another time, Raleigh hired a professional "counter" to tabulate every living body who actually commandeered a seat in the St. Paul Auditorium. It turned out that Jack had sold just 3,000 tickets to the fight but 4,400 warm bodies were nestled in the building.

"I like people, but not that much," was Jack's response.

Anyway, Raleigh hired Scotty McLean, a 70-year-old ex-brewery worker who had hung around the gym for years, as Burke's trainer. He knew the basics, he could plug a cut with a cold quarter and he knew the right things to say between rounds. When he found out that Burke's foe was named Pedro "Weasel" Jones, Scotty blinked and said to no one in particular, "With that name he'd better carry a gun."

It seemed that way to everyone at the noon weigh-in at Gallivan's. Burke scaled a turbulent 215 pounds. A two-ton boulder would have side-stepped him. Weasel Jones came in at a tight, drawn 188, but from the looks of his sparse sinews somebody must have put a foot on the scales.

Regan whispered, "Pep'd spot this guy 60 pounds and jab him out in two." Even Burke appeared to have compassion and whispered to Regan, "I really feel sorry for this poor guy. Look at those bags under his eyes. He could carry a week's clothing in them."

Actually, it was a bit pathetic. Weasel would have been no more than an even bet against Little Orphan Annie. Burke could probably win by hitting him with the back of his hand. In fact, a close miss might turn the trick.

Then something occurred on the third floor of the St. Francis hotel that might be seen as a foreboding portent of things to come, had anyone noticed. Burke did not take a leisurely nap. He only turned and tossed and stared at the cracks in the ceiling.

By the time for the Burke-Jones bout, close to 3,500 boxing fans, including 40 Minnesota football players, were on hand to see the new white phenom; part beast, part Irish, part gentleman, part killer, an irrepressible combination everyone wanted to believe was the next great White Hope.

Regan sat alone, apart from his cohorts, in the fourth row on the aisle. He began to watch a strange scene as the bout unfolded. Weasel bobbed and weaved and flickered a few faint lefts in the opening round. Paul was content to circle and circle and circle and move his hands close to his body in the fashion of a pistoning locomotive wheel. He actually managed not to throw a punch in three minutes. Odd.

Between rounds, McLean could be heard to shout in Burke's ear, "You've played around long enough! Just punch him out, Paul."

The second round was a duplicate of the first, except that Weasel landed a looping semi-slapping non-destructive right to the head and quickly apologized with a nod. At the end of this round, Weasel wore a puzzled expression in his corner. He was not worried about whether he would eventually be bludgeoned into unconsciousness, but whether he could keep moving another three minutes. At this rate he could become the first fighter in history to K.O. himself through exhaustion without being hit.

Regan began to twist in his seat while watching the stupefied expressions on the faces of the Gopher footballers. They were ready to believe their pal could unseat the Black Knight with a scowl. "Must be setting him up for the K.O.," one gridder muttered.

In round three, Weasel went down from a left jab that never got within six inches of his chin. However, the fall was so flagrantly obvious that referee Bill McCabe insisted he get up and continue. Weasel caught his breath while slumping on the second strand of ropes as the referee wiped off his gloves.

In an effort to display a sense of integrity and perhaps leave himself open to a deciding blow from Burke, the Weasel began rushing in. Accidentally, he landed three more powder puff strokes before Burke finally retaliated with a telegraphed right hand that missed by the length of Long Island.

At the end of the round, McLean could contain his anxiety no longer and screamed at Burke, "Christ kid, land a punch or do something! You could lose the fight!"

A heckler in the balcony screamed in a voice that could penetrate an armored car, "Burke, I hope it's not true you're Irish, or I'll never celebrate St. Pat's day again!"

In the fourth round, Burke managed to throw three left jabs, none of which could have been presumed to score a point even by a near-sighted man in the fifteenth row of the balcony. The crowd was beginning to jeer. Weasel, as if to say, "To hell with it," empowered his frail frame with enough energy to throw half a dozen more punches.

Even Burke's football teammates were showing signs of embarrassed agitation for their hero, yelling, "Take him out, Paul! Take him out!" He had resorted to his shoulder movements and locomotive-action forearms without, however, launching any semblance of a dangerous projectile. He was posing not poking; he was circling not cornering; he was being exposed as a fraud, not a warrior.

In response to several jabs on the shoulder from friends around him, demanding to know what was wrong with Burke, the humiliated Race now decided to move further back. By the beginning of the fifth round he was sitting 20 rows back and silently sweating himself into a pre-stroke syndrome.

Burke seemed to flurry for a spell but swung wildly, missed and nearly decapitated himself on the top rope. Weasel then clung to him as they danced a waltz to the conclusion of the stanza.

In Burke's corner, McLean was swearing quietly. He was running out of poise and inspiration. "You stupid son-of-a-bitch, you're throwing away a million dollars!" To which the puffing gridder replied, "But, God, Scotty, I'd hate to hurt this poor little guy."

On that note, Scotty gulped down his chaw of tobacco, spit carelessly into the press sections, hitting veteran writer Dick Cullum on his thick-lensed glasses, and as he carried the pail down the steps muttered, "Friggin' first time I lost a fixed fight."

Right he was. Weasel, now smelling his first victory in over four years, threw caution to the wind and winged nearly 20 pathetic punches, none of which would have brought an ailing grandmother to her knees. Burke merely blinked, went through useless motions and got off a couple of wayward blows that landed on nothing. He did manage to get tangled up in the referee's feet and, at one point, tumbled to the canvas while the crowd hooted in derision.

As the bell rang, Burke made his only aggressive venture of the fight, hugging Weasel, who was on the verge of collapse, his pathetic frame heaving in near convulsive gasps. Burke's action alone nearly crushed the dehydrated Weasel who needed the referee to hold up his hand after it was announced he had won a split decision! The judge who voted for Burke later apologized to his wife. She advised him to see an optometrist.

At the Lexington bar later that night, Regan stopped for a triple whiskey, a splash of water and no ice. In a secluded corner, he explained to Rogers and Landreville, "I just took Burke to the airport. He's so ashamed I actually felt sorry for him. Claims he just froze because he couldn't bear to hit the poor slob because he thought Weasel must be sick.

"I asked him if he was a damn humanitarian and hadn't he ever heard of putting someone out of their misery? He told me he could be a killer in self-defense but he couldn't focus on hurting an innocent bystander. I told him the 'innocent bystander' just kicked the living hell out of all of us to the tune of ten million bucks.

"Then he cried like a baby. And I actually put my arms around this big Ferdinand and put him on the plane to Las Vegas where he was going to celebrate if he won. I guess he's got this stewardess or something. Lord, the kid came out of it with five hundred bucks. Raleigh won't talk to me and the kid's afraid to go back to his classes. I hope he craps in that silk bathrobe we gave him. I've become an ogre. The friggin' world is upside down and guess what I just did coming into this joint?"

Jesse and Frenchy couldn't begin to.

"I bought a damn hot rosary from Weasel's manager. . . . three bucks. Not bad. Here, let me show it to you."

Chapter Four

Dead Fish and Lost Legs

It was time for Swede Larsen to surface at Gallivan's.

"Where the blazes you been? I thought you got hit with one of your bowling balls," Landreville wanted to know.

The always present cigarette almost leaped from his mouth as Swede explained his latest nerve-tearing experience.

"Damn, haven't you heard? I almost got blown away two weeks ago. You know that little office of mine that kinda sits right on the intersection of Concord and Robert Street? Well, God, I'm sitting there mindin' my own business around midnight and suddenly there's this incredible explosion six feet from my desk.

"Next thing I know, I'm looking in the face of a '59 Olds' hood. Lord, I thought I was had! I mean, this SOB is no more than just inches from my face. Bricks and plaster are flying and the car's engine is still revving. I'm so scared I nearly crapped in my pants!"

"Oh, no! You did it in your pants?" Landreville repeated.

"About four feet of the hood and wheels are all inside my office and all hell is breaking loose," Swede goes on.

"The bar customers are all tryin' to figure out what happened and nobody could believe it. There's dust and junk everywhere. It seemed like half an hour but I guess in about five minutes the squads and ambulances are pulling up and trying to get the driver out of the car. He's got his face diced like it went through a grinder at Peter's Meats. Blood's all over everything.

"And guess who was at the wheel? Remember Rick Zasmada, the ex-Golden Gloves heavy champ? He's the guy! Lost control coming down Concord, turned too sharp and plows into my office. Jeeze, I'd have been dead if it was a Mac truck."

Regan nearly fell off his chair with excitement. "Zasmada? Damn, he's my old buddy. We used to go to Bar Harbor together up on Gull Lake. We were single then. Good guy. We'd dance all night. A real party guy. But who am I to judge? Was he sober? How come our papers didn't report it? I didn't see a thing."

Larsen was so enmeshed in his problem that he almost chewed up his lighted ciggie. "I dunno. Just a tiny piece in your paper, way back inside. I'd have thought it was a big story . . . local boxer nearly gets killed trying to ram West Side bowling alley. Helluva story. I could have used the publicity."

"How bad did Rickie get hurt?" Regan wanted to know.

"God, I think he had something like 350 stitches just in his face! I mean this guy took some punches in the ring, but nothing like this. On the other hand, he could've wound up a Jayne Mansfield with his head as a paper weight on my desk."

"Good looking guy, too," explained Race. "Real strong athlete, too. One night at Bar Harbor we were in some gals' cabin and he was trying to pull open a jammed refrigerator door. It was a pretty big sucker and he pulled the whole damn thing down on top of him! Oranges and sausages and pop bottles were rolling all over the floor.

"The girls and me thought he was crushed. But Jeez, he just grunted and groaned and actually managed to get the big thing off and wiggle out. He was bloodied but unbowed, so to speak. I remember he had a lemon slice jammed in his ear."

Van, who had been sitting back in wide-eyed interest, noted that he, too, knew the fighter.

"Rickie could go in the street too, boys. I recall a couple of years ago when the Masher, Marty O'Phelan, came at him. Marty was an ex-Eagle Scout turned street fighting monster. He challenged Rick behind the Belmont Bar.

"Zas could punch, but each time he'd knock down Marty the big Irishman would get up and roar and spit out a few curses and a couple teeth and keep coming. Finally, he tackled Zas around the legs and threw a bear hug on him just before the police arrived. If it had lasted another five minutes, Zas would have been bear-hugged into oblivion. Marty didn't know how to box but he might have torn Zas' arms off if the cops hadn't landed."

"Well, that's where I've been," the bald Swede explained. "I'm still working on the insurance trying to clean up the joint, too. Maybe it was an omen. I told you my place is going downhill. I'd sell it to my relatives but they'd screw me out of every penny. Funny how some of my family hates me. Frankly, I don't know what I ever did to any of them."

But this was Swede's and Regan's morning. Most of the Longshots would just listen as they extolled plans for their second annual St. Paul Boat and Camping Show in the Auditorium basement. If you asked why they went second class into the cellar instead of the bright main arena the answer was twofold: the pro wrestlers had locked up the main arena on one night of their three-day weekend show. They also liked the basement since the rent was a third of what it cost to go in the main arena.

"Sure, it's a bit dingy and there are more pillars than boats," Regan would explain, "but it's the smart move. It's really a steal for about three hundred bucks a day. Old Ed Furni, the Auditorium manager, knew what he was doing when he offered us the basement."

Furni was an aging Italian, barely five feet tall. He loved Regan's column and his creativity and the enthusiasm he showed for the downtown area.

After an original boat show promoter had gone belly up at the Auditorium three years previously because he spent a ton of lettuce on a huge band along with radio personalities like Halsey Hall and full-page newspaper ads, Furni told Race, "I've got a list of all the boat people who had displays. They'll all rent again. If you go downstairs, I can show you where you can trim the cost by eight grand. That'll put you in the black."

Since Regan was used to tapping Furni for freebies to the Auditorium theater's choice stage productions, like Carousel and Oklahoma, he had a warm feeling toward any of Ed's suggestions. Swede was an eager co-promoter, since he liked boats along with race cars and could always manage a chunk of spare time in the afternoons. He also relished the idea of getting into a substantial perennial promotion since he figured his bowling emporium's days were numbered because of urban renewal projects.

Their first show had netted over four grand and Regan was elated since it was an event which demanded nothing of his sports expertise. It was worthy of good media coverage since it brought over 3,000 boaters downtown. The outdoor writers would cover it with zeal and Race knew enough to make certain each of them had a choice supply of Canadian Royal and boxes full of the hottest lures.

It was Van who put a bright new idea into their minds for the coming event. "You gotta get something special in that show; some competition or maybe even something with a streak of luck, like drawing for a trip to Malibu. Something with a dynamic twist. Two bucks at the gate deserves more than just a chance to look at a bunch of boats that most of them'll never be able to afford. It's just a parade of wasted dreams."

So it was Regan's resourceful imagination which proposed they build a large tank and fill it with live trout. Then, for just twenty-five cents the kids could fish for half an hour or until they caught a trout. The attraction might even make a few bucks, although transporting a thousand fishes from a Star Prairie, Wisconsin, fish farm was to cost two grand.

The deal was done and the night before opening, Swede and Race sat sipping gin on the rocks in the night watchman's office at the Auditorium around 10 p.m. They watched, with almost an arrogant pride, the trout being unloaded from a mobile holding tank into the elaborate 30x40 foot lake-shaped plastic pool, complete with air hoses like a giant aquarium would use.

Both men intended to sleep on cots at the scene so they could be up bright and early for the 8 a.m. opening. As Regan pointed out to Swede, "By 9 o'clock, we may have a lineup back to Seven Corners three deep, waiting to deliver their fresh green to our ticket windows."

"Jeez," said Swede on his third gin, "you paint pretty pictures, Regan. I love to hear you talk like that." Swede then giggled. He never learned to belly up a real laugh, just a fourth grade girl's giggle.

The promotion appeared certain to make a profit. Over 40 cabin cruisers, speedboats and canoes were jauntily arrayed. There was fishing equipment and an assortment of water-ski and swimsuit displays in a dizzying variety of booths. Hopeful the early March weather would turn a shade sour, Race and Swede figured nasty temps brought even the avid outdoorsmen inside for expositions of this type. It was too early for yardwork and Minnesota's huge fishing opener was still weeks away.

Swede awoke from a restless sleep at approximately 3 a.m.

"Race, wake up! Wake up! What the hell's that funny sound, like gasping or slurping? There's something haywire in this big barn!"

Shaking his head to clear the effects of four gins, Race tried to bounce off the cot and almost tumbled onto the bare concrete. He was chilly in his underwear but not nearly as chilly as the trout in the makeshift pond should have been.

"God!" Regan screamed, "I forgot something. Those fish guys told me to keep the water around 65 degrees. Oh hell, feel it! It's gotta be almost 80 degrees or more! We're going to lose a thousand trout if we don't do something. Jeeze, Bill, we'll have the biggest damn fish fry in the world if these babies all die. Not to mention the stink!"

The usually phlegmatic Swede was stunned into a rare over-statement, "This is a helluva monumental catastrophe. I think some of them are dying already. Who can we call? Who knows anything about trout dying from heat stroke?"

"Look," said a trembling Race, trying to get control of his nerves, "if it's the temperature we need ice, lots of ice. But where do we get a glacier at three in the morning?"

"I'll try the St. Paul Ice Company," Larsen answered. "Maybe they can save our fannies. But how do we get anybody at the company at this hour? By the time they get here we've got a thousand fish corpses."

"Try calling somebody!" Regan shouted in desperation. "I'll get the big net I saw in a fishing boat. Some are floating around on their backs already. I'll try capturing the dead ones."

Larsen made four calls before he got the name of an ice company official who promised to rouse a driver and get to the Auditorium within two hours with enough ice to bail out the drooping denizens of the deep.

"Hey, in two hours we're up to our arm-pits in dead trout!" Regan shouted.

"But Race, what can I do?" Swede pleaded. "And something else: it'll take them an hour or so to get enough ice into the pool to bring down the temperature. What did you say they charged us for the fish?"

"Maybe a buck a head, but that was delivered."

"What the hell does delivered have to do with it? We've got a fishy holocaust going on and there's nothing we can do. Look at 'em! Most of them are croaking. Oh, God, why didn't we just go with the boats? This mass murder'll kill our profits."

"Easy, baby," Race consoled, "if we save even a couple of hundred nobody will know the difference. If a dozen kids catch a fish the word'll be out that we've got a hot attraction."

"But if they all die and they start smelling up the joint, what'll we tell 'em?" Swede wanted to know. "That we're such dumb slobs that we didn't know that the water should be chilled?"

The St. Paul Ice Company roared to the rescue in less than two hours. By then, nearly half of the trout had succumbed as the temperatures climbed upward. Three amazed icemen managed to pull and haul and lift nearly three dozen 50-pound chunks of ice into the pool. Just to make sure the temps wouldn't rise, they poured in hundreds of small ice chips.

It was nearly six o'clock when Regan, Larsen and the icemen finally retrieved over 700 dead trout. Most of the others looked as if they had been on a three-day binge but appeared able to struggle through the show. The ice company promised deliveries every six or seven hours. The dead fish were laid in rows along a back wall. "I'll get some of the young help to put them in sacks and get rid of them later on," Regan promised.

"That's all we need, 700 dead fish to stink up the joint," Swede reminded him.

The show opened with nearly 100 ticket buyers in line. Everything appeared to go well until a tired looking deadbeat with a bent nose and gutterman's twitch demanded his two bucks back.

"Same junk as last year, same boats."

"But did you notice the nice fish tank?" Regan asked.

"Are you stupid or what?" the customer wanted to know. "Nobody's catching any fish. You probably don't even have any in the pool."

Race used all his charm to steer the guy out the door and aim him in the direction of Red Fioritto's bar. "Here's five bucks. Go have a couple of shots on us and try to be a little quiet with your complaint."

The whiner headed up the street. 'Wish I was going with him,' Regan mused to himself.

It was nearly two a.m. the next morning when Regan first noticed the terrible stench. It would have asphyxiated a bull moose during rutting season.

'Goddamn it. I was just forgetting about the damn fish and here the kids must've forgotten to get some of those greasy things out of here. What else?'

Regan looked at Swede who was snoring in a rhythm that would have made a bongo drummer sound anemic. He shook Swede's shoulder.

"Wake up, Swede. Time for another little job."

The little job took nearly two hours before all the dead fish were dragged out and deposited into a dumpster.

That Sunday night, Swede was stuffing a duffel bag with the second and final day's take of cash. "I figure off hand we made maybe four grand but lost about a thou on the fried fish. But it was a decent haul. And lucky Race, that your wife thought of lighting up all those perfumed candles in the morning to eat up those nasty odors. Jeeze, what if the health authorities had closed us up before the last day?"

Regan didn't answer. He was looking at the floor.

"Maybe this thing's getting too big for us, Swede."

As was the usual case, neither Swede nor Regan had counted all the players in the locker room. The show actually made only $614.34. The expense of the elaborate pool, the stiff trout and all the shenanigans with the ice company whacked the profit.

"It was a work of art," Race would tell the Longshots the next week. "But I'll never eat trout again."

Almost on the heels of this near-disaster, Regan got a call from Billy Ivory. He was executive secretary of the Catholic Athletic association and wanted to know where he could make a few bucks for their youth programs. Billy also wanted to help a teen-aged roost for alcoholics purchase sports uniforms.

"Try runnin'," Regan said in a matter of fact voice.

"You don't sound like the old Race to me," Billy rejoined. "What's this runnin' stuff?"

Race perked up.

"Oh, Billy, it's the new hot thing with the young crowd. Every jerk who owns a pair of two buck shorts from a garage sale wants to run. You know, distance running. Marathoning. You charge these saps an entry fee and pick a silly place to run and stick four hundred nut-heads on a course. Then give away about fifty bucks worth of plaques or certificates suitable for framing. Then you take their cash and use it for your cause. Strictly a nice lean, legit deal and you can do it every year."

"Where do we run?" Ivory wanted to know, "and how far?"

"Hey, Billy, there's 22 lakes and 200 parks in the Twin Cities."

"But there's a zillion city officials and getting permission might take all year. You know city officials."

"Hey, listen Billy, what about Midway stadium? With the Saints gone, they're dying for some renters. I'll bet you get it for a couple of hun. Just make out a course around the stadium. Have 'em run it a couple of times then romp through the parking lot and then along the train embankment and then out a couple of blocks where there are no houses.

"You know, quiet territory on a Sunday morning. You won't disturb a sleeping sheep. Hell, you can make some pretty good bucks. I can give a charity like yours a nice little shot in the column.

"And don't forget to have ribbons and poles showing the way and maybe you can get six or seven miles out of it and even invite the girls to run," Race suggested.

By now Ivory was completely sold and pitched Race.

"Would you be on the committee?"

How could Race refuse? Billy ran the CAA golf tourney and always invited Regan. Last year he had made a friend for life of Regan, who was turned in by a jealous sports scribe and links rival for using souped up golf balls. Regan had written for them from a company in New England and they were supposed to add a hundred yards to his drives. The trouble was, they sounded strange when he hit them off the tee—like a pitchfork rifling through a pile of rocks. And then there was the roll. Downhill on a warm day the ball might bounce and hop to Dubuque.

"Nobody's ball can roll like that!" cried Regan's foe, who demanded an inspection. Since they were playing for two bucks a point, this was a serious issue. The antagonist fielded a protest with the CAA committee and somebody identified the balls as a well-advertised type of out-lawed zoomer pellet.

At the inquiry, Ivory and tournament president Joe Azzone upheld Regan's ball as legitimate and pointed out there was no specific rule against any type of ball in the CAA book of golf etiquette. Regan eventually won second prize and so unnerved was the complainant that it was rumored he had refused to attend mass for a month. Regan was happy the guy didn't notice that he also kept the mystery balls encased in ice in sandwich bags in his golf bag.

"Now that," Regan whispered to a friend, "was cheatin'."

To even Regan's surprise over 500 seemingly sane men and women showed up at Midway stadium on a warm spring morn to take part in a ten kilometer mini-marathon. The race would wind through, around, in and out of the Midway stadium complex. It would then veer off through relatively undeveloped railroad properties, go up an alley and wind back around and along the fringes of the stadium, flirting with Snelling Avenue and slipping through part of Hamline University's northern campus. Then back to the baseball park where it finished at home plate inside the stadium. The route was lined with volunteers and marked with flags from used car lots which Van had found soaking in rain puddles after sales.

Ivory and Regan knew there was something amiss when the race's leaders, sighted in the final kilometer, suddenly disappeared from view before the corner of the parking lot. A spotter relayed the alarming message, "Can't find the six or seven leaders! They seem to have made a wrong turn. Maybe some kids stole the direction flags."

The usually unflappable Ivory literally jumped into the air.

"What? How can they disappear? Who the devil is leading the pack, Wrong Way Corrigan?"

At that very moment, three runners minced their way into the stadium through an uncharted maintenance door in right field, apparently believing they were leading the field. Meanwhile, back on the course, the true but bewildered leaders, who had lost track of their trek through a paucity of directional flags, had wandered nearly five hundred yards out of their way and were in danger of being run over by trucks at a Snelling Avenue intersection.

Indeed, they were lost. And as they jockeyed among themselves, they were heard to argue the merits of the event. One put it quite strongly through clenched teeth, "Friggin' amateurs."

Nearly half the field got its money back. The CAA added up the cost of printed flyers, tools of the game, security and prizes and determined it was more effort than it was worth.

"What the hell," shrugged Race to Ivory over a shot of whiskey and two onion covered dogs at the Coney Island on St. Peter Street, "welcome to the Longshots."

"The what?" a sour Billy asked.

Chapter Five

Hey, Goulet, You Forgot the Words!

There had been a fascination between Race and motorcycles since he had teamed up with Swede Larsen to stage the International Cycle Exhibition at the Prom ballroom a few years earlier. Regan always insisted it was the first of its kind. The manager of the dance emporium later professed there'd never be another one.

Over 5,000 cycle enthusiasts turned out on a couple of soggy week nights to ogle over 100 of the newest two-wheel models and some antique bikes. Impetus was supplied by a McDonalds' coupon campaign from a couple of the local hamburger havens. The show was deemed a total success with profits of nearly $3,000. That is, until the morning after the event when it came time to evacuate the premises.

Now, you must understand the respect with which the Prom on the Midway was held. This was the dance arena that handled all the big name bands from the '40s and '50s and which one night had crammed more than 4,000 dancers into a space which normally held half that amount. Of course, that was to see and hear the immortal Glenn Miller. Fire marshals chewed their nails for fear of a catastrophic stampede, but through God's intervention and the fact nobody had enough room to dance, any sort of flamboyancy, which might have triggered mayhem, was prohibited.

As a young man inheriting the job of keeping sanctity and saneness intact, Harry Given patrolled the Prom premises like a night stalker. "The floor," Harry would say with reverence, "is one of a kind. It has history in every board."

So it was with a tad of reluctance that Given finally agreed to let Larsen and Regan parade the cycles. "Only if," he cautioned unremittingly, "that they are devoid of even one drop of liquid which could mar the floor. Remember, not one drop in those bikes!"

His orders were supposedly carried out with a thoroughness that would make security chiefs at Fort Knox blush with embarrassment.

But on the morning after, Given almost screamed. There, right near the center of the floor, was a sprawling 12 by 18 foot dark splotch of something that could have caused no more horror in the heart of Given than the discovery of a boa constrictor in the women's room.

"My God!" he roared at Regan over the phone, "this is my job! This is my future! The owner's due in Friday and he'll have me by the balls. How could this happen? How could these slobs let this happen? I only hope, Regan, the owner doesn't want to sue you, too!"

Regan gave the situation only a moment's thought. "Can't you paint some pretty flowers around the oil and pretend it's a surrealistic design?"

"Are you completely insane? Ruin the best dance floor in the country? This hardwood floor is the best looking dance surface in America," Given whined.

Regan and Larsen gave a half of their $2,700 in profits to Given to get the damn disfigured boards polished—or shaved—or whatever. The ugly stain survived all efforts to remove it. And Given survived threats from his boss. But the promoters had seen the last of the cycle promotions at the Prom. Regan contended that you'd have a better show on concrete anyway; never eliminating the possibility that the cycles would ride again somewhere.

That's why Larsen and Regan were all ears when Thunder Klunder, the cyclist cult hero, invited them to a hill climb on the steep banks of the countryside near the small but sporting city of Red Wing.

As they pondered another cycle event of some sort, Jesse said he'd like to be in on any deal involving the wild young culture that was threatening to make autos disappear with their heavy influx among the brash upstarts and leather worshippers.

"Let's go to the hill climb and study those wild loonies," Jesse suggested quietly. "Maybe there's a buck somewhere. I understand that there are close to 50,000 cyclists in Minnesota. They're growing by 5,000 a year. They could be the hottest commodity on the horizon. Let's get in on the ground floor."

With Thunder pointing out the technicalities, the little group took along their wives and Thunder's fiancé to see the Sunday climb. During the afternoon over 40 rip-roaring cyclists rampaged up the sharp crest. Some somersaulted over backwards as they lost balance. Others killed their engines with a groan, caught in impossible terrain. More bounded off the course to crash into boulders or logs. It actually was a rarity to see three or four cyclists hit the top of the 200-foot course.

After the show, Dots Regan boarded a big Indian cycle and, without proper instructions, guided it deep into a cornfield. Unable to find the braking mechanism, she eventually tumbled amid the stalks.

"See, even Dots likes it!" Race beamed. "When she likes something well enough to get into it we've got a real entrepreneurial gem."

"But what kind of show?" Jesse asked.

"A hill climb, of course," Regan answered. "Only with a tougher, meaner hill and a lot more publicity. Also, bigger entry fees and a much bigger trophy. These are amateurs. We'll do it with real class. And I've got a hunch there aren't 500 people in the state who really have ever seen one of these. We'll build a course and call it Suicide Hill. Like it? Suicide Hill! I think that's got a ring to it, just like Fenway Park and Soldier's Field. It's got to have that ring."

Jesse was unprepared for such optimism, even from Regan. His business sense kicked into the scheme with overdrive. "Hey, Race, we've got to get the cycle group behind it and, I hate to mention it, but insurance, too."

"Insurance?" Regan was taken aback. The mere mention of insurance had always left Regan feeling as vulnerable as a naked cherub in a blizzard.

"Sure," Jesse pointed out. "If one of the nuts gets loose into the crowd or kicks a brick into somebody's pusser, who's responsible? Actually, it won't be as bad as you think. Maybe five hundred bucks. Lots of liability. I can make some deals. A lot depends on where it's at and if we can control the crowd. These nitwits were just lucky today."

Regan thought for a moment, scratched his neck and put his arm around Dots. He promised Jesse that he had an idea for a site which he fantasized would be beautiful. But he thought he'd have to cut the guy with the land in on the deal.

Early the next day, Regan got a call from Larsen. "Been thinking, Race," the stoic Swede explained, "I think I'll pass up the hill climb. My damn bowling alley needs resurfacing, my wife's mother is sick in Indiana and my blood pressure's going through the roof."

"Blood pressure? I didn't know you had any. I thought you were a typical Scandinavian iceberg."

"Well, I've got an idea that we should look into, Race. We'll have to work fast because we'll only have two or three weeks to pull it off. Try to get down to the alleys for lunch and we'll hash it over."

Regan also learned the same day that his paper would be sending him to cover the return fight of Muhammad Ali and Sonny Liston in Lewiston, Maine. Not to mention, one of his daughters had requested a swimming pool and the other was opting for a horse. Regan's mind was swirling. It was hectic. It was magic.

'Lord, I hope I've still got friends in the paper's credit union.'

Race decided to hook up with Swede on his new brainchild, whatever it was and postpone any action on the super cycle hill climb. Swede didn't come up with many creative ideas so Regan could hardly wait to plumb that glistening noggin. He drove over to Swede's aging pin palace.

The Swede was standing, hands on hips, legs astride a bowling lane, trying to explain to Regan the value of a new surface, better pins and brighter lights. "Got to get the damn scores up. These crackpots all want '300' scores and we've got to get ours up to challenge those fancy new alleys springing up in the suburbs."

Regan's fertile mind offered the suggestion, "Why not wind machines behind the bowlers to give them extra snap?"

Swede ignored him. "Come into the office. I think I've got a good idea. Not as spectacular as your wildies but pretty good."

Swede proceeded to point out that he had maybe 50 or 60 real racing nuts at his place and somebody was always talking about going to the Indianapolis race.

"I can get good tickets. My wife stays in contact with Jim McWhithey, who drove in the '500' of course. How about us renting a bus and taking these race fans down to Indy for two or three days? We could buy a couple of dinners and throw them a party. You know, the whole package for around two hun. I could line up 20 in one Saturday night.

"The thing is, we have to work fast. We'd only have about two weeks to promote it. But I could get at it as soon as I get back from Indiana where my mother-in-law lives. In fact, I can line up a hotel while I'm there."

"Try Lafayette," Regan was enthused. "That's where Purdue U is. I've stayed there and it's just north of Indy. Rooms in Indy'll be tougher to find than a bra in Bali. There's an old hotel in Lafayette and I bet we can stick two in a room for fifteen bucks."

Regan hummed a tune as he drove out to Hudson, Wisconsin, after leaving Larsen. He was thinking that they could get at least 40 in a bus at $200 a piece and give them a helluva time. Race figured he knew at least 20 of his friends who would kill to see the '500' up close. He figured he could even get a parking pass for the bus and that they'd get a good jump on the mob by coming back to Lafayette after the race. Jeeze, Regan thought, that Larsen could come up with some good ideas. For a Swede.

In Hudson, Regan drove past the exit and continued on to the J.R. Ranch, a sprawling 200 acres of hills and grass owned by his good friend John Rauchnot. Regan always called him "The Catcher." Simply because, Regan said, John was the "best softball catcher I ever saw. Rise balls or dippers, made no difference. John caught them all for over 20 years, including Minnesota's greatest—Johnny Vollmer."

The powerfully built, 6'2" Rauchnot was black-haired, strong-jawed, a low-keyed Italian with a beautiful Irish wife named Aggie. For years he was a hard working meat cutter in the South St. Paul packing industry. In a career change, he began catering dinners to the elite of Summit Avenue and eventually bought his choice piece of land just 30 minutes east of the Twin Cities. He turned his property into a tidy and successful eating and hotel complex, complete with indoor swimming pool, riding trails and special events.

The large, always freshly painted redwood buildings stood out. The restaurant was fashioned from an old barn and actually eight of the tables were situated in what had once been horse stalls. The swinging doors leading to each stall added a country atmosphere.

He also added a small herd of buffalo that Green Pay Packer zealots had once sprayed with green paint while celebrating a victory over the Vikings in the Twin Cities.

Rauchnot could seemingly do anything by himself. He cut his own meat, waited on tables, was a bartender in the afternoon and super-vised horse and hayrides throughout the year. As Race put it, "John could play the flute through his arse if they needed entertainment."

He also loved to dabble in promotions and never got tired of telling how one night Mickey Mantle showed up at the end of the bar in the off season and swapped stories until two o'clock in the morning. John then rented him a room.

One of John's sorties into the entertainment business was an annual rodeo in a large natural amphitheater behind his complex, just beyond his buffalo pen. Regan's mouth almost salivated when he pondered the mighty promotions that could be staged there. He thought Rauchnot was wasting it on rodeos—that is until Michael Landon, the handsome Bonanza star, appeared as a guest celebrity and the two-day event played to nearly 20,000 customers.

The shrewd Landon was a promoter's dream, helping Rauchnot with the hype at every turn. He confided to John, "You might want to spread the word around that my dad's Jewish, my mother's Irish and I've got my beautiful wife and kids with me. You never know, it might help."

Rauchnot said admiringly, "That Landon, was a helluva entertainer. He signed autographs and he kissed babies. The guy could turn a snake-wrestle into a money-machine."

Rauchnot always dreamed of putting a major rodeo in the St. Paul Auditorium and tried to get Regan interested in the investment. The writer grew far more interested after Landon's appearance put bags of moola into John's hands. However, at the moment Regan was more concerned over Rauchnot's hilly acreage.

"John, an idea. How about a motorcycle hill climb? You know, where those growling, snarling little bikes are roaring up a hill trying to get to the top?"

"Heard of 'em."

"Well, Jesse and I want to put one on out here. You get a piece of the action and the concessions. I think we'll score big. How does it sound?"

"Hey, if it brings in a couple of bucks, great! Forget the rent, just give me the food and beer. How many do you really think it can draw?"

It was the first time anyone had pinpointed the question to Race. In reflex response he answered, "At least 5,000 at a couple of bucks a head. I'll have to spend a little on getting your hill in shape. You know, that big one out there. We'll carve out a piece just to make it a little nastier."

John rubbed his forehead, scowled a trifle and said, "I think it'll work, but one thing, are these cyclists good buys or bad guys? I don't need any trouble out here."

"Hey, John, would I do that to you? They're good guys, real athletes. Besides, we can get the Hudson sheriff's office to patrol the highway. Listen, I've seen one of these. Take my word, there's no hassle. Besides, think of the bar business in Hudson. That town will want to run you for mayor."

Rauchnot laughed. "Mayor? Listen, I used to own a piece of one of those Hudson bars. But one night some tough guys tore it apart. It took two hours to get everything under control and I had to feed those cops freebies for a couple of years. Run for mayor? Run me out of town more likely."

A date in late August was picked and Regan slapped down a pair of double gins and hummed all the way back to St. Paul. Jeeze, a bus trip to Indy, the hill climb and the Ali-Liston fight in Maine. What a wonderful world. Life didn't get any better than this. And what if that dirtfest for bikers built a pool and bought a pony for the kids?

Regan wanted to make the trip to the fight in Lewiston a scenic jaunt so he rented a car in Boston. He managed to miss the exit for the coast four times and finally decided to drive opposite to the setting sun in the west, heading northeast under the influence of the powerful cocktail of gin and adrenaline.

Hey, Goulet, You Forgot the Words!

Within 48 hours, Regan had managed to reach battered old Lewiston, meet a boxing syndicate chief called Sal, and sit at a table in animated conversation with famed New York sports scribe Red Smith. A relative newcomer to the entertainment world, a singer named Robert Goulet, joined Smith and Regan.

Race had a way of insinuating himself into the hierarchy through a combination of youthful vigor, ingratiating smile and his ability to drink with the finest experts of the sauce.

Regan won Smith's admiration when he had sent him notes for a column about boxing legend, Willie Pep, winning that remarkable round from Jackie Graves without throwing a punch. Red penned a great piece on the subject. He was a midwesterner himself from Green Bay and was properly impressed with Race's candidness when he asked Race why his St. Paul paper had cancelled his syndicated column.

"Red," Regan said thoughtfully, "you're the best damn writer on the planet, but we have to be honest; your greatest stuff is when you write about deep sea fishing, horse racing and the heavyweight fights. The trouble is, Red, we don't have any sailfish or thoroughbreds or big-time heavies in Minnesota. Just a case of us unsophisticated suckers not understanding you eastern highbrows."

Red loved it and they covered a dozen subjects over the next two hours with Red concluding, "Wish you were with me in the Big Apple, Race. We could have a lot of laughs. Ever think of coming to New York?"

"Only to find a good Irish bar after the Lakers play the Knicks."

Regan was amazed that Goulet could sit mainly on the sidelines consuming three or four strong drinks with no appreciable change in attitude. "You ARE going to sing the National Anthem tonight, Bob?"

"Sure am," the dapper Goulet answered while scribbling his autograph on a pair of napkins for Race's daughters.

"Tough song," Regan advised.

"Well, I'm from Canada, so I really don't fear it," the optimistic Goulet answered.

Three things happened that night which were to make a lasting impression on Race.

First, when he arrived at the high school gym where the fight was held, a stranger in a white suit and pencil-sharp black mustache had usurped his seat, apologized for the intrusion and introduced himself as an artist from Rice Street in St. Paul. He explained to Race that he had seen his name and that of the newspaper on the press table and wanted to meet somebody from his hometown.

It was a half-hour before the card would begin so Race stepped back and watched the painter flip what seemed like reckless strokes of abandon and undisciplined flying oils at his canvas. Race shook his head and quickly surmised that 'this guy won't make it. I've seen house painters with better control of their hands.'

When the artist left for another vantage point, he handed Regan his card and explained that he was commissioned to do his first important work for Playboy magazine. The name on the card spelled out—Leroy Neiman. So what?

The second event to make an indelible impression on Regan that evening was Goulet's performance. He surmised the singer must be a little shaky when he messed up his $30 haircut on the ropes as he ascended into the ring. Of course, Goulet wrote shockingly dismal musical history that night, mangling the lyrics and tune to the National Anthem as millions heard and watched him in disbelief on their television screens.

Goulet did retain his poise as he climbed out of the ring, asking Regan, "How many around here could sing the Canadian anthem?"

Of course, the third unforgettable incident was the surprising and utter dismantling of Liston by the so-called invisible punch of Ali's that landed somewhere between Bangor and Sonny's left ear. Regan was astute enough to point out to his readers that if you looked closely at the sprawled form of Liston, his legs were twitching and trembling and moving in odd directions.

"Liston went down from an unimpressive looping right hand but he's only a shell. He'll never be heard from again," Regan prophesied. While others hinted that Liston was in the tank, Regan's perspective proved to be noteworthy. Liston was washed up. One of his brothers, who ran an elevator in a St. Paul building, later confided to Race, "Sonny's a lot older than they say. He was in jail for years."

For some reason that night, sitting alone in the hotel room, Race thought of his first date with Dots. He had taken her to the St. Paul Open golf tourney's pre-tee-off dinner at the Hotel St. Paul. The first person to ask her to dance was famed Slammin' Sammy Snead, resplendent in white suit and alligator shoes.

Race was thrilled. Later, he heard that after Sam introduced himself, Dots inquired, "What do you do for a living, Mr. Snead?" Not even his 14-inch missed putt for the Open title seemed to shake golf's idol like this query.

From that moment on, Race knew Dots was the girl for him. Sam never forgot. Year's later, he asked Race how he was getting along with Dots. "That little gal will put you in your place—and make you love going there."

Race was lonesome for home.

Chapter Six

Who Moved the Indy Track?

It was a buoyant mood that prevailed when the Longshots gathered at Gallivan's on a misty spring morning. However, Regan was still a little unsettled from an incident that happened the night he returned from the fight in Maine.

"Jeez, you won't believe this," he explained, "but do you guys realize that I might have killed a guy Friday night?"

An credulous Jesse Rogers blinked, shook his head, raised a heavy eyebrow and asked, "What? Killed a guy?"

"Yeah. Honest to God. I was supposed to make a speech at the Knights of Columbus dinner out on Snelling Avenue and there must have been a couple hundred people. This old guy named Pete came up before the dinner and asked if I'd tell an Irish joke he heard me give a couple of years before.

"It was about my grandfather falling into a makeshift grave in Erin Prairie, Wisconsin, that his wife and kids had dug. They wanted to scare the hell out of him for staying out late while he was campaigning for road commissioner. They knew he took a short-cut at night through the St. Pat's cemetery when he didn't take his horses with him. It was like an elephant trap, I guess and he landed in the mud and the dirt and passed out. Then he was supposed to have crawled up the slippery slides at dawn, shoved apart the remaining boughs and branches, looked at the dark, dreary cemetery and screamed, "This must be hell! If I meet the Devil I'll tell him I married his sister!"'

"Hey, not bad," Larsen grinned. "With your brogue, you can do it well."

"Yeah, but as I give the punch line the oldster sitting right in front of me starts laughing like a hyena. Then he tips over backwards and falls off his chair. He shakes a few times, rattles a little and conks out."

"Dies?" asked the astounded Rogers. "Really dies?"

"Jeez, yes he dies!" Regan emphasizes. "His friends are swarming all around and by the time they bring the paramedics he's gone like a tulip under a tank. His poor wife's bawling, his brother's groaning. All I can think of is, I murdered him with a joke!

"I've heard of speakers killing a crowd—but not really. Lord, I didn't have the friggin' guts to collect my two hundred. I was so surprised and embarrassed. Never knocked off a guy with a joke before. They called off the program along with my speech."

"Sad, Race," Frenchy agreed, "but it really was a pretty good joke."

"Hey, Frenchy," Regan admonished, "it wasn't funny to me. He was a nice old guy. I vowed then and there never to tell that one again."

Steaming coffee brought the enthusiasm back to the Longshots and the tasks at hand.

"Hear you're going to run a bus trip to the Indy 500," Frenchy asked Swede. "I thought of that, too. Didn't I, Race?"

"Yeah, Regan and me think we can make a few bucks. It's never been done around here. Got a bus for about $900 and it holds 40. We've got an indoor can and bar, rooms in Lafayette and Regan and I think we can get a load of good tickets.

"And the best part is we've got 30 signed up already from the bowling alley for $30 down. What amazes me is the fact that most of them aren't racing fans. They don't know an Offenhauser from an alligator."

"What's the total package?" Frenchy wanted to know.

"Just $250 and that includes a couple of free drinks, two box lunches and two night's lodging. Plus the tickets. That's not bad considering you don't have any driving cares, eh?

"We've also got a bar on the bus, boys, with the old firebrand, Regan here, bartending and telling the klutzes about the past glories of Indy. Who else includes a combination guide, history and bartender in a travel package?"

"What do you figure to make, Swede?" Frenchy urged.

"If we sell out, we can pocket maybe two grand. Mainly, it's a fun trip and Regan can get some great column material. You know, interviewing some of the locals on what they think about the big race."

Frenchy looked a little down. "Don't fret, Landreville; you can have a piece of it. I'm getting so busy at the alleys just keeping them in shape. Come on in, but bring a few customers and give us breakfast and box lunches from your new place—that Chain Link spa on Highway 12. OK, Race?"

Regan agreed it would be more fun with Frenchy along

Suddenly everyone seemed energized. Thunder Klunder was excited about a new cycle swap meet at the Minneapolis armory and eager to hear that Regan and Rogers were inviting him into their motorcycle hill climb. Landreville had hired an ex-con for four bucks an hour to paint the Chain Link.

"Got to watch the con," Frenchy explained. "He's got a druggie girlfriend and he collects guns. Some people say the guns are stolen. But he's making the new place very spiffy."

A telephone call from hockey promoter Egan interrupted the proceedings.

"Race, have I got an idea for you guys! You know how dangerous the Fourth of July is for kids? Well, how about renting Midway Stadium and putting on a nice safe, sane kiddy show on the Fourth with a big fireworks display? My wife and I were talking about it and figure somebody should do it. Could be a hulluva success!"

Egan was just coming off a hockey venture that was hot and cold.

It all depended on the coverage and what kind of action his professional team, the Fighting Saints, could generate from their blood baths with neighboring Minneapolis. Pat always had his ear tuned to the pavement for the pulse of the entertainment world.

"Love it, Pat! Love it!" Regan enthused. "Safe and sane Fourth for the kiddies. Sounds terrific. I know a guy with dancing bears and another guy with a trained chicken. I got an 'in' on some fireworks. I know I can get one of those zany radio personalities as an emcee. Want in, Pat?"

"No, you take it. But I'll buy two rows. I've got to run. I'm trying to start a five-times-a-day plane trip company just flying to Chicago out of St. Paul's downtown airport. I've got some big money lined up in Texas. What do you think, Race?"

"Love it, Pat. Love it! I know some guys who fly down to Chicago three maybe four times a week just to the races and to visit Club Alabam on Rush Street. Give 'em a good price and you're in business. Got any planes?"

"Hell, Regan, I'm not going to sling-shot them 400 miles. I've got a retired Northwest pilot whose got some great connections and we're going to get some good, cheap, used planes. I'll keep you informed."

Regan relayed the phone conversation to his buddies who were sampling some cheesecake that Gallivan had received from an old flame during his single days.

"That Egan. He's always got a tick up his fanny," observed Rogers with a half-smile.

"Well, let's get back to that Indy 500 trip," Frenchy insisted. "You've got it almost sold out? I'll fill it up."

Regan teased, "Only English speaking fans so try to make them understand you."

"Ohhh, you rascal," the chunky little Frenchman laughed. "I wanna see them race cars go 180 miles an hour. Honest to God, I don't know how they do it!"

"See, guys," Larsen observed, "everyone wants in. Next year I'll bet Frenchy runs two buses. Maybe 20 buses someday, like a caravan."

"Going to have any fishing contests on board?" Thunder needled.

"Ask Race, it was his idea."

"Screw it, Thunder," grimaced Race, "this one will be run like a church charity. We'll know where every penny is. It's got a good omen. I probably never told you but Mari Hulman, the daughter of the famed Hulman clan that owns the Indy track, took me to dinner last fall."

"What?" Thunder asked with proper astonishment in his voice.

"Listen, her husband is Elmer George, who drives her sprint car. They were at the state fair and we all went to dinner at the Parker House in Mendota. Right, Swede? And, Elmer doesn't say much. But Mari doled out the moola for the tab and the tip. Nice lady. Didn't have a lot to say but she seemed to enjoy the proceedings. Elmer wasn't getting a helluva lot out of her car and they were a bit down about that."

"And hey, they act like everybody. No put-on," Swede emphasized. "Plain as crackers."

It was seven in the morning when the crowd gathered at the Chain Link for ham and eggs. It was a jubilant, noisy group that boarded the bus to the Indianapolis Speedway. Saturday was sunny and the tour would spend the evening at the old Lafayette Hotel about 70 miles from the race and then proceed early in the morning the remaining miles to the track. Larsen had wangled a bus parking permit for a space just a short distance from the seats which were located on the notorious north turn.

Both Regan and Larsen had a love affair with the Indy race. Despite the horrendous toll, which the deaths of O'Conner, Bettenhausen and Sachs had taken of their Race Night Honors party at the Prom, they had tried to attend the race yearly although this was their first venture with a tour bus.

As the bus pulled away from the Chain Link, Swede told Regan and Frenchy they had a minor problem. Actually two problems. One was a tired old carpenter named Cooley, whose wife and daughter had given him the trip as a birthday gift. However, Cooley was an alcoholic and his wife whispered to Larsen, "Please don't let him drink or he might become unmanageable."

"Unmanageable?" Race queried.

"Well, if he gets two or three belts he gets a little silly. He might disturb the other passengers," Larsen explained.

Regan, the self-appointed bartender in the rear or the bus, asked Larsen, "But what if he wants a beer? What if he complains I'm an un-American jerk?"

"Just talk him into a soda pop," Larsen explained. "Cooley, that's him over there," Swede nodded towards a gaunt 50-year-old.

"Looks harmless. I'll watch him," Regan promised,

The second problem was Ray Klabbey, an ex-hot rod driver who all his life had dreamed of seeing the Indy Race. He, too, had a battle with the brew. In fact, at this moment, two friends were trying to lift him up the steps of the bus.

"Oh, no. Dammit, he's a pain!" Race exclaimed. But Swede shrugged it off, pointing out, "Two sour apples out of 40, that ain't bad."

"But you aren't counting yourself," Regan needled.

Finally they ushered 26 men and 14 women aboard the sleek tour bus after filling the larder with three cases of booze, pretzels, bright red apples and the box lunches.

As Regan welcomed them aboard he announced that the back bar would be open for business. "Just 50 cents for a drink and the first one is on the house," he told the passengers. He looked squarely at Cooley, whose eyes, it seemed to Regan, took on a werewolf's unnatural glow at the statement.

Race approached the driver and introduced himself. The driver's name was Benjamin Schwartz. "Just call me Ben. I'm from St. Peter. Sure glad to be driving you people. Never thought I'd see this big race."

Race pointed out to Ben that the important thing was to get there early. "It starts at eleven a.m., but to claim our parking space we have to be there no later than nine.

"Just be sure we're rolling out of Lafayette no later than six. We'll leave a wake-up call for five-fifteen, which gives them time for a quick breakfast and for us to load the box lunches and coolers."

"Sounds good to me. I've got a fine map of Indianapolis. We'll have no trouble," Ben smiled. "Sounds like a fun holiday."

Cooley was served a coke by Race but he seemed already to be listing toward port. 'Should have searched the dehorn,' Regan thought to himself.

Shortly before Madison, Wisconsin, Frenchy noticed a slight quiver and an occasional lurch to what appeared to be a rather new bus.

"Jeez, what's that?"

"Got some new rubber on the back and it might be an imperfect tire," Ben explained. "We'll just have to make do. Hope the people don't complain, but it only jiggles on certain surfaces and turns. We'll make it but it could get a little rough."

"Damn!" barked Regan from his perch behind the tiny bar. A small lurch magnified itself into a worthy tremor at the tail of the machine and the last one had sent three ounces of Jim Beam running down the front of Regan's pants.

By Chicago, Regan was nearly soaked in booze and a cigar box full of half dollars had fallen to the floor, sending coins in all directions.

"Only we could get a friggin' amateur driver and warped tires," Regan bemoaned to nobody in particular. "Next thing the damned roof will fall off and the crap can will spill out on the highway."

By and large the patrons were patient although a couple of them saw their ham and eggs again in the rocking toilet at the rear of the bus. At times the bus speed was down to 40 miles an hour, throwing all the plans off schedule.

It was nearly eight p.m. when they pulled into Lafayette and by now Cooley had fallen into the aisle.

"I dunno," Race explained to a baffled Larsen. "I didn't sell the damn fool a drink. He must have smuggled them aboard. And that Klabbey keeps kicking the seat of the gal in front of him in his drunken stupor. You know Swede, I'm not even sure about this driver. He almost pulled into the wrong lane coming out of that rest stop. Cripes, Indy traffic might bewilder him."

Both Cooley and Klabbey were carried to the elevator and deposited in their rooms to sleep it off. Regan was elated when Tom Warner, who had shared the ice dance disaster, showed up on the steps of the hotel.

"I'm down here to look over Butler University just down the road," Warner explained. "I might be moving there as athletic director. My wife heard you were coming and I checked it out. Thought we could gab a little."

Regan hugged his buddy. "God, if Cretin's football team loses you then St. Paul loses one of the best damn football coaches it ever had," Regan praised sincerely.

Sunday morning dawned rapturously as the hosts herded their tired but excited crew onto the bus. Cooley was wide awake and seemed to be negotiating without difficulty. Klabbey had already hammered himself with a third of a fifth of cheap gin and insisted on singing a bawdy rugby tune. At least he was walking and standing mostly upright.

Now the thrill show began. It should have been a short, pleasant jaunt, even in the heavy traffic to the west side of Indianapolis and the mammoth Speedway layout. But Ben, almost unbelievably, had somehow managed to get on the wrong exit on the outskirts of Indianapolis. Despite a map, which Frenchy tried to interpret for him, the bus eventually needed the help of a highway patrol car to reroute the tour, costing a valuable 20 minutes.

Later, faced with another directional dilemma, Ben suddenly found himself in a residential neighborhood that neither Regan nor Larsen, despite their many sojourns to the race, could even recognize. Ten minutes later the entourage was on a county road. Ben was apologizing because he had mislaid his glasses in his luggage and couldn't read the road map which now lay askew on his lap.

Race was fuming. "Goddamn it, Ben, stop and ask somebody for directions! We're running out of time!"

Ben pulled into what looked like a small garden farm and the bus was immediately surrounded by the farmer, his wife, two barking dogs and a seemingly endless parade of small children. All of them were naturally bug-eyed that on this bright holiday morning their humble abode would be paid a visit by a giant blue and white bus filled with strangers.

"Could you tell us where the Indy 500 track is?" Ben asked the stunned farmer.

"Heard of it. But gosh, can't right say where it's located. I'd guess Indianapolis."

"Oh, dammit," Regan was clenching a fist and gritting his teeth so hard his lips were turning pale. "Get out of here, Ben! God, let's just follow the heavy traffic. This is crazy, Swede! We're going to blow our parking space and then the garbage'll really hit the fan."

As dim-eyed and dim-witted Ben backed the bus out of the farmer's hectic yard, he accidentally hit a squealing pig that bounced a dozen feet. Now the farmer's children were screaming and crying in horror. Ben had to get out of the bus, apologize to the farmer and check out the condition of the little porker which apparently had suffered few ill effects, other than it couldn't get up.

"You're sure a clumsy damn driver!" the distraught farmer complained.

Now Regan had to get in on a piece of the action. While Larsen and Frenchy watched incredulously, Regan demanded, "What the hell's that pig doing running around without a leash?"

"I want fifty bucks," the farmer demanded.

"You'll take twenty-five for that little fat fart," Race countered. "It wouldn't make a decent sandwich for a midget!"

Settled. Twenty-five bucks. Regan was resigned and Larsen, shaking his head at the hullabaloo, guided the unnerved Ben back to the steering wheel and a more promising road and eventually into a burgeoning line of traffic, which slowed the bus to a pitiful crawl. Frenchy nearly doubled over, trying to repress laughter.

It was closing in on ten o'clock, just an hour before race time, when the bus approached the maddening maze of 16th Street. There was no time to negotiate the huge vehicle back through the bewildering flow of Georgetown Road traffic and into the designated parking area before the deadline.

Instead, Race suggested to the seemingly composed Larsen that he cut a deal with a nearby Piggly Wiggly grocery store manager to leave the bus in his parking lot. It was just two blocks from the track's main entrance. The manager agreed that seventy-five bucks was a fair price and, for the moment, the promoters had managed to alleviate the developing sense of urgency.

However, other horrors loomed ahead. For instance, they now had to move three large ice coolers full of bottles and sandwiches through approximately 100,000 late arriving race fans on the jammed narrow passageways of the raceway's west-side complex. It was a torturous mile from the nearby south gate to the north turn seats reserved for the anxious group. The temperature was approaching 85 degrees and the command, "Gentlemen, start your engines!" was near at hand.

Cursing, ranting, shoving and maneuvering, the sweaty promoters managed to bump, elbow and knee their way, along with the coolers, into their party's seats just five minutes before race time. Amazingly, no one lost their way. Only one casualty appeared on the surface—Klabbey never woke up in the Piggly Wiggly lot and his lifetime dream of seeing the Indy classic would remain just that, a dream. He would never forgive his guides.

Through all the turmoil the group seemed to enjoy a growing sense of camaraderie. The spectacle and ceremony exceeded everyone's expectations. Ben tracked down two new tires before the trip home. And the return to the Chain Link was relaxed and uneventful.

Well, it should have been an uneventful reception by friends and relatives. However, Cooley had managed to smuggle and drain a half-dozen solid belts into his frail frame, despite the prodding eyes of Larsen and Regan. He would fall rather than walk into his family's arms. They fumed at the promoters and, of course, Klabbey cursed them, too.

The trip had proven a great lesson to Regan. He intended to interview passengers for a column about what the locals thought of their great race adventure. One couple explained that they weren't married—at least not to each other. A second couple whispered that the lady was really the fiancee of her companion's brother. Another duo confessed they were naughty neighbors. And so it went, a load of strange sleaze.

Perhaps that's why nobody complained about the rough ride. They were more concerned with their anonymity than their comfort.

The bar turned a handsome profit albeit a messy business. The next morning, over champagne cannonballs at his alleys, Larsen announced to Regan and Frenchy, that they had netted a neat profit of $1,922.

"Sort of makes up for the trout," Regan said hopefully.

Chapter Seven

There's a Winner Under that Pile

The wives of the Longshots were an interesting lot. Regan's wife, Dots, was a beautiful blue-eyed brunette of slight stature with a tremendous smile. She had a complexion that would make a rose blush and a keen sense of humor. A former high fashion model, she also had enough vocal talent to sing in the Sheik's Sextet, the top Mill City supper club group and had a lead in the St. Paul Opera Workshop's rendition of the Merry Widow.

Dots could see the bright side if she were engulfed in a riot. When Regan asked her opinion of a new venture she always had the same answer: "As long as you keep working for the paper and don't miss any house or car payments, I'll never interfere."

As we pointed out, Jesse Rogers' wife was a spectacular blond. She also had an acid tongue, four fur coats, the Cadillac convertible and a weakness for shopping by mail-order. She became merely a trophy for Jesse to display on social occasions when a spouse was mandatory for creating an immediate impression.

When she kept her mouth shut she was a tolerable and pretty prop. When asked her opinion of Jesse's promotional flights away from his considerable insurance agenda, she would snap, 'He's a silly child who won't grow up." Then she would toss her long yellow tresses and order an extra dry martini.

Van Avery's wife was always more a rumor than a cornerstone. Few had seen her. It was said that nobody would recognize her in sunlight and she was never seen with Van after dark. The implausibility of this arrangement surfaced drastically the day Van and wife were invited to a Sunday dinner and he showed up alone. Nobody sought to embarrass Van by asking why he was soloing.

He flew to Hialeah and Chicago regularly for races and sporting events and explained his lonesome trips by saying, "She hates to fly." If it was a train trip, he'd explain her absence, "She hates to ride trains." Apparently motion caused her discomfort. Her close friends called her "attractive." She remained a mystery woman.

Larsen's spouse, the widow of the late race driver, was slim, sweet and sincere. She never had a negative word to say about anyone. She adored four-to-one martinis and would giggle as their ferment took its toll. But like Dots, Marie rarely became involved with any conversation pertaining to the Longshots' extraordinary and often weird efforts to strike it rich.

Marie had seen enough of her first husband's daredevil driving in Indiana to realize you can't keep a mate from the occupation in which he thrives. And Swede's bowling alley income provided a lovely home in Highland Park, quality automobiles and sufficient schooling for a daughter and son.

Digger's wife was the product of a small town family and was so busy being a mother to six children that she couldn't care less what Digger was up to when he wasn't directing funerals to Resurrection Cemetery. She rode with the punches and, in a good natured way, would chastise Digger when one of his ventures crumbled.

Frenchy's wife, Cindy, had bright yellow hair piled high on her head, large bosoms, a small dimple in her chin and an ingratiating laugh that could tickle your toes. However, on occasion, she could carve Frenchy up like a salad chef dicing the celery. The fact she worked as a waitress, hostess and even bartender in Frenchy's many saloons gave her more insight into the Longshots' operations than the other wives.

Cindy tolerated Frenchy's zany adventures but his astounding ability to disappear for two or three days at a time on a fishing excursion in the midst of a Super Bowl trip would vent Cindy's emotions to an oral volcano that could wipe out a moose herd.

On one such occasion, Frenchy slipped away on a trip into the Bay of Mexico during a New Orleans stint. Cindy promptly lifted a very large and expensive bottle of wine from a Brennan's breakfast gathering in the French Quarter, explaining, "I hope I get caught and that guy has to spend a ton to bail me out!" Later, she returned the bottle, unnoticed in the frenzy of bowl fans.

She never denied her admiration for his amazing work ethic and ability to turn shaky choices into solid business ventures. She would work alongside him as a willing helper and his customers loved her.

So it wasn't surprising that shortly after a typical debacle the women met for lunch at Frenchy's Stage Door restaurant—minus Mrs. Van, of course. They saw each other only rarely on a social level and, of course, none of them really talked about promotions of any sort. They rarely disengaged from their conversations about their hairdressers and children as Frenchy paused at their table and announced, "Race has got a great one coming up, ladies!"

"An alligator wrestling match on Seventh and Wabasha?" Dots teased before getting back to something truly important with the girls.

Unabashed, the bright-eyed Frenchy continued, "No, bigger than that, Dots. It's the Suicide Hill Climb! Jeez, Dots, you should know. Race has been talking about this one for a long time."

"I hope it costs us less than two or three thousand dollars a ticket," the quick-witted Dots replied.

"I do, too." Frenchy moved on and called Race at the paper.

"Going to Gallivan's today, Race?"

"Not today, I have to meet Larsen at the alley. I gotta know if he's coming in on the climb. I figure we can put it on in a month while the weather's still nice. Jesse's in. How 'bout you?"

"Don't have the time but I'll throw in a couple of grand. Will that help?"

'Yeah, just right." Actually, Race and Jesse decided they'd handle this on their own but what the hell, another partner only hyped the action.

Frenchy was excited. "Can I ride in it? My brother Blackie'll let me use his Harley."

"Are you nuts? This is going to be a killer! I don't want a friend of mine in the hospital for a month. Stick to the shot glasses."

Plainly disappointed, Frenchy still managed a word of encouragement. "Just saw 50 of those mad men on cycles on the road yesterday. I think we finally have a hot one, Race. Just so they don't get wild on booze and tear up Hudson. That sheriff over there is a pretty good guy but he can be pretty tough if you cross him."

"Listen, Frenchy," Race answered with an air of frustration in his voice, "this is the biggest boon for Hudson since they let in Sunday drinking. Those crazy cyclists will spend all day and all night when they're not at the hill climb just boozing away. Those bar owners should be so lucky. Waves of black leather will cut those saloon mortgages down."

A few days later, Regan talked Rogers into the fold and lined up a meeting with some earth-moving guys. He also had been expecting a telephone call from the agent of a softball pitcher who dubbed himself, "The King."

This was a guy named Eddie Feigner, who used just three players for a back-up to his pitching. He had toured the west and east for years and now wanted some advice on a midwest tour.

Regan sensed a good column and maybe a chance to do some writing for the guy's publicity campaign. Regan also knew dozens of would-be small town promoters who would be delighted to land just such an attraction to play their local teams.

The earth-moving muscle men at the Suicide Hill attraction were using equipment names and jargon that Regan could not begin to understand. The two bruising bosses, named Big Jake and Ralph, met Regan over shots and brats at the Twin Coaches. Regan figured nobody would bother them in that crowd which always included a dozen or so characters either headed to or back from the Stillwater jail.

Regan was intrigued by the cons' diverse stories of being framed. The short stocky fellow with the glasses, named Frank Eli, just six months before had penned a book, "The Riot," while incarcerated for robbery. It was not only published but gobbled up as a hot movie property. He was rumored to have earned $100,000 and Regan could only wish him well. But as he thought to himself, "He'll find it a damn sight easier in jail than out. Now the phone'll drive him nuts."

Regan showed the earth-movers a large photo of the hill at the J.R. Ranch.

"Right here's the spot," Ralph pointed at a sharp hill, leaving a mustard stain from his finger which had been clamped to a juicy hamburger.

"But that's a short hill," Race interjected. "Only about 150 feet. I don't know if that's tough enough a challenge to hold back those friggin' powerful bikes. You know, those hammer heads could chug up Everest."

"Wrong, Regan," contradicted Jake. "We'll gut out six or seven chunks that'll make 'em think they're hitting a brick wall. I can put enough holes and rough spots and rock slush along the way so they'll think they're lucky if they just flip over backwards and land with their feet in the sky."

Ralph agreed, "Yeah, Jake, we can carve out at least half a dozen booby traps that'll drive these guys nuts. Never did like those bird-brained bikers. This'll be a good way of gettin' back at 'em for all that noise and swagger they give you on the highway."

Now Regan was beaming. "We'll go out Saturday morning and take a look around. I've got to figure where the fans will sit and how long a run the cyclists will get before they hit the course. Hey, I've got a helluva idea! If I think it's a tad short, we'll dig down and make those crackpots start 20 feet down in a pit below the surface of the field. And we can muddy up the pit and make it even tougher traction. What do you guys think?"

Jake grinned, "Sounds great. Just so nobody gets to the top. That's the idea, right?"

"Hold it!" Regan shot back. "We have to have a winner! Maybe we make it so one or two real nuts can get to the top. We're going to give away six trophies and five hundred bucks. Somebody's got to win. But not many and not right away."

"Damn," Ralph grumbled, "thought we'd get a chance to wipe out the whole crazy crew."

Before they left the dismal Twin Coaches and the ornery cons, Race whispered to Ralph and Jake that when Ralph put the mustard from his finger on the photo it reminded him of the guy who was stirring his soup with his finger. A friend asked why and he explained that he had a terrible arthritis pains in his finger and his doctor advised him to put it in a nice warm place. His friend asked why he didn't put it up his rear and he replied, 'Where do you think it was before I put it in the soup?'"

Big Jake and Ralph were nearly in tears over that one as they shook their heads and headed towards their pick-up. At the door, Eli, the con, approached Race and told him he had read his columns for years. "You know Regan, I been out for three months and I can't write anything. You do it every morning. God, I gotta get back into the can to get my concentration back. Maybe I'll write a stiff check."

"Good thinking," Race replied without taking a breath.

Regan sat in his car and mused to himself, 'Exactly as I called it, Eli is a cell writer. How can I be so damn smart and so dumb when it comes to getting the right combinations on promotions? But oh, the hill climb. Thanks, God, for this winner of all winners.'

The cycle climb officials loved the idea of the exposure they presumed they would get from an entertainment area like the J.R. Ranch. They usually had to perform in some outback down the river near Red Wing or even further out of the Twin Cities.

Thunder Klunder, the cycle man, bowed out of the promotion because he was busy with three swap shows. But he introduced Regan and Jesse to all the key officials in the climbing association who showed up enmasse for an inspection tour of the J.R. Ranch.

"We'll get a hundred entries," a cyclist named Josh promised.

"That little hill?" questioned a scarred veteran named Felix. "Hate to say it but that dinky hill you're planning is a mere pimple on a bull's rump. We'll chew it up."

Another cocky young biker spit and then blurted caustically, "You'll have to stack those damn buffalo on the course to trip us up." And he gestured to Rauchnot's small but imposing herd of bison penned between the hill and the restaurant.

Regan's pride was stung by the criticism of his hill. He vowed sharply to the group, "In two weeks that hill will look as tall as the First National Bank. We're carving out a big hole at the start and we'll have more booby traps than North Korea. Just make sure you guys take your nerve pills."

Everyone laughed. The cyclists left the observation trip committed to tearing down Suicide Hill. Regan, Rogers and Rauchnot, who wasn't quite sure what to expect, pledged to make the course so tough the casualty list would exceed the prize list.

"But be sure and fill up the holes after the show," Rauchnot cautioned as the three of them gazed out on his lush 260 acres of rolling countryside, idyllic for the horse and hay rides long offered by the

J.R. Ranch. Jesse and Regan guaranteed to restore the landscape to its peaceful purposes after the hill climb.

"We'll not only fill in the holes John, we'll fill up your bleachers with fans and fill your saloon with thirsty bodies."

Preparations for the Suicide Hill Climb became a portent for disaster when Rauchnot's restaurant turned into a site where a buffalo really roamed. The near disaster occurred as earth movers began their loud gouging just a hundred yards or so from the hotel and food complex at the east end of the J.R. Ranch.

Exactly two dozen of the huge, hairy bison were quartered in the pen. For over two hours in the afternoon the beasts grew more and more agitated by the strange sounds emanating from the machinery at the base of the hill.

Suddenly, as the early cocktail customers began filing into the eatery, one mammoth and cantankerous male could stand the din no longer. With a bull-dozing thrust of his own the 2,000-pound animal burst through a weak link in the fence like a trip hammer splintering Waterford crystal. He bolted his enclosure and streaked—not for the confounding machines but directly toward the restaurant.

With little resistance the animal smashed through the screened porch, which was fortunately empty. He slammed through a sliding glass door with a rush, shattering the obstacle so loudly it could have been heard on a barge passing down the St. Croix River.

A dozen horrified customers scattered in all directions while the tormented animal rampaged through the premises. He traveled almost in a circle, crushing tables, chairs, splattering dishes and bottles in a thunderous commotion that could have cost the life of anyone caught in his angry trail. That there was no human carnage was an act of God.

An old lady managed to drop to her knees, seeking the protection of a large buffet table. A younger man leapt through the shattered glass door, hoping for safety in the open spaces. Others scrambled into the kitchen or up the stairs leading to guest rooms. In his own effort to escape, Rauchnot took refuge in the kitchen where he braced a meat cutting table against the door. He hauled down a cleaver from the wall should the animal breach the door.

"It was as if an alien army had descended and intended to blow out the whole building," Rauchnot would later explain.

The buffalo, tiring in its charge, bore out the way it entered and headed for the open range. More than an hour passed before three sheriff's deputies cornered the animal a mile away, killing it with assault weapons.

Eventually it stood still and stuffed on a five-foot podium in the restaurant's lobby. It was said that many drunks sobered up in seconds at the sight of the monstrous beast glaring down at them.

On this day, however, Rauchnot was acutely aware that maybe, just maybe, the Suicide Hill Climb was more than he could handle. And because his insurance had no fine print covering hairy monsters running amok it would cost him an estimated $3,000 in damages even before the event took place.

"This promotion's got ramifications," Rauchnot told Regan and Rogers the next time they met.

"Jeez, John, if we only had movies of the buffalo we could have made a ton," Regan replied. "But a tip, John, better pen those buffalo up on the north 40 before the hill climb starts. Those cycles might drive 'em into a stampede."

"Next time you guys pay the bills," Rauchnot growled.

Another roadblock appeared before the promotion. City authorities in Hudson voted to close the town to the cyclists the day of the event. The town's bar owners, aware that they had a big payday coming up, screamed with indignation but they couldn't afford to offend the sheriff's department. A majority of the citizens made it clear that they didn't want a couple of thousand drunken wild ones invading the little river town.

The decision was balanced somewhat by the publicity the event received in the local paper and on the radio stations in the vicinity, and the enthusiasm engendered by the tiny hamlet of Burkhardt, a few miles to the north. This burg was positively ecstatic to think its two lively bistros would certainly lure appreciable coin from the noisy visitors. "Welcome Wild Ones" became the town's buzz words.

Suicide Hill began to take on its ominous shape four days prior to the event. Thanks to a ramp leading down into the starting pit, the length was stretched for the course and made even more treacherous than hoped for. One cycle official assured Jesse that, "The less powerful bike will have a helluva time. The bigger ones might have a handful, too."

Entries totaled 85 at thirty bucks apiece and they were supported by another 500 cycling buddies the day of the event. The humid Sunday air contained the threat of rain early on but the sun splashed through on the green hills by noon, emphasizing the jagged, amber slash of the Suicide Hill challenge. It looked thoroughly dangerous, with slick logs jammed into the course, the rough and perilous rocky terrain and the starting launch hole resembling a pit from which even an anaconda snake would have trouble escaping.

Best of all, Regan reported to Rogers, the parking lot was filling fast. "I look for nearly 3,000 bodies to be here by the start of this thing. Rauchnot won't complain about anything with the beer he's gonna peddle. He'll make enough to spend a month in Denver at the national rodeo he loves so much."

The crowd was amazingly well-behaved and included dozens of children. Ten gleaming trophies were on display at the crest of the hill. The blaring country rock music on the public address system carried for acres, boosting the festive mood. The t-shirt concessions were going well and the sound of revving cycles conflicted brazenly with the languid, pastoral scene. A few minutes before the start, Regan and Jesse sat under a gnarled oak tree just off the path of action with a view of the entire scene.

"Beautiful, eh Jesse?"

"Finally, Race, a winner. We should clear five grand easy."

The competition took on a remarkably consistent but loudly vibrant pattern. A few early riders made it halfway up before losing control or veering off the circuit, sometimes coming dangerously close to the gauntlet of spectators. Others made it a little further before running out of traction or abandoning what seemed like too ominous a challenge.

"Lord, I hope they don't get loose and wipe out the crowd," Race pondered. "All we need now is seven customer deaths. I hope you got good coverage."

"The best. The policy covers just about everything except a tornado. All for about $700."

Another dozen riders hurled themselves at Suicide Hill. Some tipped, others floundered, a few simply ran out of steam. Each man in each class got two runs, which meant this display of backfiring, screeching failure could consume two or three hours.

The fans seemed to love it, cheering appreciatively as daredevil after daredevil charged the hill, only to get caught in loose stones, on an impenetrable log or old tree roots or a threatening boulder. The 65 degree angle turned away the most serious competitors within 20 feet of the top. Fortunately, half the riders in the lower-powered classes backed off after one effort. This meant the show was reaching its climax as the big, more powerful bikes mounted their thunderous challenges late in the day.

A 20-minute intermission permitted Rauchnot's four concession stands and inside bar to do a whopping business. Never had so many fans drunk so much suds and hard booze in such a short time at a hill climb.

Even the defeated, battered bikers seemed amiable, knowing that a fair number among their group would claim trophies depending on how far they had maneuvered up the hill. At the moment, the leader's flag was implanted nearly 15 feet from the top, meaning the hill should hold up even against the most valiant and juiced machines. Was the Materhorn more formidable, Regan wondered.

"Horsepower to hell!" Race shouted to Jesse, the apparently victorious promoters toasting each other with gin and lemonade in paper cups. The success adrenaline was rushing rampant through their bodies.

These were the moments promoters live for. This event would surely vindicate Gallivan's Gang in the eyes of the critics. This was pure, unadulterated success. Or, as Regan was wont to philosophize, "The rewards from Dame Fate for ignoring the blood and bruises of failure."

Part-partner Frenchy shouted down from the apex, "We make it big today!"

Jesse whispered to Race, "Damn, he would get in on a winner."

Their euphoria was distilled only slightly when an official paid them a visit from his position as starter far below.

"Don't be surprised if you have some real winners at the summit. I mean the very top," he pointed out. "These big babies are starting to find some traction. What I wonder fellows is has anybody really checked out the landing area should they hit the top?"

"Landing area?" Jesse inquired, his sleepy eyelids fighting to open against the bright sun. "You mean you think somebody really might hit the peak?"

"Yes and at a helluva rate of speed if he doesn't have room to decelerate beyond the crest."

"God, what are you saying?"

"Relax guys, maybe nobody'll even get there. Just want you to know that I'm betting on the bikes."

As the starter disappeared down the hill, Regan assured Jesse, "That friggin' starter's nice but a little prejudiced. Same as all those bikers, think they can rocket to the moon."

It was the fourth bike in the biggest class that came within six feet of capping the summit. He fell back and twisted an ankle before controlling his growling machine.

"Just like the Materhorn! Suicide Hill is holding!" Regan shouted over the din.

It was the next-to-last rider who changed the history of J.R. Ranch and brought the Longshots back to thumping reality. Some guy named Rufus Geraghty on a howling red Indian bike tackled Suicide Hill like it was a bedsheet.

Rufus was half-way up the hill in less than nine seconds, seemingly in full control. At the three-quarter mark, he went into a huge wheely but kept the power, righting his machine and sending small rocks and pebbles flying into the air in such profusion they seemed to create a wave of withering darkness.

With 20 feet to go, Rufus pounded around a greasy patch, seared a path between two large chunks of broken logs and marshaled his metal over two treacherous humps. Through his gyrations he maintained his balance and literally flew the remaining feet, while the onlookers roared their approval at his disdain for the challenge.

"Flew" was exactly the right description. As he hit a tiny landing area, he bounced once and suddenly with explosive impact rider and bike took off in the air, disappearing out of sight! His screams could be heard even over the thunderous cheers of his admirers.

"Where'd he go?" the incredulous Regan screamed at Jesse.

"I dunno! But God, is there a cliff behind the landing area?"

"If it is, it goes straight down. Oh, man! What if he's killed?"

"Oh, Lord. Our winner dead! Who gets the trophy?"

"God, Jesse, are you nuts? Worrying about a trophy at a time like this!"

There were cries and screams from the summit. Both of them scrambled through the mob trying to get to the crest. In the turmoil, the table containing the trophies was knocked over, the gleaming cups and plaques flung in all directions. Many of the awards tumbled down the precipice, which fell off sharply over 90 feet behind the ridiculously small landing area.

"Get a doctor! Get a doctor!" came the plea from the rocky embankment below the crest. By now a good share of the large crowd was shoving and stumbling to the peak, trying to ascertain the damage. Some were climbing gingerly down the rocky hilltop for a better view of the tangled bike and battered winner. His groans could be heard clearly.

"He's okay. I can see him move," one onlooker shouted.

Another echoed, "He's okay but covered with blood!"

A medic from the stand-by ambulance was now on hand, asking spectators to help him move the injured biker gently onto a stretcher. Regan and Jesse could only stare at the mangled bike and battered rider. Regan crossed himself. "Man, I hope he doesn't have a wife and kids."

Jesse wiped his face with a tissue and muttered softly, "Wonder why we didn't think of this? You know, hardly any place to land."

"That's why I named it Suicide Hill," Race tried to explain.

As Rauchnot would later say, the ramifications were just beginning. Nearly a hundred customers wanted their money back as cycle officials opted to close the hill to avert any more injuries. Certainly hill climbing is dangerous—but when a winner winds up with two fractured legs, a separated shoulder, broken wrist and broken teeth and jaw, that is considered extraordinary.

It was almost six p.m. when Regan and Jesse slipped into the parking lot. A few cyclists and their friends were drinking quietly in the restaurant. Others were headed to Burkhardt's friendly taverns. Hundreds were winding their way past the barricades onto the Hudson Bridge and over the St. Croix River.

By now only a few seemed displeased at the action. They had seen a hill sturdily and defiantly hold off the horsepower for over two hours. They had seen a winner, gallant as he was, wind up in a pile of wreckage after a spectacular crash.

Race had also seen most of the trophies smashed or stolen. Jesse was arguably right when he said the hospital bill would consume most of the profits, even if the injured rider didn't sue. Of course the insurance would cover something. But mainly it was purchased to protect the spectators. Just what clause would protect a crippled winner of an insane competition was difficult to ascertain.

In a gesture of utmost charitable dimensions, Jesse and Regan told cycling officials they would donate a $1,000 check to the organization and pay hospital bills, of course. This was to alleviate any criticism and hopefully preclude the climbers from boycotting another Longshot promotion. A disconsolate and unusually quiet Frenchy shrugged his shoulders. "Damn, that was something," he muttered.

Regan drove back alone, stopping to call his wife from the Hudson House Bar where he met Thunder Klunder, heard a report on his swap meet and digested the hill climb's events.

"We had a winner but it slipped away. More like it flew away," he reported to Dots solemnly.

Race couldn't help but recall sportswriter Grantland Rice's immortal lead, "Outlined against the gray October sky, the Four Horsemen road again . . ."

"Outlined against a soft summer sky, the cycle hero disappeared."

Chapter Eight

Big George and a Dirty Shirt

It was the exited, high-pitched voice of Landreville that stabbed into Regan's ear at 7:30 a.m.

"Race, you'll never guess who was in my joint last night!"

"Haven't got a clue. Maureen O'Hara?"

"Cut the foolin' you rascal. Just listen to this: This big black guy comes in and orders a soda pop. And then another black guy, a little skinny, older fellow, comes in and orders a straight shot. With hardly anyone around, we get to talking.

"I notice the big guy has fists like hams. He's kind of a sleepy looking guy but in good condition and I said, 'You look like an athlete.' The little guy smiles and says, 'Don't you know who this big, handsome dude is?'

"Then the little guy tells me this is George Foreman—THE George Foreman! You know, the Olympic boxing champ and top contender for the world's pro heavyweight title!"

"Hold on a minute," Regan pleaded. "What the blazes would Foreman be doing in St. Paul?"

"Easy. They know some people up here who are trying to get them in a business deal. It's one of those minority things that Uncle Sam is passing out. Don't ask me why they picked St. Paul but this is the real thing. Don't get shook up, Race, this stuff happens. Remember when I bumped into Bob Hope on Snelling Avenue and everybody thought I was nuts when I told them? Don't forget, Race, you ran into Kim Novak at Ed Mady's bar in Highland Park. You said yourself some crazy things happen."

"How do you know it was Foreman? Did he throw a punch at one of your customers?"

"Oh, you rascal. You're kidding again. Hey, they showed me their IDs and told me to come out today to the motel on Prior and University. That's where they're at. Let's go and you can see for yourself. Race, believe me, this is Foreman! He's big enough to block out the sun but he walks kinda light. Couple of people came in and wanted me to introduce them. They were sure it was Foreman.

"But this little guy with him looks kinda tricky, like a con man. Says he's Dick Sadler. Jeez, he sat at the piano and banged out a couple of tunes. He can play. Told me he used to play the ivories in a whore house in New Orleans and that he met Foreman in Houston. He said they became close friends and now he's the big guy's manager."

On the other end of the phone Regan was shaking his head. "Still sounds screwy, Frenchy. It may be a business deal but with hundreds of thousands to be made in New York and L.A. I can't see them in St. Paul."

"That is a little mysterious all right but come out today and judge for yourself."

Regan, once again interjected his doubts into the conversation.

"One thing that's still cockeyed, Frenchy, is the fact I met the Philly syndicate guys down in Houston at the Ali-Ernie Terrell fight. They insisted they just signed Foreman and owned him lock, stock and barrel. And that was before he threw a punch in the Olympics and waved the American flag."

"Hey," insisted Frenchy, "I know it does sound crazy but they weren't asking for a handout. Before they left, the guy who called himself Sadler bought a couple people drinks and he had a wad that would stuff a pig. Maybe five hundred or more. These were not hungry people. And that big guy; if he isn't Foreman, he should be fighting him. See you at noon at the hotel in the little bar. You can have a belt and I'll have some onion soup. You know they really make good onion soup out there, just the right amount of cheese. . ."

"Yeah, Frenchy. God, quit thinking about food. See you at noon. I hope your guys show up. I'm offering five to one they're phonies."

It was obvious at first glance that these were not phonies. Well, let's say Dick Sadler could have cut some strange angles in his years but there was no doubt this was George Foreman. And Vern was right. My God what a sight—well over six feet three inches, 235 beautifully distributed pounds, and yes indeed, he did fill a room.

Quiet, with a slow smile that seemed to fight its way through a large round, implacable face, Foreman appeared a gentle giant, as placid as Lake Como on an August afternoon. Regan could only think that this man, who plundered the Olympic's heavyweights, must have an enormous capacity for destruction lurking behind such a calm exterior.

When he stood up to greet Race, engulfing Regan's diminutive palm and fingers like a culvert encasing a twig, Regan was happy Foreman didn't close on his hand. He knew he'd never type again.

The entire breadth of Foreman was awesome. Here was a collection of body parts to span Grand Canyon.

Over the two-hour lunch, during which time Foreman consumed two steak sandwiches and four glasses of orange juice, the twosome regaled Race with enough information for a dozen columns. George told of being raised in the tortuous Fifth Precinct of Houston. It was there that he got in minor trouble, such as smashing windows, pilfering anything worn or left discarded by neighbors and, in general, antagonizing the cops—but staying clear of serious confrontations with the law.

"Mostly kid stuff. You know the stuff you do when you run around with young gangs and you're trying to impress them. But I was never really mean. I know if I stayed in with the rough crowd I'd wind up with real problems. Boxing brought me out of the evil alleys. The Olympics showed me that right can beat wrong. I don't think the

Lord is mad at George," he concluded. He was young but endowed with simple wisdom beyond his years.

Sadler listened, intoning "Hallelulia!" at intervals. When Foreman stopped speaking, Sadler would riddle the conversation like a machine gun. He expounded on George's "Rapier punches. . ." "the grace of an antelope. . ." "power that could drop a water buffalo. . ." "strength that could pull a two-ton auto out of a ditch."

God, Regan thought, this is unbelievable. Frenchy kept interjecting his "I told you, Regan," verification with regularity.

It seemed strange to Race that throughout the conversation nobody could explain just what Foreman, ranked number three in the world boxing ratings, hoped to gain from his sojourn in St. Paul.

Sadler tried his best to explain. "These men, Mr. Holmes and Mr. Taylor, contacted us in Houston and flew us up here to St. Paul. They are gonna sell us a computer-type business with an office on Lexington and University. Is that a legit location, fellows?"

It certainly is.

"They figure if we can invest maybe fifty to one hundred thousand dollars we'll double our money the first year. Then we'll expand. We're going to look at it tomorrow. Meantime, George has some numbers in Minneapolis he has to call, like friends of friends of his. Maybe a blind date, huh? You young lothario."

George appeared to force a slow grin. He was either a strong man, always under control, or a lazy man burdened by his new responsibility. Regan tried to figure the big guy.

After the surprising conversation, Race was bursting with energy to explain to his readers that this calm giant of a man they might meet on any street corner could easily become another Jack Dempsey or Joe Louis of fighting lore.

"By the way," Sadler whispered in Regan's ear as they headed for the door, "could you do me and George a couple of favors?"

Without thinking, Regan was pleased to answer, "Sure, whatever you need."

"Could you find George a nice car that he could buy at the right price . . . and also get him a fight? The car doesn't have to be new. And I can find an opponent if you can find a building and a promoter. I don't want George to go stale while he's waiting for one of the top heavies."

"No trouble," again Regan answered. But this time his brain was cranking out messages like the publicity shill of a political convention. He'd get George over to his pal, Dick Long's Cadillac dealership. Then he'd call Emmet Weller, an amateur boxing promoter and protégé of Regan's old friend, Raleigh. Together they'd put on a Foreman fight. With George's Olympic and professional fame, it could be a rouser.

At that moment Regan's thoughts did not include Frenchy. But Frenchy's did. "Count me in on everything, okay Regan!" Landreville insisted firmly. "Don't' forget, I found these guys."

"You're in," Race signed. There was room for everybody—just in Foreman's hands alone.

Now Regan's mind was firing like pistons in the Indy 500 pits. He'd line up a car for Foreman, make a fight and take any profit to the best Chinese restaurant in town. There he'd order enough kettles of elixir to keep a hot supply of Chow Cones going for 10 days at the state fair. Chow cones . . . he couldn't get them off his mind.

"Oh, you lovely entrepreneur," Regan thought to himself as he slashed away at his typewriter. He was pouring out an informative and fact-filled column on the exploits, background and promise of Foreman. He still wasn't quite sure why big George was in town but he knew Pat Egan, who had a hand in bringing professional hockey back to St. Paul after a seven-year lapse, had also been mentioned as a Foreman benefactor by Sadler in a quiet aside as they ended lunch.

Pat was happy to elaborate over the phone about Foreman's presence in the Saintly confines.

"This big hitter named Ox has plans to get George a future. A lot of fighters wind up with nothing. I'm trying to help with the location and start-up plans.

"If George's crowd comes up with an even fifty grand, I think we can get the government to just about match that on a minority deal. We've got George a great little office.

"I've got an idea Race, why not come out when we show George and Sadler the office tomorrow? We're trying to make this guy some solid money and not see him lose everything like most fighters do. Our group figures to help him man the business and we can make a few bucks on it, too. It's a printer-copier type operation with some good equipment. Everybody can make a buck."

Sounded plausible. All of Race's suspicions were put to rest. Pat and whoever his partners were apparently had George's welfare at heart. Office equipment was the wave of the future. For the moment, George's boxing career had been stalled, mainly by the caprices of Cassius Clay, who was in the process of changing his name to Muhammed Ali.

At the moment, George was merely a valuable ornament in the heavyweight division, despite the fact he terrorized most potential foes. Regardless of the money, most of the would-be opponents must have figured they'd risk permanent disfigurement from his boulder-like fists. And Regan surmised the Philly syndicate was biding its time until Ali ran out of gas and George could be their trump card.

But first Race must find a car for George. Frenchy picked up Race and they drove to Long's glistening Cadillac lot on West Seventh. Long was a former Chicago railroad security man who had moved into the car business at the urging of his brother. His sibling happened to own one of the world's largest General Motors franchises in the nation on the outskirts of Chicago.

Long never pretended to be a particularly imposing businessman. Figures bored him. He did know how to dispense authority and absolutely charmed the St. Paul populace with his low-key insertion into a variety of popular charities.

"Get Long and you've got a winner," was the standard suggestion for anyone trying to raise funds.

Within minutes, Long had Foreman behind the wheel of an elongated canary yellow two-year-old Eldorado. What set it apart was the hood ornament, which would have done justice to a world soccer cup champion. It had to stand a foot high and no Roman piazza was graced by a form more fanciful. Regan mused that in a January wind the ornament could capsize even this two-ton juggernaut.

"That's your car!" Sadler almost shouted to Foreman. "Big enough for comfort and bright enough so they'll all know it's you—the coming champion! And no dents. George, no dents!"

George agreed quickly as he settled his huge frame into the soft black leather driver's seat. He grinned and admitted, "Sure feels good." When he heard the thunder of the high-powered engine, George beamed, "Never thought I'd have something like this for my own. Sure beats thumbin' a ride from the old neighborhood in Houston."

George was so decent that Race found himself saying a silent prayer that the big Texan would never have his faith or body battered by the cruel game of pro boxing. The Philly mob was capable of anything.

Sadler did a little two-step as he worked his way with agility and glee through the rows of glistening used cars to Long's office. Long dropped an arm around Sadler's shoulders as he introduced him to his business manager. "Be sure I get a lot of tickets for your next fight, if it's in St. Paul."

His words were not lost on Landreville or Regan, who smiled at each other. While Sadler counted off $2,800 in cash and handed the bills to the business manager, Landreville guaranteed the Cadillac boss that there was going to be a fight in St. Paul very soon.

"We'll certainly see that you get the choice seats, Dick." In his mind, Frenchy was figuring Long might buy perhaps 20 ring-sides and suggested that to Race.

Regan whispered in his ear as they walked out of the office, "Hey, you got it wrong. Not 20, but maybe 200. Dick loves to promote. I'm sure he can use every one of them." Race knew whereof he spoke and knew Long's methods. Long happened to be one of his talk-show sponsors on WLOL radio.

That evening Foreman and Sadler picked up Regan for a drive to a restaurant in Savage on the southern fringe of the Twin Cities. The eatery was supposedly financed by Twins baseball club president, Calvin Griffith, along with other elements of his family. Regan, seated next to Foreman, got a little edgy on Highway 13, a narrow, well-traveled strip of two-lane asphalt along the Minnesota River.

"George, you're only going 25 miles an hour. The traffic's backing up behind us," Regan reminded the big fellow.

"Race, this is the nicest car I ever drove. I'm gonna make darn sure I don't break it up the first night. I sure don't want any dents in this sweetie."

Regan had anticipated correctly. Within minutes the flashing lights of a highway patrol car signaled for the sleek yellow machine to pull over. The young officer grinned when Regan introduced him to George Foreman, world title contender.

"For sure?" he wanted to know.

"I'm Regan of the Pioneer Press," assured Race, as he flashed his press card. "George just got a new car and he's driving very carefully until he gets the hang of it."

"Yes sir, the hang of it," George agreed pleasantly.

The officer was understanding.

"Well George, step it up a little. We don't want a parade back to the Mendota Bridge," the officer smiled. "You might want to try a side road if you don't feel like going a little faster."

"I'll go a little faster," George promised and put his hand out through the window for the officer to shake.

"Tell you what, George, just follow me and we'll pretend like it's a funeral procession. Try to stay as close as you can. We won't go too fast. By the way, I hope you win the title, George. I'm sick of that Clay character or whatever he calls himself."

"Me too," George agreed cheerfully.

Regan was thankful that Sadler, sitting in the back seat, had not said one word. He finally muttered to no one in particular, "George is real quiet for a kid from the wrong side of the tracks. He's got some class."

Before they got to their destination in Savage, George had only managed to push the speed of his new Caddie up to 30 miles an hour. As the cop and George turned into the parking lot, more than a dozen agitated drivers were in their wake.

"You'll never get arrested for speeding, George," the young cop shouted to his new acquaintance.

'But at that rate you won't catch Clay, either,' Regan thought to himself.

The trip to Foreman's potential new minority business was enlightening. Taylor, Egan and another sharp type had outfitted the modest one-story offices with white carpet. You had your choice of phone colors, pink, blue or white. The desks were white and new. Sadler's eyes were bugged and his senses boggled. Foreman swiveled in a large tan leather chair, lifted a pink phone and observed almost solemnly, "This looks like a successful business already."

Regan was quite sure what the venture was, namely to put any moola George possessed or could borrow into the hands of creative workers. He had figured out that Egan was merely the tool that brought the mysterious promoters together. The perfectly groomed Taylor, in a dark blue suit and graying temples, guided Foreman over to a duplicating machine.

"Basically George, your company will be turning out duplications of plans. We think one of the first clients will be a Minneapolis hospital which is building a new addition. When the original plans are finished, the George Foreman Company will turn out vast amounts of copies, hundreds, for the various contractors and sub-contractors and city officials.

"Millions of plans," Taylor emphasized, "are produced for all sorts of projects every year and you'll be on the ground floor for business because you'll have the name and the publicity and the best equipment money can buy."

"What about those new-fangled computers?" Sadler wanted to know. "I hear they'll be the coming rage in three or four years."

"Good thinking. You'll be getting up to a dozen of the latest. People who can't afford them will come in and rent them right here for their use and probably pay about ten bucks an hour for the privilege. They're going to be too expensive for the average company to buy. Can you imagine, George, ten people using your computers and you getting $100 an hour from them? I mean that's big money!"

Taylor was almost trembling in his anticipation of what Foreman's copy and computer conglomerate might become.

"Now, the best part; of course we'll franchise. Just like McDonalds. Your offices could be in 500 cities, each one making you hundreds an hour as the demand goes up."

"It sure beats playing piano in a whorehouse," Sadler nodded solemnly.

Everyone laughed.

Foreman was in dreamland. "Always wanted to run a big chain. I'd love sittin' in an office. Don't get any knocks in the face doin' that kind of work."

Regan shoved his hands in his pants pocket. 'Sure glad I'm not promoting this,' he was thinking. He had the feeling somebody was going to get screwed—and it wasn't going to be Taylor. Pat put another 'potential' together but apparently bowed out before anyone could ask who Ox Taylor and friends really were.

The Minnesota State Fair held a special allure for promoters of all types. It drew well over a million onlookers in ten days, mainly because of its accessibility. Located in the Twin Cities' urban core, it was one of the three or four largest in the country.

The fair was the home of the fastest sprint car auto racing track in the nation. Its sprawling midway show area was the largest in the midwest. It had just installed an overhead sky ride and grandstand celebrities like Al Hirt and Red Skelton regularly drew huge crowds to their stage performances.

The battle for choice locations was incessant and fair authorities were under constant criticism for giving "outsiders" better positions than locals. For instance, the Abominable Snowman and Boss Trucks from California always secured rentals near traffic lanes. Regan was content to start his Moonburger concession on a dusty corner on Machinery Hill, an area which became a graveyard after 8 p.m.

Now, Race was hopeful that a well-run concession would and could demand ore advantageous location as the years progressed.

So it was with joy that Race learned that the fair officials had given him a relatively lively corner near the main entrance from which to dispense his Chow Cones.

This move may have been attributable to the fact Regan and Gallivan had become friends with many of the fair's guiding lights over the years. Gallivan knew how to entertain the out-of-town fair directors at his restaurant. Regan had become the foremost authority in the area on auto racing, which would draw crowds as large as 25,000 on five or six days. John Libby, the fair's director, often ate at Gallivan's and he admired Race for the coverage he afforded the races.

Regan had hired a couple of college boys to serve the Chow Cones. If trade became intense, Regan himself could step in and he felt he could always call on wife Dots to fill the breach.

Race had gotten the idea for his new venture from a vitamin pill peddler who just happened to mention that nobody ever put chow mein in a portable container, to be eaten while you walked.

Chow Cones would become the rave of the fair, Regan thought, as he looked over a shipment of 2,000 cones he had ordered and was storing in his garage. These were double strength ice-cream cones, durable enough, the bakery promised, to handle the extra weight of the hot chow mein. Preliminary tests of a few quick nibbles had titillated Regan's tastebuds and he was delighted that one of his ventures had unlimited potential. A natural for franchising.

The main ingredients of the chow mein were ordered from Wong's on the corner of Selby and Western Avenues. It had been in operation for nearly five years and had built up a large following. Regan had ordered six large kettles of chow mein, which the chef insisted would fill over a thousand cones. The chef agreed to make as much food as needed to keep pace with the expected torrent of customers.

"Cool weather is the secret," Landreville explained to Regan. "Cool weather and you'll sell a zillion, you rascal! Hot weather and you better figure on delivering a large load to the city dump."

"Yeah," Regan answered plaintively. Frenchy had dropped by Regan's house to offer encouragement and good wishes.

"If you get in trouble with long lines, Cindy says she'll help. She really likes chow mein."

It was a bright, crisp morning for the fair opener, with forecasts of temperatures in the high 50s. Regan's mind and heart sang with anticipation. Jesse called Regan to offer encouragement before he left for the fair.

"I'm going out and bring my kids. They're all going to slobber down Chow Cones," Jesse announced.

Race asked Jesse if he thought he should open by nine o'clock in case somebody wanted Chow Cones for breakfast. The usually dour Jesse couldn't help but smile to himself and suggested that Regan might want to stay open until two or three in the morning, since they might be ideal for party snacks for the homeward bound night clubbers.

Regan's young help was in place by ten a.m. They were all sharp students at St. Thomas College, had practiced operating the cash register the night before and had the large vats on a warming grill a full hour before serving time. The plastic spoons and cones were all accounted for.

The signs were in place the day before the fair opened. Race loved them. "Chow Down with Chow Cones. . ." "Chomp on Chow Cones. . ." "Not a Big Cone—A Small Meal. . ." "Chow Cone Chompers are Delish. . ." "You Can't Lick Our Chow Cones. . ." "Champ Chinese Chow Cones."

Race raced from the paper to the fair, elated to find that everything was in place. Each kettle, one at a time, would simmer on a portable electric plate with back-up kettles refrigerated in the giant cooler of the Beer Garden. If this venture caught on Regan would petition to trademark the name Chow Cone on the first air mail leaving town Monday morning.

One of his helpers suggested that they take a picture of the first customers. They happened to be a middle-aged couple from Owatonna.

"We'll spend our first fair money with you," the stout man, named Ted, smiled. His wife said, "Ted's a real big eater. He had breakfast only an hour ago but he just loves chow mein."

You could tell he loved anything edible from the way his yellow sport shirt and tan slacks caressed every ounce of extra lard.

"He'll never want to eat anything else after he tries the Chow Cone," Regan guaranteed, while patting Ted on his shoulder. Then, while Danny heaped a huge spoonful of Chinese goop into the cone, Alex took a picture of Regan and Ted and his double-chinned spouse.

The little Chow Cone family watched happily as the couple moved around the corner and were engulfed by the crowds as they headed for the agricultural building.

"There goes the start of millions!" Regan told Alex and Danny. "You guys are seeing the launch of a huge enterprise. Stick with me and Chow Cones will make us a mighty company," he enthused.

"Right on," exclaimed Danny.

"Yeah, an enterprise!" agreed Alex.

Three more customers lined up and Regan's mind was pounding. 'If we sell 2,000 a day at 50¢ each, we'll clear about four hundred, after paying the fair and help. That's four thousand in ten days. Ten fairs next year and that's forty thousand. Twenty fairs in two years and that's eighty thousand dollars! Oh, God, this is too good to be true.'

It was.

"For Christ's sake, you nitwits, look what you've done to my clothes!"

There stood red-faced Ted from Owatonna. Chow mein—juicy, liquidy, slowly creeping chow mein—was engulfing most of Ted's frontal self. It was dropping out of the cone's bottom so rapidly that Ted could not control the damaging flood even with his wife's handkerchief and another handful of napkins.

The goop was on his chin, his neck, pooled in the creases of his shirt, even down there on his knee. The stuff was staining every inch of space it claimed. Godzilla couldn't have ducked the spreading wave.

"Look! You've ruined my goddamn pants! You've ruined my shirt!" Ted was storming and his pleasant little wife had become a veritable jungle beast.

"Do you people realize Ted hasn't got another change of clothes? You idiots have ruined our whole day! God, you people shouldn't be allowed in the fair. I'm calling the Attorney General's office and telling him you are frauds. And the State Fair Board is going to hear of this!"

Race tried desperately to placate them. Finally, he reached into the cash register and gave the man a $20 bill. "Look, this will take care of the dry cleaning and more. Something must be wrong with the cones."

Of course. Regan had failed to test them, counting on the seller's assurance that they would indeed not buckle under the liquid elements of the chow mein. He had considered a paper liner but that would detract from the taste and preclude the melodious mixing of the cone and chow mein.

For the moment, Regan seemed to assuage the disgruntled pair. But out of the corner of his eye, Regan saw three more young customers heading his way. Their heads down, mopping chow mein from their shirts and sweaters which were already badly stained. Mud wrestlers did not look more in need of clean-up jobs than the Chow Cone victims.

After guaranteeing enough cash to cover the damage and noticing that the Owatonna couple was hunting for a security guard on whom to vent their venom, Regan ordered Danny and Alex to close shop. Again, he doled out $20 bills to the latest angered customers.

Danny tore down the signs while Alex began to cover the kettles and disconnect the heating plate.

"Could I take some of the chow mein home?" Alex asked.

"Take the whole friggin' kettle-full and all the cones you want! But be sure and eat that crap in the shower!" Regan shouted.

"You're something. How can you still joke after all that?" Alex asked.

"I've had worse than this happen," Regan answered dolefully.

Like a hill-climbing champion flying over a cliff.

Chapter Nine

Cruisin' for a Bruisin'

Members of the Longshots were sitting on the deck of a luxurious 48-foot Chris Craft which nobody seemed to know who owned. This was not unusual. Yacht parties continuously sprang up on the shores of the St. Croix River. The owner of the ship mattered little. Some boats were owned, some rented, some were crafts of mystery.

"I suppose Krueger . . . you know Krueger, the slot machine guy. I think he's got a piece of this one," Jesse said cautiously while tapping the side of his orange blossom drink with his long, thin fingers.

The rest of the 'Shots—Regan, Landreville, Van, Rogers and Larsen—stared at the lush green banks behind little Prescott, one of the many Wisconsin harbor towns along the river which became the Mississippi and separated that state from Minnesota.

The early fall scenery was just beginning to kick in and the dark reds and soft yellows of a wondrous autumn were framing the tiny town, located just downstream from the Twin Cities.

"Jeez, this is neat," Race mused as the group waited for their host, who was picking up groceries for the late afternoon gathering. He was a breezy little fellow named Sammy. None of the group seemed to know much about him, except Race who marshaled the group.

"Who needs to have a million to live like a millionaire when we keep coming up with days like this? Am I right? My executive editor, you know, George Edmond, well, he's got 82 pairs of golf slacks. Not even a car but the pants make him feel like a millionaire."

"Right, Race," Landreville agreed. "If you got friends with a boat and somebody else who owns a cabin and you, Race, with all those free golf passes, you've got it made. I say we all have. Right, rascals?"

"I've got a boat, a sailboat," Jesse mentioned. "Keep it at White Bear, but hell, when do I get to use it? My wife can't sail, even though she blows big with the mouth."

Everyone chuckled.

"Tell you something else," Regan pointed out, "you've got a boat and you're always worried about leaks. You gotta cabin and you're always fumigating for bugs and fixing the rotting docks. You got a foreign car and you're always looking for parts. Got that racehorse and you're always calling the vet. The idea is to enjoy all these things but let your friends own 'em. I've got the swimming pool and it leaks and my daughter's horse wears out more shoes than Gene Kelly."

"And something else," Jesse opined, "you let others use the stuff and they screw it up. I've had a drunken relative virtually tear the wallpaper off the bathroom of a little cabin I've got up in northern Wisconsin. Let the kids drive the car and they strip the gears. I had some nutty neighbors who got the sailboat anchor hooked onto a dock and before everything was through it cost me three hundred bucks for repairs.

"Hell, I'm ready for a monastery. The monks have it made. Really, nothing to worry about but saying a few prayers and growing cabbage. I wonder if they know how lucky they are."

"Well, not really," Race interjected.

"One thing that we've got that nobody can take away is that special feeling when we make a promo go. I get a tingle when I hear people talking about our event and we see that first ticket buyer and we hear the rustle of change.

"That's a high the monks never know. Never mind that we haven't made any big bucks. Fact is, you really can't beat the anticipation, the thrill of making something out of nothing. Hell, if we never hit we're living the fantasies that most people only dream about." Regan emptied his glass of gin and orange juice.

"And you know those monks, they'd love to be sitting around here today and quaffing a few and pondering the problems of the excessive wealth we'll have one of these days."

Van was into the conversation, pointing out that nothing had more godliness to it than the little guy coming back from the parimutuel payoff window with the rewards of the 20-to-1 shot in his hand and the look of a man who has just seen a miracle.

"And I've seen that look on the face of a father buying his daughter her first old red convertible for her graduation gift. There is a special sanctity to the moment. We can't knock things too much. I agree with Race; when I've got a good seat for a world title fight, the contestants are coming up the aisle and the arena's charged, man, you can cut the tension with a baseball bat. Well, those are feelings the monks never get."

Larsen's feet had kept tapping during the conversation.

"You guys are kinda philosophical, but how about mentioning the Indy 500 auto race? Imagine, 400,000 fans from all over the world, all shades and nationalities packed into one place. And the best drivers on the planet get the word, 'Gentlemen, start your engines!' And the roar of the engines and the crowd screaming. Don't tell me a monk wouldn't give half his crops to be there. Lord, I've seen the big show over a dozen times and I still get so excited I nearly crap in my pants when those cars hit the starting line and all hell breaks loose."

Regan was analyzing their words carefully and scripting a few of their opinions indelibly on his mind. He agreed with Van that a major fight would be a near zenith production. And why not some day get the boys to buy an Indy car? It would be a thrill they'd never forget.

Race disappeared below deck to the lounge and poured himself another double gin, this time tempered only by a twist of lemon and an almost invisible splash of water. Regan figured an Indy car could be found and right at hand was George Foreman. Why not Foreman in that fight in St. Paul as he waited for his title shot? Regan walked back up the stairs, an imperceptible glow on his face and his heart thumping a little quicker. More games at hand.

Returning to the group, he was quickly brought back to reality by Jesse's question, "How did you settle that Chow Cone debacle?"

"Oh, I dropped eight or nine hundred for dry cleaning bills and the food and concession costs. But more important, I think I qualify for a Guinness Book of Records entry."

"What record?"

"The shortest run of any concession in a fair's history. Know how long we were open? Exactly 16 minutes! In that time, we officially sold nine customers. Five of them had gunk drop all over their jeans, two of them almost from stem to stern. The only really bad thing was when some smart creep asked why we didn't test the cones before pouring in the chow mein."

"I told that jerk we were up until midnight all week and the damn factory practically guaranteed us the heavy-duty cones would hold the Chinese slush. I should go back and stick those thousand cones up the noses of all concerned."

"I know some guys who'll bash the windows at the cone company for fifty bucks," Van winked.

"Listen, Van, I've got my own guys. Ever see my new bumper sticker on the Dart? Says in small print that I'm a lifetime member of the Hell's Outcasts! They told me they'd tear up anybody's lawn or smash any windows, any time, any place for me."

"How'd you get so lucky?" Swede asked.

"Well, remember a couple of weeks ago when I told you I expected trouble from the radio show where I panned Cassius Clay for changing his name to Ali and the Moslems jammed all my lines? And then came the Hell's Outcasts out to the station with the snakes around their necks and the brass knuckles? Hell, they scared the guts out of everybody. Later on, I took them for beers over at Andy's and they made me a lifetime member.

"That's because when Jesse and I threw a motorcycle show a few years back at the armory we hired them for security. We gave them $500 for their treasury. They were cheaper by far than off-duty cops and they did a better job. Nobody dared touch any of the equipment with them around."

Jesse agreed. "They were damn good—if only they'd trim some of those dirty looking beards. They look like somebody whose been sleeping under a pier in their clothes for a month. I don't know how they stand each other. To me, they all smell like rotten liver."

Would you believe that their leader is a U of Iowa grad, Jesse?" informed Race.

"In what, turd gathering? They did the job for us but the customers must have thought we were all opium fiends to have garbage like that enforcing our no-touch rules."

"I like them better than those Muslims," Race snapped back. "The Hell's Outcasts may puke on their leather but they came to the station shot-fast, and lord help the Muslims if any showed up."

By now Sammy was back from the grocery store, hauling a wagon load of food. Behind him trailed a large man in a white mechanic's suit, his graying hair and dark glasses setting off a pudgy, deeply lined face and unkempt mustache.

Sammy, an acquaintance of Race's for years, was an earthy Norwegian from south Minneapolis, who traced his antecedents back to Roosevelt High which was also Regan's alma mater. Sammy had been in various businesses, including a stint as a midget race driver and pilot. Like the Longshots, he played promotional games and dabbled in everything from far-out inventions to theories of perpetual motion.

His latest adventure was a new and supposedly unsinkable speed boat with a revolutionary engine designed by a friend. This was the large man who suddenly appeared at the side of the boat and was introduced as Spike Northolme.

"And why you are here as guests of Spike and myself is to let you see and ride in our new experimental boat," Sammy explained.

A couple of Longshots looked around, assuming the boat was either being towed beside the large yacht or perhaps ensconced in the bowels of the ship.

"No, it's not here," Spike said in more of a growl than a sentence. "This is still a highly secret commodity. We have to keep it under cover. The press release isn't even out yet and, Race, we hope maybe you can help us with that. Anyway, we'll take a jaunt down the river to a spot just this side of Red Wing. And we'll give you a view and a ride.

"You fellows tell us what you think. It just holds four passengers. We'll take a couple of rides and show you the maneuvering capabilities. Everybody'll get the feel of the next revolution in pleasure boating.

"I think you'll be as astounded as we are. Briefly, it can back up, turn on a dime, explode to 30 knots an hour in seconds and the jet-type engine is 10 years ahead of its time. The boat has such capabilities both in safety features and sheer agility that even if you don't care about these things I think you'll be highly impressed."

Sammy couldn't contain his enthusiasm. "God, guys, it's wondrous, just wondrous."

"You know about this?" Larsen whispered to Regan.

"Hell no! Do you think I'd have worn my lizard loafers and new linen jacket? I can't swim or even float. I'll let you take my place. You like speedy things, Swede."

"No, you're the key man, the guy who's going to write about this super innovation. For a few free yacht trips, I presume. By the way, I wonder if Champion Motors knows about this."

"They could sabotage us," Race grinned, trying to relax.

In 20 minutes the yacht was anchoring in a narrow inlet. A small garage-like structure at the end of a long dock housed the watery wonder.

"This is something the CIA'd love!" Landreville almost shouted.

At that moment, as the group approached the gray tin building, Larsen caught sight of an angry cloud formation to the west. "Cripes, look at that sky! We're supposed to get a late summer roar today. Hope they get this baby in the water and out before the storm hits."

Sammy and Spike were now opening the doors to the building, inviting everyone in for a look.

"Looks like a regular speed boat, only smaller," Frenchy observed.

"Too damn small for my taste," the always candid Jesse critiqued, comparing it mentally to his graceful 30-foot sailboat on White Bear Lake. "Should be in somebody's bathtub."

Regan only stared, privately praying that the storm would unleash its fury quickly and postpone the launch until another day, preferably one from which he could bow out.

Two other well-dressed strangers appeared at this point. It was assumed by the Longshots that they were potential investors.

"Let's get this into the water," Spike ordered, as he pulled the tarpaulin off the blue and white creation.

"If you all can give me a hand, three on each side, we'll just lift it up and carry it to the end of the dock and set it down gently. Won't take but a couple of minutes. You'll be surprised how light it is."

That was encouraging, Regan thought.

Actually, the 300 pound package of wave rider provided no great chore for the hands guiding it to the water. The motor rose up in the rear, preventing it from dragging on the dock. The boat was soon bobbing like a happy duckling.

"I want a vest. Can't swim," Race requested firmly.

"I'll take one, too," said Larsen, who volunteered to take the first ride with Regan, Sammy and Spike.

The water was getting choppy as the storm's pre-winds began to blow gently but consistently. The dangerous clouds still appeared to be miles away and everyone agreed the test run should be completed well before the storm posed a danger.

Comfortably, but tightly packaged in, the foursome roared away from shore toward the middle of the St. Croix. The boat did the usual twisting and turning, trying to make a friendly adjustment to the waves which seemed to grow larger as the little craft spaced itself from shore.

Over the roar of the gutsy 125-horsepower engine, Regan shouted to Sammy, "Rides fast! I suppose you're saving some tricks . . . ehhh . . . oh! Chrissssst!"

Spike had made a sharp run to starboard and the boat appeared to be lifting itself toward the trees on the steep Wisconsin bank. Larsen was engulfed in a wall of spray that wanted to drench his very soul. Regan was breathless and could only scream, "Ohhhhhhh . . . phhhh!" If he wasn't encased so closely, he'd have made the sign of the cross. Instead he considered an act of contrition.

Spike settled the boat down. "How high were we?" Sammy calmly asked Spike.

"Oh, up a couple of feet, but we aren't going that fast. This thing is as close to unsinkable as we can get."

Even though Regan had confidence in the ability of Spike to handle the craft, he remembered they had said the same thing about the Titanic.

The worst was yet to come. In a few seconds, before Regan or Larsen could steady their entrails, Spike cut the forward switch, veered a bit to the right, and with a varoooom began backing up the boat. A monstrous black barge appeared, perhaps 200 yards away! Anything in its path would be obliterated. Regan recalled that just a couple of months previously a runaway barge had wiped out three blocks of docks in St. Louis.

"Good for our back-up test," Spike informed the foursome, "now let's let it rip and see what this little baby can really do!"

Suddenly, the tiny craft bucked and lurched and headed backwards at what felt like a frightening pace.

"God, not again!" Regan screamed, his white-knuckled hands grasping a small rope on his side of the boat, giving Regan the barest amount of security. He squeezed himself as close as possible to Larsen, trying to prevent any movement of his body. He loved speed but he wasn't ready for an immersion procedure. You could drown at five miles an hour.

The backlash of the reverse movement propelled more water over the occupants. When the craft churned and reverberated perhaps 90 feet, Spike let out a whoop and turned the throttle full speed forward, certain they were out of the barge's course.

This time the spray was so heavy neither Regan nor Larsen could see the small windshield in front of them. Regan thought, 'My God, I'm going to drown inside a boat!' Larsen thought, 'I'll go down choked on a trout. It's the ghosts of the boat show's dead trout seeking vengeance. Oh, my God!'

Race was sure the little boat was rattling apart. Every seam was stressed. Suddenly, Spike spun the boat almost completely around, yelling, "Let's see if this little SOB can or can't sink!"

"The micro-head's a maniac!" Race screamed at Larsen.

Spike only laughed and continued a circle pattern, the incessant spray of which soaked everyone. The frightening spin turned the waters around them into a tempest while the boat flailed and roared in defiance at Mother Nature like a Yorkshire pup yipping at a mastiff.

Regan knew this was the end. Larsen was pretty sure. In fact, Regan wasn't certain the boat was even above the water line. He was drenched to the skin and his eyes were mere slits trying to peer through a greenish veil of water. Larsen tried vainly to find some humor in this situation, wondering aloud if Spike and Sammy were escapees from a mental institution.

Eventually, the man-made storm subsided. For the next 10 minutes Spike took them on a joy ride. Lest they perceive any timidness on his part to test the craft, every few minutes he would gear up the boat and whirl it around or make some horrendous and sudden veer that drew in enough waves to almost engulf the tiny cockpit.

The sky continued to darken. As they headed to shore waves began to pound the small craft with a steadier and more resounding force. Regan felt like a ping pong ball in a wind tunnel. By the time they were within 20 feet of the shore, Spike shouted, "Going to make one more great move!"

He managed a complete rotation at top speed, only this time the boat tipped so vehemently to its port side that Spike lost control and the game little puddle-jumper capsized. Race and Larsen were thrown free into the water which, fortunately for Race, was only three feet deep.

Spitting and flailing, he managed to come within a few paces of shore, where he regained his feet and waddled close enough to be pulled out of the water by a hysterical Rogers and Landreville, laughing until their sides ached and they were bent like safety pins.

Larsen, a stunned but capable swimmer, followed Race onto the dock. Sammy and Spike retrieved their slippery little creation and, with the help of the speculators on shore, corralled and roped it to the dock.

Van's eyes were as large as frisbees. "Damn, was it supposed to happen this way?"

"Are you nuts?" Larsen moaned at Van. "This silly little bastard isn't worth a counterfeit nickel! No wonder they keep it under wraps. Anybody finds out about it and they'll have those two peckerheads arrested! They're a danger to society." Larsen began spitting and coughing.

These were strong words from the usually docile Scandinavian but they seemed to reflect the opinion of all the Longshots.

Race was so shook-up he was speechless for one of the few times in his life. He would admit to Dots later that evening on their patio,

"Just looking at our pool makes me nervous. I heard the Lord calling today."

Sammy's two potential investors could only shake their heads before heading toward their Cadillac. "Where did you encounter those crazy weirdos?" one investor could be heard asking his friend. "Bona fide psychos."

It was a silent cruise back to Prescott and the Longshots' waiting cars. Race and Swede were buried under beach towels. At the pier, Sammy apologized for the dozenth time, "Sorry guys," Sammy kept saying. "I don't know what went wrong. Spike thinks it still has a few problems in shallow water."

Sammy offered to buy the 'Shots dinner at the Steamboat Inn but nobody accepted. Damp rags and fiery tempers don't make for good company.

Before they parted ways, the Longshots learned that the storm had indeed been an explosive one, blowing out windows and creating havoc on Main Street in Red Wing, just downstream a few miles. The episode could have been tragic and they all leveled blame on Sammy for his ill preparations. Sammy wrote personal apologies to all the Longhsots and escaped a nervous breakdown.

Race summed up the experience by casting Spike and Sammy as "Stupid micro-brains. I'm so friggin' cold my balls will be blue for life." Larsen, too, was shivering from his saturation but he supplied a brief bit of levity by whispering to Race, "I don't think I want a piece of this one."

Chapter Ten

The Bullfighter Hates Blood

I suppose it happened after Race awakened from a dream in which he was a matador in Spain and was thrown into the air, screaming "Aaaarrraaagh!" in a nightmare of despair. Dots had shaken him awake while scolding, "You're having another one of those terrible sleeping fits. You can't keep eating and drinking so late. It's going to kill you!"

"No, no," Race pleaded, while trying to shake his head clear. "You've got it all wrong. I just got a terrific inspiration in that dream. It's something we've been talking about, a bloodless bullfight!"

"Bullfighting is illegal, isn't it?"

"If they kill the bulls. But there's no rule against pinning a rose or a ribbon on the bull in this country. And I've read stories about how they're trying it in a lot of border towns. And would you believe, they're staging one in Wauwatosa, Wisconsin? Can't you just see another one in Hudson at the J.R. Ranch? Dots, at least 10,000 Twin Citians would drive 20 miles to see something like that. It might be their only chance to see a matador."

"Great. And where are you going to get a matador? At the South St. Paul stockyards?"

"Jesse mentioned that he's heard that they're bringing them into this country from Mexico. Not the real greats but I'll bet none of the turkeys around here would know the difference. Besides, most of the crowd'll be pulling for the bull. You know the old slag, 'Minnesota Nice.'"

Dots closed her eyes. The last time Race had awakened from a nightmare that violent he'd come up with the idea to put a tight-wire rope act on for cyclists, extending from the First National Bank building in St. Paul to the Foshay Tower in Minneapolis. Hopefully this bunch of bull would vaporize, too.

The idea refused to go away.

"Got an appointment to meet Hector Martinez in Wauwatosa Saturday evening, ten days from now, at the hotel where he's staying." On the other end of the line, Jesse could not instantly fathom just who the hell Hector Martinez was until Race finally clued him in.

"So you're really serious about this bloodless bullfight thing?" Jesse asked cautiously, almost hoping it was just some kind of joke.

"What the devil, of course I'm serious. You brought it up and Digger O'Halloran seconded the idea when we had a few out in Mendota at the Colonial the night we talked about another motor-cycle show.

"Damn Jesse, are you getting the weebies? I've found out all the key stuff, the dates of the fight at the fairgrounds over there and the hotel and matador's name. By the way, it's Hector. That's kind of a sappy name for a bullfighter. Maybe we ought to change it to Tyrone or Raphael. Something romantic. How the hell did he get a name like Hector?"

"Maybe he killed for it," Jesse offered. "But how big is the show and how do they pull it off?"

"Well, I talked to one of the officials at the fairgrounds who inked it through some show biz bookers in Brownsville, down in Texas. This guy tells me they send a batch of big red posters, like you see in movies. They bring in some bulls, not really tough ones but nice smart little bulls that chase anybody in tight pants and a cape. They also bring a mariachi band, a couple of gals who do Spanish dancing, and, oh, yes, he says they've got a red-hot cornet player who really blasts out those great bullfight songs.

"Now listen. They've also got some assistants who pretend they are picadors but they just excite the bulls with poles that don't draw any blood. The whole cast is about 15 strong and they bring six or seven bulls. God, can you see the publicity around here? Bullfighting arrives!"

"Are you holding something back, Race?" Jesse questioned.

"The cost. You would bring that up."

"Well?" Jesse prodded.

"Frankly, I don't know. Yeah, I asked but the guy at the fairgrounds said the agent told him every place was different. Two Saturday shows are costing them about three grand."

"But Race, that's Wauwatosa. When they find out we've got over a million people around here don't you suppose it'll go up a few bucks? If they're booking from border to border they must have a few street smarts."

"That's the reason for the conference down there a week from Saturday. We deal first-hand with whoever is there. The agent or the fighter or the manager. Really, who knows what a matador carries around besides his cape and sword."

"I imagine a jar of Vaseline for his hair," Jesse concluded.

It was an intriguing conversation that engulfed the threesome on their drive to Wauwatosa. Regan was regaling them at the moment about how a bullfighter might have saved his skin.

"Where and how did that happen? In Spain?" queried Jesse.

"Not Spain, in L.A."

Digger looked dumbfounded as he tooled along in the Lincoln through Wisconsin's lush Dells. "There's no bullfighters in Smogville," O'Halloran snipped.

"Well, remember when Wes Fesler took his Ohio State Buckeyes to play Southern Cal in the Rose Bowl—the game in that nasty rain?"

"Yeah, you were there," Jesse agreed.

"Well, the night before, on New Year's Eve, I got tired of listening to the Buckeye band blow its brains out in the Biltmore's lobby and headed outside for some air and a prowl around the loop. So I hear this great Mexican music coming out of a second story window and decided to see what the party was all about.

"You guys know I love any kind of Latin music. Before you know it, I'm ordering a martini at this long bar outside a big ballroom. Halfway through I realize I am the only non-Mexican in the place! It also dawns on me about the same time that Pachuco wars between the Mexes and our servicemen have been all over the papers.

"By now a big Mexican in a white zoot suit comes up to me and demands to know what I'm doing at an obviously Mexican party. I hold out my hand and tell him I'm Race Regan from the St. Paul papers out to cover the Rose Bowl, and that I love Mexican music and that I've got many nice Mexican friends back home on the West side.

"He looks doubtful but tells me he is Jesus Christi Montanez. Then he wants to know that if I'm truly a sports writer who do I think was the best bullfighter of them all. Now this guy is still looking very menacingly at me, like he's ready to pull a shiv and make me the entre at the dinner they're obviously getting ready to eat.

"Now would you believe that five or six years earlier I got intrigued with a book about Juan Belmonte, an honest-to-God Spanish bullfight hero who appeared a couple of times in Mexico. I told Jesus about his sad death when he came back to the ring once too often and how he had invented the Veronica pass, and how he left his wife and family one of the greatest ranches—and where, to this day, they still raise fighting bulls.

"My lord, the reaction. You'd think he'd seen Pancho Villa ride by on a mule. Jesus embraced me, really squeezed tight. Then he asked me if, by chance, I was Catholic. I showed him the rosary that I used to carry all the time to garrote would-be critics. Jeez, he squeezed me again.

"Next thing you know he brings me to his table where about a dozen of his relatives are partying it up. He asked a couple of his cute little nieces to dance with me and there I go, with them showing me dance steps I thought only Fred Astaire knew.

"Before it's over, they invited me to their grandmother's house for tacos. All the time I'm thinking they're setting me up for the big stab. Instead, they wind up taking me to my hotel about three in the morning and giving me half a dozen addresses so I could write to them.

"So, you ding-a-lings, don't laugh when I say a bullfighter saved my skin. Without Belmonte, as sure as I sit here, they'd have sliced and diced me like a fresh tomato. I never told them I'd been in the Army. I think if they had known that I'd have been left in ribbons."

"You have the damnedest stories, Race," O'Halloran observed while shaking his head and causing cigarette ash to flutter over the steering wheel.

"What are some interviews you really remember?" Jesse interjected. "Give us a little insight into the low-down stuff you thought was the best, really human yarns you ran into."

Race pondered for moment and said, "How about Johnny Blood, you know, the all-time Hall of Fame footballer, a guy who lived up to every inch of his legend status."

Jesse interrupted again.

"Did you know Blood is dating my aunt and they're talking about marriage? I hear he's got to be the ladies man of all time but a little screwy," Jesse interposed.

"Not screwy, Jesse, a wild spirit. Did you know that in the late thirties he coached the Pittsburgh pros for Art Rooney while playing a couple of positions?

"Golly, what a character! One night he told me that he happened to be at a bar listening to the radio after practice and heard that Rooney had sold his quarterback. Blood called him and asked why and Art, a great gambler, told him he lost him in a craps game and needed the bucks. Then he told Blood he could play quarterback better than the regular. So Johnny wound up playing quarterback, safety, punting and coaching the mighty Steelers who were called something else. I think the Iron Men.

"Oh, and here's an angle: Blood got his name from a marquee on the Astor Theater in Minneapolis, advertising 'Blood and Sand,' the movie about bullfighters. His real name is McNally but he didn't want to lose his eligibility in college at St. John's by playing semi-pro ball on Sundays at Parade Stadium."

Digger was impressed. "I heard he really did have brains. Was he smart sounding when you talked to him?"

"Smart? Like a genius. He taught at St. John's in Collegeville but was on such a different mental plateau that the kids were bewildered. His best buddy is Whizzer White, who became the Supreme Court justice; only guy he says who can carry on an intelligent conversation with him.

"And he looks right through you with those black eyes. He told me one night in a saloon that he's certain he's got the devil inside him. Calls himself a true black Irishman.

"And something else, right this minute he's angling for a professor post in economics at the University of Minnesota.

"I once saw him stretch a 250-pound loudmouth with a six-inch punch. He could have been a heavyweight champ. But Jesse, if your aunt marries him, she better watch out for the gals. When they meet him they've got to touch him. It's like he hypnotizes them with those black eyes."

"You're nuts about Willie Pep, aren't you, Race?" O'Halloran asked.

"Well, you know about him beating Jackie Graves in Minneapolis and not throwing a punch in the third round. He still won the round on all the judges' cards. Fastest hands, feet and reactions I ever saw. Mike Gibbons called him the best he'd ever seen. Pep once told me the only things that caused him problems were bad dice, slow horses and fast dames. The experts thought he didn't train. Crazy. He told me that after the parties or craps games that he'd run back to his hotel room or home or whatever. Four or five or even seven miles. He was always in shape. The absolute zenith of boxing ability. I'd pay to watch him skip rope."

"Bet you guys don't know how I won the best 'action sports story' award of the year a couple of months ago?"

Digger was enthralled by all this and plied Race for more inside information.

"This one you'll never read. Anyways, I was covering the Lakers in New York against the Knicks in the playoff finals. The game is early afternoon. Some new acquaintances say we should run out and see Belmont Race Track; that it's beautiful and we can get a drink and nibble and still get back for the game. Sounds great to me, so we take a cab out and nobody's paying much attention to the time.

"We're lathering up pretty good and I must have had maybe three double gins and what the hell—you can't leave Belmont before the races, can you? So we are really enjoying the sun and flowers and great grandstands and then watching the horses getting the leather put on in the saddling ring.

"Pretty soon, it's the third race and the fourth and then I finally look at the time and damn, the game's been going on for nearly an hour and a half! My first thought is horror. I'll be canned from the greatest job in America! But then somebody points out it's an hour later in New York then the Twin Cities, so if we get back I can still turn out some kind of yarn for the first edition.

"God, I arrive just as the teams are leaving the court. The Lakers win, too, just closing out the Knicks. So I go into the locker room and one by one I grab Slater Martin and Jim Pollard and buddy Vern Mikkelsen and, of course, George Mikan and Bobby Harrison, who always liked me.

"I asked each guy the turning point, when they thought they had it under control; when they were a little scared and shaky.

"I wrote it just that way, including Mikan saying the officials were protecting the home team and Slater Martin telling me he'd like to go mano y mano with Dick McGuire all day. I write the game story just that way. Best basketball story I ever wrote. So I win the sports story award on a game I never saw! Gentlemen, that's talent!

"John Kundla, you know, the Laker coach, told me later I'd better never let the paper find out or they wouldn't spend the bucks sending me out of town. I could cover games from the office. Dammit, the story was great!"

Jesse's laughter pealed from the back seat. "Regan, you are a screwy SOB. Is that called creative juices? Or is it fantasy?"

Regan grew almost teary when he paused for a moment and thought of Kundla. "Most underrated coach in pro basketball. He deserves a medal for just keeping his collection of super-stars together.

"Imagine, Martin got sore because Kundla wouldn't let him blank Bob Cousy from the field in an easy win. Mikkelsen still tells me he could always use the ball more often. Big Mikan is the terror of the league but he has his bad emotional periods and a pretty good temper. Pollard, the Kangaroo Kid, can do it all but I think he gets jealous of Mikan's publicity. Fact is, running a winner is tougher than a loser.

"I owe a lot to Kundla. He took me to my first stage show in New York three years ago to hear Ethyl Merman in 'Hostess With The Mostest.' He introduced me to the Blue Room in New York and Peggy Lee joined us after her session. She loved the Lakers. And we got the waiter captain at the Copacabana on a Saturday night to give us a table right on the dance floor, next to Johnny Ray's piano. Imagine, me, a young kid from nowhere, feeling Ray's perspiration flying over me—we were that close!"

"Damn, you liked that? His sweat on you?" Rogers interrupted.

"Yeah, I didn't mind when the Copa chorus started dancing five feet away either. They say every one of those beauties married millionaires. Anyway, in a booth just another 20 feet away, Jackie Gleason was sitting with June Taylor, the dancing darling of his show. In walks Mrs. Gleason and, in a voice loud enough to wake a hibernating bear, she calls the two of them every dirty word in the book. Gleason? He just sits there nibbling that long cigar and staring at her. That marriage can't last. But the action petrified everybody in the place.

"That Kundla. He did more for me introducing me to the big time than anyone ever did. The last few trips, we always took along Dave MacMillan, the old university coach. He sits with John as a kind of assistant. You gotta remember, the U of M didn't hire Catholic coaches for decades. But Dave told all his Shriner buddies that Kundla was a good Mason. At the same time, I think John was taking up collections at Holy Cross.

"I swear, when Peggy Lee sang 'Lovers' just for our table, old Dave looked 30 years younger."

The Digger glanced sideways at Race. "You can be sentimental, can't you?"

Regan half-smiled and suggested that he was talking too much. One thing, however, he wanted to know, "Did Jesse really get lost in the underground tunnel trying to sneak off with test papers in the history course at Notre Dame?"

Digger lit another cigarette and nodded. "Yeah, Jesse tried to pull it off in the heating vents. But he didn't come back for over an hour. We all thought he got lost. Can you imagine what would have happened if they'd turned the heating juice up?"

"Yeah," Jesse recalled, "I couldn't get the grate off in the classroom. If I had stolen the test I'd probably wound up graduating from Silo Tech. Imagine, Notre Dame threw out Jumpin' Joe Savoldi for getting married in his senior year! They dumped another guy I know for buying an old car."

"Hey, the school's emblem isn't a crucifix for nothin'!" Digger replied.

Regan laughed and volunteered his best story along those lines. "Seems Abe Goldstein was thrown out of every school he attended for bad conduct. His parents finally sent him to Notre Dame for discipline. He looks at the crucifixes and figures this place really creams you if you foul up.

"Anyway, his folks don't hear from him for three months and finally send him a wire: 'Don't forget Yom Kippur starts tomorrow.' And he wires back, 'Frankly, folks, I've never heard of the horse. But put two bucks on his nose and I'll say three Hail Marys for him!"

O'Halloran asked Regan to talk about the wild TV sports panel shows Jesse had missed when he was out of town, "The ones with boxing champ Joey Maxim and that wrestler, Vern Gagne."

"Oh, the Maxim show was back there, well before the wrestling debacle. On the boxing show, I needled Joey about his grab and hold style. I told him the only way he'd ever knock anybody out was to suffocate them. Then I made the mistake of telling the over-rated slob that he couldn't stop his wife in the kitchen with a two by four.

"He jumped up and made a pass at me and yelled, 'You flinty-eyed little piece of mackerel. I could tear you apart with my little finger!' And he stormed right out of the studio, slamming the door and leaving poor Doc Kerns, his manager, staring at the ozone. We kept photographing Joey's empty chair for laughs."

Now Race was wound up and the miles flew by as he enthralled Pat and Jesse with his experiences.

"You know, when I was a really young cub I used to broadcast the wrestling and boxing matches for WMIN, sometimes steady when Marty O'Neill was doing the ball games. I had the only two honest wrestling matches in the Twin Cities.

"In one, Cliff Gustafson, who is supposed to win, wrecks his back when he falls wrong while he's attacking the champ, Sandor Szabo. Szabo is supposed to take the fall that night and come back again to regain his title in St. Louis two weeks later. Szabo has mastered the Hungarian Whiplash, one of the most feared holds—along with the Backbreaker of Cowboy Dick Raines and Bronko Nagurski's acclaimed Airplane Spinner to deaden the nerves and, of course, his Shoulder Block of football antecedents."

Jesse interrupted, "Jeez, you sound like a believer."

"No, I'm just titillating your visual imagery as I describe the scene of gory combat. Of course, I knew beforehand who would win and when the action would be hectic or slow so I could read my Snyder Family Liquor Store commercials . . . 'For courteous and reliable service and the finest in domestic and imported wines and liquor, stop in at 95 South Sixth Street.' I always wanted to add, 'and bring in the kids, they're certain to have a good time at this family store.'"

"Anyway, Gustafson was a former AAU wrestling champ but he had no more color than a loaf of stale bread. He had a helluva following from Gonvic, a little potato town up north. All his relatives and friends are there, about 200.

"Well, when he crashes down on my announcing table—as a result of Sandor's excruciating whiplash—he snaps some vertebrae. But nobody knows that, including the ref, little Wally Karbo.

"Wally panics and so does the mob. Now get this: there are over 7,000 fans in the Minneapolis Auditorium, all pulling for the local hero and to a man they figure Szabo has pulled a dirty trick.

"First thing I know, some 200-pound plow jockey from Gonvic has grabbed my microphone and climbed into the ring, intent on killing Szabo. By the time I get up chasing after my mic, the farmer had clobbered Szabo with my equipment and there's blood streaming down his face. At least 20 people are in the ring, cursing and swinging and trying to get at the champ. Karbo is down and nearly trampled!

"Four riot squads finally get things under control. They had to shut off the broadcast and Gustafson wound up in a cast for over a month. To this day, Gagne and Karbo and their lard-ass crew know that I grew up in all this crap. Occasionally, a little honesty creeps in purely by accident.

"One night at the St. Paul Auditorium theater section, Nagurski is meeting Abe Kashey and it should go to a 30-minute draw. Both guys are big draws—hero against villain. Well, the St. Paul ring is on the theater stage right next to the orchestra pit. This is dangerous so they tie a few ribbons on the ropes above the pit so nobody will fall in that direction.

But halfway through the match, the Bronk gets Abe above his head in a spin and would you believe, he heaves him right over the wrong side of the ring, into the orchestra pit, about 12 feet below!

"Abe screams, the crowd screams and I scream! Abe is crashing to the pit! For a few seconds I wondered if some venerable vendetta between the two antagonists had surfaced in a raw, uncontrollable moment of honest ferocity. But, naw. . . Bronko's a sweetie. And after you got under the hundred pounds of black hair on the old gorilla, Kashey was a jokester.

"But, hell, he plummeted down into the concrete pit, broke a shoulder and wrist and was out for six weeks. You know, Bronk has that funny high-pitched voice and he was explaining for a week, 'I just got a little dizzy and didn't see the ribbons. I hope Abe doesn't hate me.' If Abe had a gun that night, he'd have blown Bronk's head off!"

Race continued his non-stop monologue.

"One of the best stories was told to me by the guy they called the Prussian General, the man they said couldn't see humor if Bob Hope was playing tailback. That would be Bernie Bierman, the U of M's great coach. But he has a beautiful soft side that few knew.

"One night after a press conference I asked him how the Gophers happened to lose 7-6 to unrated Notre Dame in '37 in Memorial Stadium. He stunned me when he said the turning point 'came around Snelling and University Avenues.'

"Then he explained that the Gophers were riding in from Bayport in their new high powered bus with a police escort blazing sirens. At that corner, they passed Notre Dame, which was riding over in a couple of dilapidated St. Thomas College buses.

"The windows were down and as Bernie said, 'I think we may have made some rather disparaging remarks about their mode of transportation, reflecting, of course, on the capabilities of the team. That was a bad mistake from which we never recovered.'

"Oh, yes, Bernie could chuckle. We got to be great pals. A really loyal and misunderstood coaching legend."

It was late in the afternoon when Digger finally drove into the parking lot of the Wauwatosa hotel where the bullfighter was registered. Race didn't know what they'd encounter. "Maybe the guy's taking a nap after the afternoon show. I still don't like his name, Hector. Sounds like a creep."

Hector Montantez was the only guest registered from Mexico. He was ensconced in a second-floor room. Race figured that meant he'd negotiate by himself.

"Good, no damn agents trying to give us the shiv," Jesse pointed out.

As they knocked on Hector's door, they heard moaning, like the agony of a wounded animal.

"Jeez, maybe Hector's been gored and he's lying in there all bloody and beat up," Race volunteered.

The door opened to a scene that would have done justice to a B-grade Hollywood flick. Peter Lorre must be under the bed, Race thought.

"Enter, señors, I am Hector, the bullfighter."

Hector turned out to be a smallish, dark-skinned Mexican with a large nose, tiny mustache and shiny black hair that would have claimed him a position as a gigolo on a cruise ship. The moans were coming from the bed.

"That is Angel, one of the boys who help me with the bulls. He ees hurt in the side by a horn thees afternoon but I don't teenk his ribs break. He ees good strong boy. Little whiskey fix him up good for next fight. The bulls are leetle but very, very queek. Eh, Angel?"

Next came the visit to his shrine on the dresser. Seven little candles and one "Beeg one for the long prayer to Our Lady," Hector explained. "Even in bloodless bullfight, you need a little help from above. I teenk Our Lady hears all prayers."

The stained five-buck statue of Mary sat behind the candle. Race wondered if this Virgin was the one he prayed to before the hill-climb, when he asked for good weather. Which he got. But which came with a flying cyclist going out of sight over the top of the hill. He couldn't remember if he had prayed for a favor since then.

Hector explained that his Mariachi were playing for a picnic but would be included in our show. "They play loud, beeg sound. Oh, so romantico." Like a Salvation Army outfit with sombreros, Race thought.

Digger O'Halloran was getting restless with the flickering candles and groans of the injured kid on the bed. "We have to know the cost for two or three shows over a weekend. We'll handle the publicity. You take care of travel, bulls, your cast and the music. Figure three shows. Oh yes, in three weeks, if you're open."

Oh, Hector was figuring all right. He was sitting on the edge of the bed now, knees crossed, with a dark glass of brandy between his thin thighs. On a small piece of wrinkled paper he was trying to hold steady a three-inch pencil. Just the sight of this frayed looking little man was turning Rogers' guts to rocks.

Jesse was pacing a six-foot area, flicking glances at the tiny shrine and then at the wounded youngster laying on the bed next to the matador. 'Isn't a dime's worth of class in the whole room; if we pay this jerk more than 500 bucks for the whole shebang he'll be over-paid,' Jesse was thinking. Then he wondered if the kid had any medical coverage.

"Tres shows . . . tres shows . . . big music. Six keeds working bulls. Hmmm . . . hmmm . . ." Hector was certainly not fast on the figures but he was beeg on the totals. "Si, si. We can give you the whole teeng for tres thou . . . ou . . . thou . . ." words failed him.

"Shit! Three grand for your collection of phonies? You've got to be kidding!" Rogers almost growled in disdain. "Listen, Hector, you ain't Belmonte or whoever. You are a fourth rater! Regan, show him the Associated Press story about flunkies like him sponging off the suckers. Hey, if you said $1,000 or maybe even $1,700 but three grand? I could dress up a few actors in three hundred bucks worth of costumes and fool the people just like you're doing. Nothing but a sleazy con game."

Hector was on his feet, his jaw jutting. Obviously he had been insulted and he was a man of Latin honor. He spit at Rogers just as Race managed to leap on him. Race wrapped an arm around his neck with his own version of the Sleeper Hold while Pat managed to force Hector back down on the bed. Naturally, the jolts cause the poor wounded kid to moan even louder.

Jesse wiped his face off and stormed out of the room, shouting back, "You're a phony nothing! You couldn't kill a bull with a cannon! Get back to the glass factory!"

Race managed to quiet Hector. "Just a little misunderstanding. We appreciate your job and we know it is very dangerous. Mr. Rogers just doesn't understand all the . . . the . . . implications. You know, the band, the dancing, all the show. Maybe we can get him to understand where you're coming from. Si?"

Hector searched Regan's eyes with his own, a glow of innocent candor shining bright. "I give very good price. I come down a leetle but your friend, he is no-good, señor. He comes to my room and insults me. I hate heem!"

Digger was patting Hector on the back and telling him, "I love your shrine to the Virgin. I pray to her a lot. We will watch your fight tonight and talk to you about terms after it's over. We'll see you at the arena."

"Buenas noches," Race managed to stammer.

"The guy's insane trying to get three grand," Race advised Digger once they were out of the room. "I've seen better looking athletes in the gutter on Jackson Street."

They found Jesse in the dining room, sipping a shimmering martini and nibbling on a grand pile of shrimp, but he was still infuriated over Hector's value of himself.

"What an a-hole. I can't believe the price. I wouldn't pay a counterfeit two-buck bill to see him operate. No wonder he doesn't kill the bulls. He couldn't dent a piece of Swiss cheese with King Arthur's sword. Even suckers wouldn't put up that miserable piece of garbage. He alone is enough to give Mexico a bad name. And that poor kid. If he's a picador, the bull has to win every time. He looked like a sack of worms. And that shrine! Who does Hector think he is, the archbishop?"

Race was surprised by Jesse's demeanor. He was usually Mr. Sleepy Eyes Calm. "Easy, Jesse. I never saw you blow your cool so fast. You are usually Mr. Ice. What's got you so ruffled?"

"Jeez, the whole scene! Here's this little ant trying to be a big shot. He's insulting our intelligence. No matter. I spoke to the manager and told him we were Mr. Montantez's agents and that Hector just asked us to sign the check and put it on his hotel bill."

Digger grinned, "You didn't!"

"I did."

The three of them spent over an hour putting away $52.75 worth of shrimp, prime rib, greens, and, of course, an entirely adequate supply of gin and whiskey.

En route to the arena the threesome naturally became lost. A large crowd on the lawn of a sprawling yellow farmhouse framed by a maze of cars seemed the logical place to ask for directions. But the offer of drinks at the wedding celebration and wild rhythms of an exuberant Polish polka band were enticement enough to drive from their minds any wayward thoughts about negotiating with Hector this evening.

They decided to stay at the party where the splendid hosts were certain that these were more relatives from Susan's hometown of East St. Louis. Digger even danced with the bride and told Susan how proud he was that she had found a true man of the soil in big Tony.

"Looks like a gentle giant to me," Digger complimented.

Rogers was busy telling anyone who'd listen about scouting bloodless bullfighters at the county fairgrounds.

Regan was excited over the band, informing the leader that they were just what he was looking for in a worldwide battle of polka musicians he had just conjured up while being mesmerized by their proficiency. "We'll call this one 'The World's Polka Challenge'. I can see it drawing 50,000 people!"

"I kinda thought we were good, maybe even the best," the leader said.

Race smiled, "I'll drink to that!"

Chapter Eleven

Beware of Falling Stocks and Boxers

Enter Paige Donnelly, the "Bewildering Barrister," as Regan called him.

You could never say Donnelly's credentials were suspect, just vastly different and amazingly versatile.

At the age of 24, he had opened the first completely social pool hall in the state of Minnesota on the main street of Mankato. Meaning that men, women and children were all welcome. He even equipped the six-table parlor with lacquered white and pink cues for the ladies and ball-rackers with Disney characters imprinted on them to stimulate the kids. Signs that warned, "Beware, Cue Tips and Childrens' Eyes" were everywhere. No cussing was permitted.

Regan observed of Donnelly, "He's either the smartest man I ever met or the most eccentric. But he's a winner."

Perhaps a little of both would be the fair appraisal. In fact, he was bright enough at age 32 to write a teaching guide for professors of law. Two years later he had a staff of seven and professed to have never failed to free a client charged with a drunk driving violation through his first 200 cases. He was already becoming a legend for his impeccable preparations during injury trials. He even hired a private investigator he called "Mannix."

But it was in forming fast, glamorous local stock issues that Donnelly truly excelled. By the time he neared 40, his office staff had doubled and he had produced half a dozen over-the-counter stocks while friends at the Capitol made the issues almost impervious to legal restraints or challenges. Not that Paige ever doubted the integrity or promise of his issues but his unflappable commitment could over-sell the potential of the product. And he always put his green where his mouth was.

For instance, he raised $800,000 for an early detection kit for breast cancer that had the St. Paul community fighting for shares. The stock opened at $4 and rose to $7.25 in a week.

Paige's reputation was such that the mere mention of one of his cocktail party stock sells at the St. Paul Hotel would be enough to signal a stampede for invitations. Nobody ever seemed to question the validity of the stock's worth or the substance of the enterprise's potential. Indeed, Paige's shrewd appraisals generally were on the bull's eye. He had made large sums for many of the young and restless pin-striped suit brigade.

In one inspirational burst, Race told Donnelly that he should issue a rodeo stock. "Those cowboys hustle around the country for virtually nothing—pennies. They get bruised and cut and broken up and all of them are bow-legged. We should get a few rodeo stock companies together and issue a solid rodeo issue. I know that 3,000 cowboys would buy in."

"Why don't you get started on it, Race? I'll set up the wheels. No trouble. But be sure we get 20 percent of the stock for our work. It's new and it's different. It might mean early retirement."

So Regan promptly flew to Phoenix where a major rodeo was going on. He sought out the largest rodeo livestock company on the grounds. This outfit, which supplied bulls, bucking broncs and calves for rodeos all over the country, was owned by a millionaire cranberry grower from Wisconsin named Boots Simpson. He preferred the cowboy life to the executive's. His wife was a barrel racer.

This meant that if Race and Donnelly could persuade the livestock company's owner to shift a few of his cranberry company holdings onto the value side of a rodeo issue, a major cowboy stock might

be gracing the business pages. The rodeo man was definitely interested and the next meeting was set for a tiny southwestern
Wisconsin hamlet where Boots owned 200 acres.

This was the place where he brought his tired performers like
giant Brahma bulls and powerhouse bucking broncos to recharge
their batteries. It was on this moonlit night, while leaning against a
fence in the fields listening to the occasionally whinny of a horse,
that Paige and Race felt they were within an eyelash of triggering the
first rodeo stock issue on the face of the planet.

Boots and his wife had been talking over the venture for a week.
Frankly, he had some doubts. "I just can't see shifting parts of our
successful cranberry operation over to the stock business which can
be very hairy at best," Boots explained.

Boots' wife, Judy, leapt into the conversation, urging him to do
something a bit reckless for the pure joy of it. "God, Boots, we've got
enough money. Let's have some fun on Wall Street!" she pleaded.

Boots insisted that his aging father would disinherit him and the
deal never came off.

Paige and Race rode the train back to St. Paul, dreaming and dis-
cussing what might have been.

"Don't worry, I've got some others. Want 500 shares of Hank
Meadows?" Paige teased.

Race studied the short, plump man with the round, rosy face and
devilish spark in his eyes that made you respond with a smile even
if he was pulling your leg. Paige never cursed and his even-tempered
gentility was always a source of amazement to those who had heard
so much about the bombasticity of lawyers whose arrogant verbosity
carried so many to the top.

Nonetheless, Regan was taken aback by Paige's mention of
Meadows who Regan had always regarded as somewhat of a clown
chef; a guy who hyped crowds in various supper clubs. "You mean
the Hank Meadows of McGuire's, the chef?"

"Why not? He's been talking to me about re-opening a vacant

restaurant on Lexington and Larpenteur. You know, he wows 'em at McGuire's. I don't really know if he can even cook but Lord he shakes more hands than the governor. This place used to be Chinese but he wants to make it a steakhouse. He claims it can do $300,000 the first year. It's kind of weird that a Chinese eatery ever had financial problems. Must be a first. They must've been tossing cat's tails into the soup to blow a Chinese place."

"Don't tell me about Chinese. Remember Chow Cones? The damn things cost me a good spot at the fair. I hate anything Chinese."

"But what about steaks? Meadows says he can get cheap publicity all over town and you know he's always on the TV or radio with those dizzy tips."

"Helluva talker," Race agreed. "How much are you going to raise?"

"Oh, I'd say $300,000 should do it. Half of that will go into fixing up the place and taking out some ads. Hank really knows tons of people. So I thought we' do some direct mail. He claims he's got hundreds of addresses of McGuire's customers."

"What will the stock cost me?" Regan wanted to know.

"Why don't you just write me a check this minute for $500 and I won't cash it. I'll throw it into the issue and we'll just see what we can get with it. The insiders' shares might be a buck and half and you can hold it for a year or so and I think you'll get back five grand. Nice profit. No worries. And we know how hard Hank'll work."

Race wrote out the check. By the time the train reached St. Paul he was dozing off while dreaming the sweet fantasy of Meadows' new restaurant chain. It would be a giant conglomerate of 4,788 steakhouses from coast to coast. The stock would soar to 80 bucks per share and Race's initial five hun would be worth in the neighborhood of $35,000. A nice neighborhood which he was thoroughly enjoying when Paige jabbed him in the elbow and said, "We're home."

During the next few months Regan realized the harsh truth about stocks. Even insiders can't predict the whole story, not even when the entire issue sold out in 30 minutes at one of Paige's parties.

Two weeks after Meadows' steakhouse opened, Regan invited his wife and two sets of neighbors out for dinner, offering to "Buy the best steaks you ever tasted." He figured any flaws would now be ironed out.

Moving through the rain, Regan's party had trouble finding the restaurant's opening in the small shopping center, mainly because there was no opening. A faded, rain-soaked poster had been tacked onto the doorway informing the public that: "Meadows Has Been Temporarily Closed. Watch for Announcements Prior to Reopening."

"What the hell?" Regan spluttered to his sodden, hungry guests. "It must mean license problems. I know it can't be the food."

The truth was that Hank never really got the restaurant going after opening night. Regan missed that because of a sports assignment. But the first night's verdict was flawed. Poor service, inconsistent food and a general lack of organization. Well-done steaks were fried to the pan and rare meat looked like a brain transplant.

The trouble was that Hank was a great hand-shaker but a dismal businessman. He was so exasperated at trying to cope with all the ramifications that he had taken leave after the first eight days. A reported Arkansas sighting had him cutting whiskers on a catfish farm.

Before Regan could vent his disgust on anyone, an apologetic Paige graciously offered, at no cost, a chunk of his new venture: Mille Lacs Industries, named after the giant lake in the central part of the state.

"Forget Meadows, the place may come back. But this Jim McNerney from Montana has a great little company," Paige explained. "His top product is a hot, new three-wheeler with big tires, kind of a little land rover that can wheel over hills and really rugged terrain at good speeds with amazing balance. Just don't growl at me or call me any names," Donnelly pleaded.

"No problem," Race agreed. "What kind of 'chunk'?"

"I'll get you a couple of hundred shares no matter what it costs.

You've always been a good friend. I'm really sorry about the Meadows thing but who knew he was a terrible businessman? A pretty good chef, great talker but absolutely no organizational skills. I guess we can't be all things, right?

"Yeah, I suppose . . ."

"But this Mille Lacks Industry item is really a good one. This guy's done his homework. Could raise a million. It should be out shortly. I'll call and you be sure to come to the party. At least you'll have some good meatballs and some topnotch gin."

In the meantime, Regan interviewed former boxing legend Joe Louis at a golf tourney at Mendakota Country Club and asked him about Rocky Marciano. "Bet you wished you fought Rocky when you were at your peak, Joe?" Race asked.

"Hey, Race," answered the always pleasant Louis with a grin. "I'm just happy I met that guy before he learned to box a little. He hits like a freight train on a downhill grade. When he knocked me out of the ring, I thought I was flyin'."

Regan asked Joe about Foreman.

"I liked what I saw in the Olympics. He's got the size of a grizzly bear. Don't move too much but if he hits 'em, they'll stay hit."

"Can he be a champion?" Race asked.

"If he stays in shape and gets someone to coach him a little. Needs to move, shuffle a little."

The conversation with the Brown Bomber left Regan so energized over the production of the coming Foreman fight in St. Paul that he woke up Frenchy at 6 a.m. the next morning.

"Let's get to work on the fight," Regan urged.

"Sure, sure. What fight?" the still groggy Frenchman inquired.

"You goofy Frog, the Foreman fight! Joe Louis thinks he's going to be the next great one with that wicked punch. We'd better get him on a card before he leaves St. Paul or has a wreck in that yellow Cadillac."

Now was the time to get Foreman's signature on a contract. Within the next two days, Landreville secured papers and an Auditorium date.

In a week, Weller lined up the preliminary card. Regan set up interviews between boxing writers and Foreman. Sadler agreed to an opponent of his own choosing—a pretty fair trial horse named Charlie Boston out of New York who supposedly had sparred with Marciano at one time. Foreman would get a $2,500 guarantee and another $500 for training expenses went to Sadler. George would also get 40 percent of any profits.

Van Avery, who loved fights as much as red used cars, agreed to announce the weigh-in and also the match although long-time public address favorite, Spike McCarty, was demanding time on the microphone, too.

When the notorious Harold McAvoy, a loyal ringsider and bar owner, ordered 30 choice seats at ten bucks each, Frenchy and Race knew they were heading toward a bonanza.

Two nights before the fight, Frenchy and Race huddled with Jesse and Van in the bar at the Lexington restaurant.

"What do you really think we'll do?' Frenchy asked Race.

"We've had good ink and this Foreman is kind of a mysterious guy. You know, what's he really doing here? And does the Mafia really own him? And who really is Dick Sadler? And why isn't Foreman getting some really big-name opposition? And how come he doesn't have a regular routine at the gym? Want me to go on?"

"Yeah."

"And who is the mysterious girl he's seeing in Minneapolis? And how come he moves around from one motel to another? And how come a nice guy like George has a manager who maybe isn't so nice? And if Foreman looks this good why's he fighting for a few shekels here when he could make ten times the amount in Chicago? I'll say he's really a mysterious guy. But mystery guys do sell."

"But hey," Jesse tried to slow Race down, "let's suppose he's a young fighter who hasn't been recognized outside the Olympic crowd. And his very shrewd string-pullers in the East want him to just stay healthy until the big title chance comes and Sadler needs a little more walking-around moola and George'll plaster some guy who's not very good and not much of a threat. Foreman gets to work up a sweat with no threat from the rival and Sadler's got some lettuce in his pocket and the world goes on. St. Paul sees a future champ. Nothing so mysterious, boys. Just adds up—I think."

The rest of the figuring was done over soup at the Stage Door. Emmett Weller took out a crumpled sheet of paper with a series of columns and a maze of notes.

"Got to figure at least $10,000 in expenses," Weller said slowly while poking a ball-point pen into each figure.

"Damn boxing commission always wants a dozen freebies. Ring costs $200 and Auditorium security about $300. Prelims and the rest of the printing for posters and tickets and handbills and flyers and other crap plus the gloves, referees and rest comes to around two grand. Throw in the doctor, taxes, rent and all the little crap and it hits close to ten grand. That's purses included and includes $1,500 for Foreman's foe, whoever Sadler's bringing in."

Race interjected, "But if we do 2,500 customers at seven bucks a head we can come out of it pretty good, right, Emmett?"

"You would think so. But I don't like Frenchy's giving that Sadler 300 ringsides to peddle. That's three grand. What do we know about that quick-talking little piano player? He might be a quick walker, too."

"Hey, take it easy, Emmett," Race admonished. "First, Sadler and Foreman can't afford any bad publicity. And where are they going to hide? You could hide a dirigible in a closet easier than hiding Foreman. I trust the guy. I think this Foreman is a real decent kid. Sadler leaves me shaky. George is an innocent gem."

The ticket-buying pace stepped up the morning of the fight. Boston appeared for the weigh-in but looked fat and flabby and had circles under his eyes that made the Vesuvius crater look like a tea cup.

Van was in rare form, performing and posing for the hundred or so boxing types who shouldered into Landreville's Stage Door saloon for the laughable scale ceremony. Van grinned his Cheshire cat lipper and asked Regan: "Heard about the guy who never procrastinates? He never gets around to it." Van could hardly wait for the action. Not since his days agitating his chickens in their gory business had he been this aroused about a battle.

"Phones are going crazy. You guys might have the winner of the year. But tell me, Race, does this Boston guy look a little goofy to you? Could he have just been released from the vegetable farm or maybe a tuberculosis ward? Is he really the twin brother of Weasel, the guy Irish Paul Burke fought?"

"What's he weigh, Van?" Regan asked.

"What do you want him to weigh?" Van smiled. "I can get the doc to play tiddly with that scale."

The weigh-in managed to come off without incident and Foreman's glistening 225-pound frame looked Goliath-like against the pudgy, almost yellowish-hued pear-shaped flab of his foe. The only place Boston could have fought recently was in the back yard with his mother-in-law.

"Seen better bodies in Jake's junk yard," Van said dolefully, shaking his grey thatch. "Oh, well, wait'll the mob sees me in my rented tux. Cost me fifteen bucks, but my daughter said I look like Cary Grant."

Late editions gave the fight the front page cover, pictures and all. That was always good for 500 tickets. The radio stations had taken up the chant, albeit a little late. Two television stations covered the weigh-in for the evening news shows. The weather was good. The prospects bright, although Sadler seemed a little more nervous than usual. He would leave the restaurant every five or ten minutes and return more jittery than a cat in a room full of rocking chairs.

During dinner at Gallivan's, enroute to the match, Frenchy was visibly upset. The little guy was concerned that Sadler had not turned in any money for the advance tickets he was carrying. "He was supposed to meet me at my joint at three o'clock," Frenchy said, agitated. "I called him but he's like a friggin' mouse in a cheese factory. I can't track him down here, there, anywhere. If he tries to make a run with that money . . . oh, that little rascal!"

"Relax," Race urged. "The guy has to show up at the fight. He shows up and we settle up. What's he going to do, skip town and leave George behind?"

"Still wish we had that money in our hands—or the tickets."

Everyone in sight seemed to be mauling the 16-ounce steaks Gallivan served. The bar was alive with fans, including the usually heavily rouged divorcees who seemed to always appear at loop sporting events, hopeful of finding just the right guy who'd at least buy a few rounds.

"Here's my guess," Regan said as he pushed a small piece of white scrap paper in front of Jesse with the figures '$25,000' written on it.

"Think it'll go that high?" Jesse asked.

"Why not? It's catching on. Foreman's a name. I just hope Boston manages to last at least three rounds. Can't afford a diving contest."

Race's worst fears became a factual nightmare. In front of nearly 3,000 fans, who were prepared for the best, the bout turned into the worst.

For one thing, Foreman's foe had trouble getting in the ring, tripping over the lower strand of ropes. After the introductions, he couldn't find his seconds and went to the wrong corner.

As the fight opened, he appeared to be searching for a trap door that would release him to safety. When George tossed an experimental left jab he did everything but scream, "I give up!"

It was an exercise in purgatory for the promoters. Regan could not swallow. Landreville had his chin lowered in his hands. The commissioners had turned ashen. Promoter Weller, who was working the corner of Foreman's pathetic opponent, appeared to be looking for an intervening angel. The six commissioners figured they'd be hearing from the governor who was sitting just six rows behind them.

Foreman's foe had trouble raising his hands. It appeared he had never been in the ring. The Viaduct Bar produced better looking prospects any Saturday night. Mercifully, Boston, or whoever he was, splashed into oblivion in the first round from one casual punch and three invisible ones. The fans didn't know whether to jeer Boston or cheer Foreman. Nobody seemed more surprised at his foe's pathetic demise than George.

"Damned impostor," commissioner Jack Gibbons growled to Race. "I'll nail that Sadler. Whoever that bum is he sure as the devil hasn't fought much, if ever. I feel sorry for George but this crap is going to hit the fan. I can't believe that tub of goose grease is the real Boston!"

Nobody had any idea of how much crap or how large the fan. Within two days the mess had made sports pages from coast to coast. As it turned out, the foe was not Boston but somebody apparently named Smith, a rumored dish-washer out of North Carolina. Sadler evidently made a deal with him for far less than even a mediocre opponent would cost and everyone figured he pocketed the rest.

The authentic Charlie Boston was threatening lawsuits. Within 48 hours Sadler was mysteriously summoned out of town, supposedly by the sinister Philly crowd. They had ways of demanding explanations.

And poor Foreman. The genial giant had been ready to slay a dragon and instead met a paper clown. George just shrugged his wide shoulders and explained, "I fight whoever Mr. Sadler gets for me. The one he got was pretty bad, huh?"

Bad? Miserable. Indefensible. Race actually felt sorry for Foreman who would fight a gorilla in a box car for fifty bucks.

Naturally, that was the end of Foreman's St. Paul boxing career. The fight grossed about $18,000 and Sadler came back to pay for about half of the tickets he was issued.

"Just couldn't seem to find the right people to buy them," he explained.

Profits totaled $1,745 which, after being split among all those involved, amounted to about 98 cents per hour in actual payroll time. And after the state's cut and what seemed like a never-ending list of minor to major extras, the insiders were suggesting that maybe boxing was dead.

The commission was shaken up and banned Foreman and Sadler from any more fights in St. Paul for a year. Frenchy said that he could have knocked out Smith or Boston or whoever the hell with "a slap of my hand."

For once everyone agreed.

Race tried to philosophize, "Look at it this way, we got to see a future ring great shadow box at a reasonable price."

Van corrected him, "A shadow would have been more dangerous—and cost less."

Undeterred by the bad press following his victory over the no-name opponent, Foreman told Regan a few days later that "I'll still fulfill my destiny, win a title, get married, make a lot of money and give praise to the Lord."

Toward that goal, George fell in love with a Minneapolis girl whom he married soon after. Financially, his posh University Avenue office was a drain, reportedly to the tune of fifty grand. George left town.

But he continued to visit St. Paul. After all, wasn't this where the Longshots fixed him up with his spiffy yellow Cad?

Chapter Twelve

Famed Red Foley's a Washout

It was at Kermit Johnson's resort, an idyllic retreat called Sherwood Forest on Gull Lake, that Regan's intramural plans began to take on a cosmopolitan grandeur. Blame it on an accordion-playing Norwegian named Thornsten Skarning of Minneapolis.

But first you must picture Sherwood Forest, where a towering, genial, white-haired Kermit likened himself to Robin Hood. "Taking a few shekels from the rich and spreading it around us poor." That's the way Kermit explained his philosophy of running a resort in probably the most highly competitive business in Minnesota.

"Keep the roofs from leaking and make sure their cocktails are clear and cool and let them beat you at ping-pong. That's what it's all about. Make sure you have a wife like Natalie, who makes certain everybody meets everybody else and that everyone thinks the other one is a huge success."

That was Kermit's formula for keeping his sprawling 24-cabin operation in the black ink. "Oh, yeah, you gotta have a big fireplace and it has to be going every night, even it it's 60 degrees outside. Atmosphere is everything."

The towering two-story rock fireplace in the lodge was a gathering spot after dinner. And Natalie had her job down to perfection. The little, agile, brunette, a picture in perpetual motion, would flit from table to table introducing, "Ted and Grace Jones, you know, the Joneses who are on the Roseville school board—I want you to meet the dearest people, this is Jim and Vivian Olson; they're the Olson's who own that adorable new nursery in White Bear, the one with the huge sign. You two successful couples must have a lot in common. I guarantee . . ."

Incredibly, nearly 90 percent of the time, Kermit and Natalie could pick out the right combinations to pair off for dinner. Many of the couples would return on the same dates and some would even continue the relationships back in the Twin Cities.

The Johnson's bolstered Regan's ego by insisting he act as bartender on the large screened porch before and after dinner for two hours of sports conversation each night. Regan's family got complimentary housing.

But it went a little deeper. Regan purchased cars from Kermit when he ran the sales department of a Chrysler agency and both of them enjoyed each other's company, particularly in the late evening when they would huddle up in the darkened lodge's kitchen. There, Kermit would make Regan huge cheese sandwiches and hot chocolate. "If anybody knew how good this tasted we'd never sell any booze," Kermit confessed.

They would talk until nearly dawn about people and promotions and sports. Kermit once coached a small high school's basketball team. And he was a master of cutting to the core of situations in the fewest possible words. He was completely familiar with Race's many ventures in the entertainment field.

"As I see it, Race, you have a small flaw in your thinking: you are slightly too impetuous. And that leads to one fatal mistake in each venture. Like not knowing how powerful the cycles were in the hill climb. Or not knowing that condensation would wreck the dance show in the ice arena. Or not knowing who Foreman was really going to fight. See what I mean? One flaw eventually kills each promotion, even if you've got 90 percent of it right. And those trout dying by the hundreds at the boat show, you should have known everything there was to know about trout."

"Oh, hell, Kermit. What was I going to do? Spend three months talking to the damn fish to find out what temps they liked in the water?"

"No, of course not. But why not spend some time with the guy who owned the trout pond? Why not ask a real cyclist expert how much room he'd need to land when he hit the top of the hill? You just presume too damn much. Know why? Because you are a creative mind. You are not a detail man.

"The truth is you should hire a nuts-and-bolts factual guy who is a smart fine-tuned expert on the technical things you are trying to put on. Remember the silly camera guy you had at the fair? He needed 20 pictures to get one that wasn't fuzzy. If you'd hired a real camera expert you'd have made a killing."

"You've got something on your mind besides advice," Regan smiled slowly, not looking up from the large wad of mustard he was applying to the slab of Swiss cheese between halves of sumptuous dark rye.

"Well, I have. You are perceptive, too, Race, along with that creative mind. If you were just a little more detailed . . ."

"Cut the Swede horse crap," Race admonished, biting so deeply into his cheese and rye that mustard curled up and around the corners of his mouth.

"Well, have you heard of Thorsten Skarning, my finely tuned accordion player with all the Norwegian twinkle? Did you know he's not just an accordion player, a run-of-the-mill musician?"

"What is he, a magician too?"

"Don't be a wise ass. The guy's a real smart cookie when it comes to promotions. He goes all the way back to Lawrence Welk when he was just starting. In fact, he claims he gave Welk a ten spot to buy dinner when Welk was just getting going in the St. Paul Hotel 20 years ago. Anyways, he's been around, a real insider who has brought in everything from saxophone players to jazz bands. Thorsten has a knack of knowing what the public wants."

"Listen, Kermit, I don't know a thing about the music business."

"What did you know about motorcycles or food people like Hank Meadows?"

"Okay, okay. I'm bleeding. Take it easy with the dagger."

"Anyway, Race, Thorsten wants to talk to you. He's got some guy named Bob Utech, who puts out a hockey paper and they want to do something pretty big. You might be interested."

"Utech? Utech? Yeah, I know who he is. But what's hockey got to do with accordions?"

"I don't know. But let's meet Thorsten tomorrow after lunch. Won't cost a nickel to hear him out."

"Listen, Kermit, I appreciate the adventure but let me tell you how little I know about music. I'm the guy who told the Flamingo Club's owners to get rid of John Denver and keep the Turkish belly dancer. She died overweight after eating chocolates. You know about Denver."

"The real John Denver?"

"Yes, the real John Denver. Jeeze, I don't know how he ever succeeded, singing through his nose the way he did."

The next day over double Cabin Stills and tall scotches, Race and Skarning hit it off amazingly well. They met at the Rendezvous, near the Gull Lake trails.

"You see, Regan, timing is everything in music. And now is the time of the big country name. The Twin Cities and the state have more country music nuts than most places but really no big-name acts come in consistently. Well, I've got the name and the place. All I need is about twelve grand."

"Hey, who's the name?"

Thorsten smiled, his pale skin almost breaking in anticipation of Race's curiosity. "Red Foley and the Ozark Jubilee."

"What! The Red Foley? The guy I catch now and then on television?"

"The one and only. And he'll bring his band and four other singers—including the hottest new guy, Marvin Rainwater."

"Yeah, I've heard of him. Got a new record about smoking."

"That's it. 'Smoke, Smoke, Smoke' I think. These are heavies. I got a Sunday night date in four weeks at the Met ballfield. We could 'yump 'em good,' as we say in Oslo."

"How'd you get him? He's sure no Swede or Norwegian."

"It was easy. I know people he knows. I used to play down in his part of the country. And here's something else; Foley's son-in-law is Pat Boone. I don't know what his schedule is with all that TV. But if he flew in and we knew about it in time and could get him to sing a number or two, we'd do 10,000 customers."

"Cripes! That's something. But a question, Thorsten. If this is so good, how does a humble little guy like me get cut in?"

"Utech suggested it. He'll come in for a third. Said you really get into a lot of promotions. We can get Red for about $7,500. And my plan is this: if Red makes a bundle for us, we plow it right back into another big one. We could become the dominant country western promoters in the Twin Cities! And as our reputation grows, the big guys are calling us."

"You said maybe we hit 10,000 customers. But let's be realistic, what do we make if we draw half that?"

"Well, we charge four bucks, which is about the average for shows like this. That would be a $20,000 gate. After all expenses, we'd make eight grand. But if it catches on, wowee!"

"God! I love it! How do we advertise?"

"That's the beautiful part. We buy a few spots on WDGY, you know the country station. Then we paper about 150 country western bars and dance halls in a 100-mile radius of the Twin Cities. You understand, the country music fans spread the word by mouth. It's more infectious than lockjaw. One guy always tells ten others. And Foley hasn't been in these parts. He's hot."

"No chance he'll cop out?"

"Foley is Mr. Integrity. Anyway, I'll meet Utech next week at his home in Bloomington. I'll give you his telephone number and address. Bring along four grand if you're interested. I'm figuring on doubling my money."

Regan agreed to the meeting. He also could hardly wait to tell his decision to Dots and see if she had any intuition on the subject, since she had been a professional singer and loved theater.

Dots was amazingly brief and to the point when Regan asked her advice. "Foley? Maybe. Pat Boone? I'd pay."

Honestly, Regan was thinking, he hadn't heard that much publicity about the Sunday evening show. But then he really didn't travel in country music circles. Both papers had rather small items in enter-tainment pages and he had caught a couple of radio blurbs. But three days before the event he had his nerves jangled a bit when Thorsten called and asked what he thought about rain insurance.

"Rain? God, I never gave it a thought. It doesn't rain that much in early fall, does it?"

"Well, the long-range forecast is for clouds and showers Sunday afternoon. You know these country music types don't buy in advance. We've only got about two grand in the till. I figure a huge walk-up crowd but it's just a thought. For two grand we could buy ourselves about seven grand's worth of insurance. It might be a safe bet."

Race's buoyant attitude couldn't have been deflated more quickly if somebody had rammed a jack hammer into his buttocks.

"Hey, I just borrowed the four grand from the credit union for a home improvement loan. They think I'm putting on a new kitchen nook. In fact, they want to come out and look at my kitchen, figur-ing after all these loans it's got to be the showplace of the nation."

"Then you'd rather forget the insurance?"

"Let's take a chance. If it does rain it may only be for an hour or so. Our 7:00 p.m. start could be set back a little, right?'

"Maybe. I don't know how tough Foley is on things like this."

Sunday dawned clear and a little crisp. A sliver of fall in the air on this late September date.

As usual, Regan stopped at the office, wrote his column and then slipped around to the Parker House in Mendota for a burger enroute to the Met. The bartender, a gabby little Greek called Cheater, asked Regan if he was going to hear Foley. Regan's spirits immediately picked up. The weather was still good, temperatures in the low sixties and he began to beam with the anticipation that maybe a lot of people like Cheater knew about the Jubilee.

"Are you going?" asked Regan.

"No. Just feeling sorry for the people who bought tickets. They tell me it's going to rain all night."

Regan shoved aside his burger. "It doesn't look bad outside."

"Coming in from the southwest. My cousin, Art, just called from Albert Lea and says it's rough down there. But I suppose the promoters have rain insurance."

Race swallowed a rock. He refused to admit he had anything to do with the show.

By the time Race left the Parker House, half a burger was doing hand-stands in his belly. He called home to tell Dots to put on rain gear for the show because the sky was turning off its light switches. A long black blanket of ominous clouds was drifting in from the direction the bartender had prophesied.

'Damn! If only I had gone in for the rain insurance. But what the hell, it could clear in three hours.'

It never cleared. Small clusters of potential customers huddled around the entrance and maybe three or four hundred more sat in cars, trying to make up their minds. A lot of seats behind home plate were covered by the over-hang but the stage would be sitting in mud. The overall dark, damp atmosphere had to demolish any customer's enthusiasm. Again, God had made a fist, Regan philosophized.

Nobody would ever know how much the rain hurt but only about 1,700 gathered inside for the show. Thorsten estimated another 2,000 drove into the parking lot, looked around and refused to walk 200 feet or so to the structure in weather that had spasmodically turned into a noisy cloudbursts.

Before throwing his wallet to the sacrifice, Race shuffled around a concession stand, trying to pick up the mood, maybe learn something about this strange breed of music follower. What he heard in one corner turned his spine to cactus.

A fat, bearded, semi-ape type was asking a question of two smaller pick-up truck aficionados. "Hey, how come you guys didn't show up at Pine's River Club in South St. Paul this afternoon? You could have heard Marvin Rainwater belting songs for two hours for free!"

Regan was absolutely stunned. He had to interrupt the group of ugly strangers and inquire about their conversation.

"Sure," the beefy guy in the New York Yankee jacket explained, "these guys sing all around for maybe a hundred bucks on days like this. Probably more than they get from Foley. I've heard of at least four shows in the Cities where somebody from this outfit even sang for ten bucks. These guys just like to sing. They're like gypsies, always hustling a buck."

The bastards. The cheating, friggin' bastards! Regan rushed with this news to Thorsten and Utech. "How can these jerks do that? How can they call themselves professionals?"

Thorsten tried to explain. "I really can't believe it either but you've got to remember, Rainwater and a couple of the others started their careers around here and probably figured they owed it to a few saloon keepers who hired them when they were breaking in."

"They should be outlawed," Utech complained. He was a tall, raw-boned, heavy-eyebrowed guy with a face like a sack of potatoes who was an expert about the high school and college hockey players in the state. "They could have cost us 1,500 customers or more. You'd think Foley would have some control over them."

"Hey, they're not his children," Thorsten said defensively.

"Speaking of children," Regan interjected, "did we ever have a chance of landing Boone?"

"Naw, he was singing at a concert in 'Frisco," Thorsten explained. "But we had a winner if it hadn't rained and those guys hadn't gone out and given it away for free, like a nymphomaniacal whore."

"What do you think we lost with the rain?" Race asked meekly.

"Not more than six grand," Thorsten quickly answered.

"You sound like that was a triumph," Race complained.

"I've been in dozens of these and you don't get discouraged. You just learn."

Regan thought back to Kermit's assessment of his promotions—"You don't get the experts"—this friggin' Thorsten didn't know any more about music promotion than a bricklayer. Maybe there were no experts!

After the concert, the promoters met Foley at the Black Cat supper club in Bloomington, a few miles from Met Stadium. Red explained that he thought the concert was as good as could be expected, under the dismal circumstances, and that the audience was certainly lively.

"What there was of it," Race observed solemnly.

Foley was given a check for $6,000 and he didn't complain about the missing $1,500. In fact, he offered to pick up the group's dinner tab. "You guys got hurt. I understand," he nodded.

"Tell you what," the weather-worn Foley told the down-hearted group, "this was a major success compared to some of the shows I did in the early part of my career. I've sung before 20 to 30 people a lot of times. And you can't really blame some of my people for singing out there to pick up a few extra bucks. They're still struggling. Hell, we're all struggling."

Everyone had to admit Foley had put on a tremendous show. His group sang their hearts out in the rain.

Dots had opted to stay home.

Regan had the wipers on and music blaring from his car radio as he headed toward Roseville. He'd have to call Jesse and Frenchy and Larsen to tell them about the fiasco. Because of their individual personal situations during the past week, none had even asked about the show. Jesse was fighting with divorce attorneys; Frenchy was launching another dinner club; Larsen was talking about buying a sprint car and Digger was talking about buying into a pro hockey franchise or maybe creating his own.

Regan had to smile to himself when he thought about telling Dots how much her ticket had cost this time. Another loss. How many more could she take with such gentle, philosophical aplomb?

He remembered her saying after the hill climb to thank God the flying cyclist hadn't landed in the St. Croix River. After a putting game flop at the Fair she had said that the kids loved the brown stuffed prize monkeys more than anything in their playroom. After the heavyweight boxing fiasco with Irish Paul Burke, she had told Race that he should say a prayer that nobody got hurt.

Race wondered if she would think $2,000 was about right for a hamburger steak at the Black Cat.

Chapter Thirteen

A Fast Dream, Real Cash

Regan put it bluntly to his wife, Dots. "Honey, how far do you go with a dream?"

"Depends on the dream. We've had a few nightmares. You're not thinking of re-treading the putting contest, are you?"

"No. Much bigger."

"Will you risk the house and children?"

"Dots! Have I ever hurt you or the kids? You know better than to ask a question like that."

"Then go ahead with the dream. You won't be quitting your job will you?"

"No. But if it goes like I think it can, we could be moving on to the national scene."

"Oh? Let's hear it."

"Well, Kermit Johnson may have said it best the last couple of times I talked with him up at the lodge. He says we all think too small. That we nickel and dime ourselves to death with two-bit operations. He says if it's a good idea to shoot for the stars. I don't mean hock the house but I mean make it impressive enough so it carries an impact.

"In the past, we thought too small. We didn't have enough of an advertising budget. Or we counted on people to get the word out and they failed. Or we didn't look at the logistics. Or we were hurt by bad locations or bad dates. But there is a right combination. And we've got a big one if we want it. Frankly, I think it's the best we've ever had."

"Well?" Dots asked, ignoring the load of ironing.

"Recall Dayle Maloney, you know the inspiration clinic guy who is knocking them dead selling leisure trailers and stuff? Well, he can get a top flight Indy 500 race car, the one Bobby Unser ran to second last year. It's called the Olsonite Eagle and it's a beaut. Red, white and blue and a burner."

"You mean a real race car? Won't that cost a fortune?"

"Listen, Dots, not as much as you might think. Dayle can get the chassis for about $90,000. We can get three new Offenhauser engines for about $40,000 each. With the set-up, garage, driver and a good mechanic and even a lot of unforseeables, the whole project will cost only about $200,000."

"Lord, Honey, you could build five nice houses for that!"

"But wait. Dayle's going to put in fifty grand and he's got two other silent partners who will go about the same. One, I hear, is a big-time bar owner with tons of green. I know Jesse will want in and I can probably get a good piece for 20 grand. O'Halloran, the undertaker, is pleading to get in and so is an ex-racer."

"Hold on, hold on, sweetie!" interrupted a now wide-eyed Dots. "Do you realize $20,000 is approximately what our first house cost? And what happens if the car doesn't win? Who's going to buy an old rebuilt Indy car?"

"You have hit us where it hurt. But let's say we finish even fourth or fifth or sixth. We could pick up about half of the investment back in prize money. And I'm betting , like Dayle says, that we get a dozen sponsors who give us big bucks just to put their names on the machine. Most of these cars are getting covered with decals. Dayle claims his boss at the leisure-vehicle company would put in 10 grand to have his face stamped on the cowling."

"The cowling?"

"Imagine what we get for the hood and sides! I envision this baby getting maybe as many as 20 sponsors that could bring in over 100 grand. From there on it's a cake walk. We take the car, no matter what it does, to all the little county fairs and maybe the State Fair. Every kid in the state will want to touch the car that ran at Indy."

"Suppose it runs only 50 miles. Will the kids still want to touch it?"

"Listen, Dots, won't you be proud to say you own a piece of an Indy car?"

"Who's going to drive it? Some local hot rod kid?"

"Just let us worry about that. It'll be a competent driver, a real pro."

It was a gathering to be remembered. Regan had written a column explaining the adventure in speed and suggested the name, "Minnesota Invader." He pointed out that Minnesota hadn't had a machine in the big merry-go-round since Bob McManus, a soft-drink mogul, placed his racer in the glamour event back in the late '30s.

"Minnesota Invader" was on everyone' slips when the noisy little group met in a corner at what had been Napoleon's and was now under new ownership and re-named The Blue Horse.

"Great name, Race," the wide-faced Maloney smiled as he wrapped a heavy arm around Regan's shoulders. "You know how to name 'em. Invader—that's the powerhouse word! And Minnesota has to appeal to the locals who take so damn much pride in all these lakes."

"Yeah. That's what I thought," Race nodded.

Jesse, toasting with an extra dry martini held high, affirmed the choice to challenge for the Greasy Grail. "Here's to the new speed age and Minnesota's first triumph in a major sport!"

"Yeah . . . how about it! . . . done deal! . . . on our way! . . . to speed and the fast guys behind the cars! . . . to the Invader, may it conquer the world!" Everyone of the seven investors was saluting the thrill of being "500" entrants.

Egan was already on a trip to Chicago, looking for more heavy investors.

"Why not more right here?" someone asked.

"Too big for just Minnesota," answered Dayle. "Every big hitter who ever owned a fast car will want to get in on this one. We're talking about $200,000 expenses. I'm talking about $300,000 above that from sponsors."

Dayle's eyes sparkled behind silver-rimmed glasses and his considerable belly jiggled like Santa's. His bass voice seemed to echo through the premises.

Another toast: "To the Sponsors!" Race shouted. And he was joined by the happy throng, all anticipating the big kill. No venture had ever begun with such unanimous agreement over a promotion which everybody knew so little about. But if you mentioned that to anyone of the group, be prepared to fight.

Regan explained to Terry Malone, the bartender, "We've got everything a good promotion needs. A couple of big, silent hitters. A promoting fool in Maloney. He'll have us on every radio program and TV show in the state. Egan knows how to find big hitters from around the Northwest. Jesse can get us all the cheap insurance we need. We've got Digger, the mortician, who can bury any mistakes. I can certainly get the paper hepped up on a little better race coverage. Every guy contributes—either cash or deeds."

The bartender had the audacity to ask, "Anyone know anything about engines?"

Jesse was silent—but only for a moment. He responded almost casually, "God, we hire that done. We'll have a couple of good mechanics and a top flight driver. We start interviewing the drivers right away. And those Offenhauser engines, all top mechanics know about them. But those drivers, how about A.J. Foyt or Roger Ward?"

"You nuts?" retorted Race. "We're not giving away the house before we put on the roof. Those guys want your shoes. We want a young, hungry driver who'll take some chances."

"What kind of chances?"

"I don't mean rupture the wall. We want a guy who'll charge when there's an opening. I've seen that race. You don't win it on the first lap."

"Thank you, Tony Hulman," Malone cracked.

"Get your nose back in the lime bottle," Regan needled jokingly as he mingled with the now loud and boisterous group. They had been joined by a tiny man who was introduced by ex-race driver Al McChesney only as "Little Felix." McChesney owned a piece of a small Wisconsin strip and also sold leisure vehicles with Maloney.

McChesney was in for a small piece and so was a large, red-faced and unkempt husky named Red Carlson. Carlson hailed from Fulda, a sleepy farming community and he was supposed to be the mechanical whiz who would oversee some of the engineering challenges posed by Offenhauser engines.

On hand but strangely missing from the financial structure was Swede Larsen. His assessment, "I've owned enough sprint cars to know you can't buck the big money corporations at Indy. They'll swallow up the little guys. I've always wanted to get in the big one but I need deeper pockets."

"What about your friend, Jim Hurtubise? He's been in the chase, running his own rebuilt cars right out of his garage," Regan inquired.

"Sure but there's only one Little Hercules, Race. You know that. Jim could take an Edsel and put it in the fourth row but he won't drive for you guys. He's too independent. He'll want to call every shot, from the nuts to the color of the car. Plus, he's still banged up from all those burns from his last accident. You'll need a top flight driver," Swede offered.

"Got any ideas?" Jesse asked.

"Art Pollard might come. He's a good one. Been in the grind. Knows the track. And I hear from my wife's friends in Indiana that he's fed up with his sponsorship. Might cost you fifty Gs but he'd be worth it."

Race stiffened. "Fifty Gs, Swede, is slightly over our budget. We're thinking more like ten and the usual 40 percent of the earnings."

"Better forget Pollard," said Swede. "But then again, maybe you'll catch him getting out of the right side of the bed. He might be in the mood to try something new and fresh like this if he sees you've got some money and a good car."

Regan asked quickly, "Isn't Bobby Unser's car from last year a good one? Hey, second place. And running strong at the finish. The Olsonite Eagle is ours if we move fast. And it's a helluva looking piece of iron."

Larsen interjected a sobering note:

"Last year is like the Civil War at Indy. The aerodynamics change as much as 25% on the good cars. Be prepared to experience shocks and bring along enough motors and tires. You go through tires like piss through a storm sewer.

"Engines? Better have three or four. You're bound to blow. And make sure your driver's not a drinker. Indy isn't wide enough for hangovers. Only 60 feet wide down the stretch. It's just a ribbon. Remember, you want a steady guy with a heavy foot and lots of engines and tires."

"Dammit, Swede, you sound more pessimistic every day. No wonder Ingemar Bergman, or whatever the hell his name is, makes so many movies that look like he filmed them under a sewer cover. Bet you wish you had some nice red Irish blood. Tell me you do!"

Swede looked at his dangling cigarette for a few seconds and responded with a typical understatement, "Race, I doubt if you know a piston from a jock strap."

Overhearing those mincing words, Van Avery, who had arrived late after a midnight sale at the auto pavilion, wiped his glasses, readjusted his hat and surmised, "Race, you asked for that. Swede's got stability. The rest of us are just pipe dreamers. I still say you guys should have bought a horse."

"Race cars don't eat or need new shoes," Race snapped.

"No, they just blow $40,000 engines," Van countered.

Time was flying for the little group of dreamers. The Longshots were involved in so many small fires that they were having trouble concentrating on the real blaze—the Indy car. It was as if now that they had the monster in the cage they were a little afraid to confront it for fear it would sneak out and tear off their arms.

The Olsonite Eagle Chassis would be purchased in a matter of days. It was the Longshots'. But the $90,000 expenditure seemed to awe them all. For the moment, they again were scatter-gunning their energies.

Regan and Rogers, over their third martinis of a soft autumn evening at Gallivan's, decided that there were at least a dozen St. Paul figures who deserved testimonial dinners. They decided this upon hearing that an old acquaintance named Dick Mangini had opened a beautifully decorated restaurant on the East Side and was looking for special events to distinguish his location.

He had installed a bocce ball court under lights at the rear of his place and hoped the understated beige and maroon and mahogany furnishings would make this a gathering spa of distinction. Mainly, Regan and Rogers found out, his price was right.

From behind large, stylish horn rims, Mangini was saying, "For you old friends, just bring me some big dinners, fill the place on my quiet Mondays and you can have a huge Italian-American buffet for seven bucks. The rest you keep or give to your charities.

"Did I tell you Yogi Berra was in here? He's a pal of my cousin in New York. But you guys can do me a job. Remember just seven bucks, you get a great deal and tremendous meals. All you can eat."

And so the testimonial service of Regan and Rogers was born. The first one had to be for Gallivan, saloon owner extraordinare. "A very daring, honest man," Regan suggested.

"The best," Rogers agreed.

But the opening dinner got a little out of hand. Once word got out, the Chamber of Commerce wanted in. Celebs had to be involved. And instead of a cozy outing at Mangini's this testimonial grew into a 700-plate dinner at the Hotel St. Paul.

It was a success of sorts. The $12 tickets went almost overnight. But what kind of gift do you give a man who has everything? That was solved when a Finnish legislator named Mont Torson volunteered a rare hunting gun someone had given him years ago.

Presumably it was the only Winchester rifle ever built in Tokyo after Japanese industrial spies stole the plans from the American factory. That made it a very valuable collector's item. In fact, the case in which it was kept would make most Stradivarius violin boxes look like Sears shopping bags.

So much for artistic success. When Rogers and Regan counted all the players in the locker room, they came up about $400 short. Kansas City sportscaster George Higgins was brought in as a guest speaker. Gallivan was so touched he actually shed a few real tears.

"Well spent. Gallivan's a helluva guy," Jesse offered.

"Hope he tries out that gun before he uses it hunting. Could be booby-trapped by the Japanese," Race suggested quietly.

But the testimonial venture caught the imagination of this Longshot pairing. Race nominated a softball pitching star, who promptly believed they knew something about his health they weren't telling him. They had to get him drunk before virtually hauling him up to the podium. But after giving him the small silver service tray, the event produced a neat profit, which quickly went to pay mounting bar bills at Gallivan's, The Blue Horse, Frenchy's establishments and Swede Larsen's bowling lanes.

Rogers came back to nominate an old boxer for another testimonial. Then it was a Gopher football coach. Then it was an old hockey star. Next came humble sportscaster Marty O'Neill, who couldn't show up because of illness and whose live presence was replaced by a life-size photo.

Marty's stand-in photo got such a hand that when he heard about the ovation he promptly ran for city council. He took a terrible beating at the polls. Van Avery pointed out, "Everybody loves you, Marty, it's just that they don't think you have the know-how to improve garbage pick-ups."

Even a floundering boxer was honored at Mangini's and given enough money to offset his training expenses for a fight abroad. It mattered little if anyone really cared about the recipients of the testimonial or who garnished the speaker's table. Family and friends always jammed Mangini's and the crowd always left complementing the owner on his food.

Regan served as MC and managed to introduce at least 90 percent of those attending the fetes. If you weren't introduced by Race, believe me, you were the object of humiliation among your peers. All of the galas provided a little extra spending money for Regan and Rogers, along with the satisfaction of doing something a tad noble for the unappreciated. As Regan said, "If we didn't do it, it wouldn't be done."

The dinners led to some touching emotional moments. Even Rogers had tears in his eyes when prep star Dave Winfield, heading for pro fame, praised his granny for helping his blossoming career.

Profits meant little. One night, in a gesture of charity, Race gave all the clear moola to a tiny old violinist who had played at a number of sporting events in his "fashionable" fur-collared tuxedo.

Rogers didn't object. Mainly because he was paying himself at this particular time more money than his insurance business was taking in.

And though Race was drinking a little bit more, he still managed to arrive on time at work and continued to win attendance honors. His family was still intact, albeit showing signs of nervousness. This potential problem was definitely filed away under the heading of 'Minor adjustments to be dealt with in the future.'

Over cheeseburgers at Frenchy's Stage Door supper club, Art Pollard, a ruggedly handsome race driver, was making his pitch to handle the Minnesota Invader. Yes, he knew the car. Yes, he thought it had a chance. Yes, he was experienced in molding a set-up crew and pit men who knew the tangible and intangible vagaries of the famous Indy 500. Pollard dissected and analyzed the proposed operation and was frankly enthusiastic.

"With the right mechanic and people in the right places, this car can make a run at it," Pollard told the meeting. "But I'll want 30 grand up front, a decent hotel for six weeks, expenses and the regular 40 percent of the winner's share. That might be $50,000 this time around. And you fellows would clear about $300,000 or so. For that, I give you my abilities and all my expertise. I don't have to tell you, I will charge when the time is right. I stay away from traffic for 400 miles and then let her rip."

Pollard's reputation was one of a lead foot with brains and pizzazz. After the meeting, Maloney, Egan, Rogers and Regan huddled well into the night. After closing his bowling alley, Swede joined them at Mickey's all-night burgerarium on Wabasha Street.

"A lot of dough. He's good but Lord, he's expensive," Race observed.

"But he runs like a jet propelled tiger, I hear," Maloney offered.

At this point, Jesse spilled his coffee all over himself, jumped from the table and shouted, "Damn, it's hot! Screw it! I don't care who we get but let's move on it!"

Swede advised the group to think it over for a week or so. Obviously, Pollard was searching and didn't have his race connections set. Swede turned to Maloney and suggested, "Why not talk to Larry Dickson, the Michigan kid? You know him and I've seen him run. He's a sweetheart. Fast. Gutsy enough and he's been whipping their asses in the fast sprints all over the midwest. He also wants a piece of Indy."

"Hey, you've got something," Maloney agreed. "I took a bunch of guys to Michigan for a race meeting and happened to catch him. He just blew everyone away. And he's never been to Indy. He should work cheap—if nobody's got him."

It was agreed that Dickson would be interviewed before any choice was made.

It was 10 a.m. at Gallivan's and Van Avery dropped in, greeting his friends with a typical spiel, "My new Fords give you far more room, fellows, by removing the big bulge in your wallets."

Regan was feistier than ever. "Van, you just don't give up. I think you actually believe that car crap, that Detroit is making better cars every year. If they are, how come they're doing away with fenders and running boards forever? Gosh, the guy who designed my old Hudson Hornet with the step-down entry, would be chewing on his bones in Calvary."

But Van stuck to his guns. "This year's American automobile is the product of the century. Just peddled 11 last week, which means this'll be my biggest year. And all of them had motors!"

"Today we decide who's going to drive the Invader," Maloney stated, while doodling with his pen. "We talked to Dickson and he's hot to go. We get him for five grand and expenses compared to all the money Pollard wanted. On the one hand, Dickson is young and hot and cheap. On the other hand, he's inexperienced. Pollard's got a big name, obviously an Indy star and damn expensive. Let's vote on it."

Super hustler Egan, always the fashion plate in double breasted blue wool blazer, put it bluntly with his vote. "I go for the big guy, what's his name, Poppard—no, Pollard—for the job. I don't know crap about racing but I'd rather sell our sponsors a big hero than an unknown."

That was the last vote Pollard got. Race said, "Get me Dickson. I like 'em young and with fire in their belly. He'll eat hot dogs and the other guy'll be ordering filet mignons. Remember what Jack Dempsey told me, 'Hungry guys try harder.'"

Jesse agreed. "We'll have 200 grand in total in this thing and Pollard is declaring himself in as a partner. Forget him. I say let the kid have his chance."

Carlson, the blurry-eyed mechanical whiz, opted for Dickson because , "I don't want any big star trying to run the whole show." His buddy, McChesney, another small shareholder, went along with the majority.

Digger opined, "Go with youth. No fears, no guilts."

"Sold. It's Dickson. May he run hard and heavy," Race blustered. He told the group he could hardly wait until his talk show that night to tell the world. "And if I can get Larry on the phone, we'll hook him into the show. How's that for a kick off!"

Jesse and Swede decided to switch from coffee to Bloody Mary's, just because of the importance of the occasion.

"Here's to gutsy guys," the monotone pipes of Swede saluted. "I almost wish I was in. But two bruisers from the Flats tore out a window last night. The urban rebuild creeps are pressuring me to move and I got some bad boards in alley No. 4. I don't need the crunch of an Indy car. But remember this: the big, fast thrill of my life was when I rolled out my red Number Seven at the State Fair four years ago. It finished dead last but while it was running I was hemorrhaging in my heart."

"Friggin' Swede," Race shook his head. "If you were hemorrhaging in your heart you would also be throwing up on your shirt. What's so good about that feeling?"

"If you ever wheel your iron onto the starting grid you'll know," Swede promised.

Race had more thrills in store for him that day. Two quick trips at this moment to two downtown banks, asking for two loans of $12,000

each. He had solid collateral—the new home was worth nearly $80,000 and he only owed $35,000 on the mortgage. But he always hated to ask for loans. It was like you had failed and needed bale-outs.

"Bullshit, that's crazy. You're a millionaire when you owe a million! The more you owe the bigger success you are. They don't lend money to losers," Minneapolis truck magnate Bob Short told Race while negotiating to buy the Lakers pro basketball franchise.

Short was right. Both of Regan's bank negotiations went so quickly and effortlessly that he was walking the streets by noon, feeling like a man reborn. All they needed was to look at his past record, paying all his loans back quickly and completely on all of his ventures. The fact that he would borrow from one bank to pay off the others kept his accounts radiantly unblemished at the seven banks with which he dealt.

Also, the fact that he had given a half-dozen tickets away on the fight card featuring Foreman to directors of the respective banks' lending departments may have helped.

Race's happy thoughts were dashed over dinner at home when Paige Donnelly called concerning the 300 shares of Mille Lacs Industry stock that Race owned.

"You won't believe this," Paige said quietly over the phone, "but Jim McNerney, the guy who started Mille Lacs Industries, just got killed up north. Would you believe he rolled over in his new over-land rover creation. Broke his neck."

Race didn't even think about the stock loss. "God, that bright young guy really had a future."

Chapter Fourteen

A. J. Is Only 40 Miles Ahead

As time trials approached for the Indy 500, the spicy little group of backers and kibitzers began showing tension in various ways.

Egan began looking for solid race car investors and seemed nervous over a product about which he knew little. Larsen got in a knock-down, drag-out screaming match over the family's finances. Jesse took a five-day trip to South Bend to see Notre Dame play a 48-minute basketball game. Van Avery, involved in the race only emotionally, lost a month's mortgage payment on a New York fight. Maloney got hooked on a pyramid club scheme but on the night he was to hit the big share he had a few gins, got lost and couldn't find the payoff house location in Minnetonka. Digger O'Halloran got involved in stock futures that threatened to deposit 75,000 eggs on his front lawn. And Race, naturally, turned to a couple of off-beat efforts, which collapsed so quickly they were almost painless.

The first was his "Rent-a-Relative" venture, begun when he attended the funeral of an acquaintance in Minneapolis where only six people showed up. "Even the guy's wife wasn't there," Regan explained to Dots. "That's a crying shame. Too bad they don't have a rent-a-relative business."

"A what?" Dots didn't believe she'd heard what she heard.

"Why not a rent-a-relative business, so you wouldn't have such crappy funerals? Think how nice it could be with three or four well groomed, nice looking mourners showing up and introducing themselves as cousins or aunts from California or Texas. Man, it could have made all the difference in the world. The mortuary could add it to the cost or close friends could shell it out."

Dots doubled over with laughter. "You're kiddin'. You've got to be."

"Heck no. Look at it this way, for confirmations you could bring in a retired colonel. Think of the prestige. For a guy who liked sports, some old All-American from Alabama could hang around. It would be terrific for weddings where only a couple of square heads show up. For a couple of hundred bucks you could rent any kind of relative . . . war hero . . . Navy cadet . . . policeman . . . judge . . . fire chief. I'll bet a lot of people would love interesting characters like this for conversation at parties or first communions."

When she stopped laughing, Dots placated Regan. "It's original. I'll give you credit for that. Where do you start!"

"With Glen Olson. He's vice president of a bank downtown. Glen pulls crazy stuff like this all the time. Remember, I had him play Santa."

"Can he do anything else?"

"Well, I know he imitates waitresses at sports dinners. Jesse and I had him for a hockey dinner one night. He looked like an ugly broad with big, stuffed bosoms and he'd lean over the table and put his fingers in the soup or coffee. I think it was the assistant chief of police who protested to the restaurant owner and said he should be ashamed to hire such a klutz—and so terrible looking at that. It broke up the place."

Hardly had their conversation ended when Regan had Olson excited about the possibility of millions of entertainment dollars. Next he called an amateur theater director who said he knew of a couple of actors who might be interested in working on the days when they weren't on stage. Race knew most actors in the Twin Cities were unemployed most of the time.

Finally, Race took out two small ads in the personals section of the newspaper. "Rent-a-Relative for that special occasion when interesting guests liven up the proceedings. Capable, trusted 'relatives' for all family events, including graduations, funerals, anniversaries, etc."

"Good ad for only a few bucks. We'll run it on the weekends and see how the action is, Glen," he told Olson. "What do you think we should charge? Don't be cheap. This could be real important to the client."

"Well," mused Olson, a little man with balding head and laughing eyes set in a rounded 50-year-old face, "I suspect they'll try to cheap us down. But I'd go for $40 and a free meal."

"Forty bucks, hmmm. The company, that's me, would require $40 to pay for the ads and a small profit. But if we send out four or five 'relatives' each trip and get 75-100 specials a year and maybe more with Christmas holidays, well I think we could gross maybe 30 grand over the year. Hey, maybe twice that, depending on the demand. Of course, the franchising would be huge. We could retire."

Olson, who never could keep a straight face, had another idea. "And if they don't like the looks of the corpse, why not a quick casket opening and one of our people can play the role of the deceased! Whoever saw a good looking corpse?"

Race and Olson were overtaken by laughter. They happened to be in Glen's small office in the bank and the ruckus soon attracted the attention of the working force.

"Sorry," Glen apologized to his minions. "It's a business deal. Strictly business. But it's got some funny angles."

The ad ran in the personal pages of weekend editions in the two Twin Cities papers, a total subscribership of over 800,000 and drew exactly three responses. One came from a lady in a senior rest home who was tired of her "friends" in wheelchairs and wanted a "new look around the place." The second came from a farmer near Eau Claire, Wisconsin, who "thought it was kind of like an advertisement for a wife. I'm a lonesome old man." And the last was from a ring-a-ding morning show host who thought the ad was hilarious and wanted to talk to someone about it.

The downcast Race went on the air and vowed to the interviewer, "It's only the beginning. Someday we'll rent customers to sporting events to fill up the stands to make it look like a sell out. The Miami Dolphins could have used it their first two years in operation when they only focused TV shots on a couple of sections. Owner Joe Robbie told me that."

Regan filed the obscure venture away in a drawer with the vow that some day when he had a little more time Rent-a-Relative would be launched in a whirlwind, big-time national media campaign.

Dots was relieved. She believed and quite rightly, that Race would have rented her out as a former Metropolitan Opera singer at a wake and ordered her to give out a few verses of the corpse's favorite song. Race did get a lead for Olson to give a humorous talk to a mechanical engineering dinner. He lectured on the coming of portable shopping marts built on huge cables. Prior to intermission, he invited questions, excused himself and walked out the door.

You could almost slice the growing intensity of anticipation over the Indy 500 venture with a butter knife. Particularly the enthusiasm of Regan, which reached an apex when Swede and Race brought Indy hero Eddie Sachs in for their annual party at the Prom honoring local speed stars.

Sachs was a bundle of personality. After the program and enroute to Eddie's loop hotel, the three stopped in front of the capitol building. Sitting on the steps overlooking the St. Paul skyline, Eddie poured out his feelings about racing.

"Faster, younger guns coming up all the time. I passed out in the cockpit at Milwaukee last year. But I'm feeling a lot better now. Sponsors want more speed all the time. You drive under constant pressure."

Regan popped the question everyone who knew Eddie had been pondering. "Eddie, when you were leading with just a couple of laps to go, why did you pull in the pits and change tires, blowing the race? I heard it was because you promised your wife you'd quit if you ever won the Indy and you couldn't bear to stop driving."

The candid, likable driver stared into the distance. "Maybe what you've heard is right. But I could never admit it. Some things just get in your blood and you can't even think about giving them up."

The Minnesota Invader was hurled onto the scene with a large investment party just a few days after the stock issue was okayed by the state commission. The Invader issue sold for $5 per share and $200,000 was raised within two hours at another of Paige Donnelly's cocktail parties. The Minnesota Invader now had approximately 200 stockholders. The original partners maintained 51 percent of the issue. But three new Offy engines cost $105,000.

"Now we can take a deep breath," Race told Jesse.

Jesse agreed wholeheartedly. "And now is just the start. If this car makes the race, or better yet, finishes in the top three, we'll sell twice this issue for another car next year. The beauty is that everyone will want to stay in the act just to say they own the car. If we ever win, we can offer to pay them off. The perfect set up."

"Sounds almost too good to be true. Finally we're in the big time!" Race enthused, slapping Rogers on the back.

Jesse was enthralled. "We might become as big as Roger Penske, the guy who puts a couple of cars in the race every year. Hell, we might even have three or four."

Unfortunately, as Indy practice opened, the Invader, driver Larry Dickson and the crew were experiencing far more difficulties raising speed than the owners were having raising the lettuce.

Race was on the hotline to driver Dickson the fifth day of practice.

"How's it going, Larry? Making any good times?"

"Well, Race, not yet. But we're getting the feel of the car. I haven't had much experience in the big Offenhausers and I'm just getting to know the tires and responses. We're thinking a lot and I know we've got a good machine. Kinda feeling out the track and the car."

"Good, Larry. Don't take any risks."

Three days later, Regan was calling again. "How's it going, Larry?"

"Little better. Had her up to about 145 today. But it takes time. We're doing what everyone else is doing, you know, getting to know the groove, getting in touch with the car and the track. But it sounded good today. Might have hit 150 in the straights. Needs some chassis adjustment but it's going to be okay."

"Keep your foot on the gas, Larry. Keep pushing. But stay healthy," Race advised.

A week later, almost the same story.

"Think we got around 155 today, Race," the driver informed the now-agitated and slowly simmering Regan.

"Christ, Larry! We've got to shove it harder than that. If we don't hit 165 pretty soon, we can kiss this baby good-bye. So keep trying. Don't get reckless but you know, start pushing that baby."

Two weeks into practice, Race was having trouble sleeping. A sports blip had come across his desk pointing out that A. J. Foyt had just turned in a steaming 180 mph test run. Regan could hardly wait to red-line Larry in his garage again.

"Little engine trouble? Goddamn, Larry, Foyt just hit a 180 without trying! It's not funny, Larry, but we're already 40 miles behind Foyt! Start hammering it, Larry. You must have the feel by now. Lemme talk to Red Carlson, the engine guy."

Carlson was low key as usual. "Had to put in another engine today, Race. This might be the one. We're dickering for another engine tomorrow. How much? Maybe 35 grand—but it has just a few miles on it. Got to keep at least three healthy engines. But relax, Race. Larry Dickson is a helluva driver. He's getting better every day."

Regan was chewing on his thumb. "Hope the sucker doesn't hit his peak the Fourth of July. Does he know the race is Memorial Day?"

Regan was beside himself. His two-martini lunches had become three-martini lunches.

"Jesse, Dayle, we've got to do something!" Race blurted over a beef sandwich and a gin straight at Toppie's. "Seven of those friggin' stockholders called my home in the last three days wanting to know when they'll see headlines of 'their' Minnesota Invader in the fast time. Now they all want to see some good publicity. Even my numskull sports editor is asking me how the racer's doing. If this thing flops, we'll never hold up our heads again."

"Relax, Race, or you'll have a heart attack," Maloney advised. "Truth is, you're upset because Dots' brother bought a couple of grand of the stock and you're afraid he'll think you jerked him around."

"Watch out, Dayle," Race spat back, "I'll stick that fat face of yours up an exhaust pipe if you ever say anything like that again. What I'm asking is how is your boy Dickson doing? Maybe the kid is only good for the little tracks. Maybe Indy is too big and too fast and he's scared crapless. Does he know you've got to hit 190 in the straights?"

"I'm glad you don't own a racehorse. If it threw a shoe you'd accuse the nag of aiming it at you. We can't be all bad or A. J. Foyt wouldn't have come over to ask if we needed any help."

"Damn, Dayle, we should have asked to use his car. Or at least to slow down a little."

"Easy guys," Jesse intervened. "It's still nearly two weeks before the first trials. Lord, maybe everything will fall into shape in a couple of hours. We know we've got good equipment. But I do have a little bad news, I tried to get Alan Page, you know, the big Viking and Notre Dame hero, to pose for some publicity stills with the car. But his agent wants too much—like a grand or so."

Race snapped like a bull whip. "That's the least of our worries.

Did you find out if Page drives a car? I'll bet he can go faster than Dickson."

Just in time, Swede Larsen dropped by to ease tensions. "You guys are going through what every race car owner in the country goes through. I call it the time trial terrors. Look, there are 60 cars trying to get into 33 places. Some come back every year and miss. This is your first year. You've still got time."

Regan patted his chest in mock sanctity. "Mea culpa. I'm so relieved our great white father has spoken. In reality, Swede, we've got a screwed up ship. We've apparently hired two mechanics who couldn't start my Dodge Dart in July. We've got three engines and nobody can get any of them up to speed. And we've got a driver who's satisfied traveling in slow motion. Maybe he should be plowing my driveway."

Maloney advised the group he'd be going down to investigate by the weekend. Jesse said he'd join him. Digger was on the phone and said he, too, would go.

Pressure was going to be put on the Minnesota Invader crew. The following weekend, the group got back and told Regan that it looked promising. But they also pointed out that if Dickson didn't get the Invader's speeds up by the time trials, it was possible to look around for another driver.

"Maybe Foyt will take pity on us," Race said happily. "Maybe he'll switch cars, just to prove he's really a helluva competitor." Then Race looked around at the little group and grinned his devilish black Irish smile. "If this was a Mafia operation, we'd break Dickson's arms!"

The first weekend's trials were a disaster. The Invader never got over 160. The bad news was that it was slow and growing slower. The goods news was that it hadn't hit the wall.

While stockholders fumed, it was apparent to insiders that their pride and joy was never going to make the grade or the grid.

"Lord, we've got a quarter of a million buck investment that isn't worth the decals pasted on it," Race complained to Jesse. "What now?"

"Well, Penske's blown some engines and he could use one of ours. Maybe two of them. We can pick up close to $50,000."

"Great! Take what we can get," Regan advised.

Maloney tried using his inspirational clinic techniques on himself. "When you're down get up! When they step on you, wipe off the footprints and charge back! This isn't the end of the world."

"You'll think so," warned Race, "when the stockholders want their money back."

"They still have the car," Maloney pointed out hopefully.

"Yeah, very impressive. An Indy 500 car sitting in the garage with no engine. Bet they'll all want to take their kids over to see that. Maybe sit in it on Sundays," he mocked.

The Invader never invaded. It actually began running slower. No flame. No fame. No starting position.

Nothing the backers could envision equaled what actually took place that Memorial Day at Indy. The late, great Mark Donohue, pride of the Penske stable, drove one of the Invader's engines to victory in the million dollar glamour go-round, while the Longshots looked on in sadness and despair. Donohue's average time of 162 miles per hour also set an Indianapolis record.

Now the Longshots were faced with either engaging in a running war with stockholders, the majority of whom suddenly realized there was no value to an Indy car that didn't make the big chase or digging into their own pickets and paying back some pretty monstrous sums. Naturally, a vote was taken, and it turned out 7-0 to scrap the latter idea and try to placate the shareholders.

"Better hire a helluva attorney," Jesse opined.

"We've got Paige Donnelley, the best stock guy in the state. He can hold off claims for the next 50 years," Regan proclaimed.

And suddenly, three days after the meeting, an enormous ray of hope beamed out of the western skies. It came in the form of a telephone call from Egan.

"I know this sounds a little strange but I happened to be calling on some pharmaceutical people out here in Phoenix and I mentioned about the Invader stock issue. I think they want it! Unbelievable, huh? But if they do take it, of course they won't need the car or anything. We can dump that. All they want is the blue sky stock issue. It's for their own company so they can push some big new products. It's too difficult to start a stock issue out here from scratch. And they're serious. I met with the board today."

"There's only one catch," Egan chuckled over the lines. "The finder's fee—shall we say my little gift for diligence. It should be worth at least 10 grand. Is that too steep to pay for the biggest selling job since somebody convinced a newspaper sickey in New York that Paul Bunyan was a real life giant?"

The word from Jesse was relayed to the Longshots and before the vote was taken, Race nominated Egan for President of the United States.

"The deal is on!" Rogers almost shouted to Pat. "Ten grand. And for God's sake, lock it up quick!"

The Longshots agreed to peddle the Invader chassis to county fairs or rent it out to strip malls for promotions. Hell, if the Phoenix pill pushers wanted it for a hustle, they'd make them a gift of it.

Drinks flowed that afternoon . . . and on and on. . . for about two weeks. Then came the hair-lifting news from the stock commission's capitol offices. Paige delivered the ominous warning.

"Maybe you fellows can't swing this one. There are a lot of legal ramifications. The commission questions whether a firm can take over a stock issue, pay all the debts and then move with that issue into a completely different field. I don't know, but it may go before a judge."

The technicalities of the issue boggled everyone. The drinking slowed to a trickle. Lunches became quiet. Even Van's bright observations such as "Religion is the only thing that keeps the poor from murdering the rich," drew only dull, mumbling responses. It was as if resurrection day was nearing and nobody dared look at the calendar.

Nearly six weeks later, a federal judge, named Miles Lord, ruled that the Minnesota Invader stock transaction with the Phoenix firm was completely legal. Shouts of joy from the Longshots could be heard in Winnipeg. Regan's house was sturdy again. Jesse lunched at the Athletic Club without untoward glances. Maloney, Digger and the rest of the Longshots got back to inspiring and burying people. Egan was the only outright winner— but the St. Paul restaurant owner, who had no papers indicating the cash he skimmed off to pour into the speed machine was legal tender, threatened to sue everyone. But that court case would be in the distant future.

And now a relieved Regan was free to invest some time in the career of Ed Feigner, king of the softball diamond.

Chapter Fifteen

Manhattans and a Growling Con

It was a cloudy Saturday afternoon and Race had shaken off the affects of the Indy 500 debacle. After due negotiations, he was face to face in the Lowry Hotel bar with the King himself—famed softball pitcher, Ed Feigner. This was not just another softball pitcher, Race had found out through six sets of letters and calls with Feigner's agents and the King himself.

Feigner was perhaps the first of the true touring sports phenomenons. He considered himself a greater attraction than the Harlem Globetrotters and the House of David. Part Roller Derby racer, part six-day marathoner, part incredible egomaniac, part genius, part tough guy and 100 percent athlete. At 6'2" and 225 pounds, the crew-topped Feigner had the chest and shoulders of a Marine drill sergeant. He also had a right arm that was nearly twice the size of a normal adult's and a hand that could squeeze a soccer ball into a watch pocket.

An orphan from the Pacific Northwest, Feigner had defied the odds for the past seven years by traveling with a three-man back-up crew that included a catcher, first baseman and deep-positioned shortstop. In that time, he had won an average of 200 games a year, lost only a handful, averaged 16 strikeouts per seven-inning game and played before crowds as large as 30,000 in major ballparks.

Even Yankee Stadium had showcased his wares and Feigner had responded to the roar of the crowd by pitching from second base, blind-folded and between his legs. He had boasted many times that he could strike out any man with a bat in any era and backed it up at a sportsman's show by fanning, in order, Willie Mays, Harmon Killebrew and Roberto Clemente. That night, Babe Ruth would have looked like a mouse swinging a wet noodle.

Now Regan and a fellow sports scribe, Mark Tierney, managed to sign him for a game with a collection of St. Paul softball luminaries at Dunning Field, a cozy confine holding 1,800 seats. This was part of a playground complex, which in those days was home field to urchins of all ages, including at the time three promising graduates named Paul Molitor, Dave Winfield and Jack Morris.

Regan and Tierney rented the lighted field for 40 bucks and agreed to pay Feigner $1,000 plus 50 percent of any gross receipts taken in over that figure. If they drew 1,500 customers at two bucks a head, it was a worthwhile little venture.

Feigner's presence at the bar was everything Regan and Tierney had hoped for and, in fact, beyond their wildest expectations.

Striding in behind a handshake that could pain a gorilla, Feigner said in an arrogant tone with a direct-eye glare that would frighten mountain goats over a cliff, "Me, I'm the King! But before we talk, I want a double Manhattan!"

Ordered. Regan glanced at Tierney. Both were casually sipping the tantalizing fringes of four-to-one martinis. It was 4 p.m. and the game was scheduled for 8 p.m. Both Regan and Tierney thought the same thing—that this guy must be something if he could imbibe a double Manhattan and still dazzle the batters. And they hoped he didn't order any more, after the second arrived five minutes later.

But within 30 minutes, while regaling his hosts with words of his astounding deeds, Feigner had ordered his third double Manhattan. An order of fries were divided among the three, as Feigner pointed out that this could be a glorious association if the promoters didn't screw him.

"Within a few seconds I can tell within 99 percent how many customers are in the park. Never, never try to play games with me," Feigner warned.

Then he told them of his personal life, his pending divorce, his son, his greatest nights, his airplane, his speedboat and his travels all over the world, where he had played for the edification of princes and kings.

"Some day the Pope will want to see me," he vowed. "I've been clocked at 104 miles an hour! I've won 94 percent of my games for seven years! And I've been asked to try out for major league teams. But I can make more than most of those guys and call my own shots. Some day I'll own my own sports college, where I'll teach young people fine points of all sports. You know, I can shoot near par golf and I can bowl 200 plus games. I could probably be a box-ing champion."

"Not to mention tight end," Regan enthused.

"A given."

"Are you interested, Ed, in the kind of team you'll face?" Race in-quired. "We've got some pretty good guys."

"Doesn't matter. When I get through with them they'll all look like girls."

With that, he ordered his fourth Manhattan.

"You train with those?" Tierney asked softly.

"Four or five Manhattans never hurt a well-trained athlete. Hell, I could throw with a pitcher of them in my gut and it wouldn't make a difference. Not when you play over 200 games a year. Know some-thing? I once pitched and won four games in a day—all at different sites! There never has been or ever will be another King."

"How long you gonna pitch, Ed?" Race asked.

"Forever. At least until I'm 60."

Race shook his head, thinking he's either nuts or the Manhattans had him. Forget pitching until 60, Regan thought, just get one more game in—tonight.

Both Tierney and Regan pictured the rest of the team dragging the plastered Feigner out on the field by the legs, while the customers jeered and demanded their money back.

As the threesome left the hotel and headed in opposite directions, Tierney glanced over the loop buildings in the direction of Dunning field, five miles to the west. "Lord, Race, it's getting dark over there. I just hope the rain stalls for another couple of hours."

It was nearly 6:30 p.m. Regan and Tierney met again a half hour later on the street running past the field. They sat huddled in Race's car. The western skies were ominous and there was an occasional light drizzle, the kind that forced Race to turn on the wipers.

"Jeez, if we do play, I hope that dizzy muscleman finds the park with his team. He said they all drive together in some big red, white and blue van. But how in hell do you suppose he can pitch on four Manhattans? And what if he stops for a couple more?"

"Strange thing, "Tierney pointed out, "they really didn't seem to affect him. He was an arrogant bastard coming in and the same going out, but no louder. He wasn't sloppy or getting silly. And he walked like he was leading a Roman brigade."

"Maybe he's a freak, like Babe Ruth. The Babe could be out all night, hung up on booze, full of stale hot dogs and still produce. And look at Harry Greb, the boxer. I heard he took babes to his training quarters. I saw him fight on an old fight film and he was a killer."

Tierney agreed that there were people like that. But what was more amazing than Feigner's physical disposition was the fact that a steady line of cars began driving by the park. With only 15 minutes until game time, even in the damp circumstances and threatening atmosphere, the stands were nearly filled and another 200 customers were in line.

Race clapped his hands and dropped an arm over Tierney's shoulders. "Whee, maybe the guy's magic. Look, there's his big van and he got out all right!"

The rival players, secured from municipal league volunteers, had shown up and were cavorting during infield drills, despite the now near-steady rain. If they could just get four innings in nobody would have to worry about refunds.

But that was too much to ask. Five minutes before starting time, lightening and thunder ripped and roared. Sheets of rain that became near-torrents sent the crowds scurrying toward their autos. Race had the announcer blare through the loud speaker that patrons should keep their stubs and there would be a rain date. That, of course, was pure speculation. Feigner was heading for southern Minnesota the next day and then into Iowa for 20 games.

They met Feigner again at Connelly's bar on Lexington a few minutes later and he agreed to come back. "But this damn park's too small. I'll get back here in six weeks but you've got to get me into Midway Stadium. We'll do 5,000."

Regan and Tierney now were convinced that despite the drinking and braggadocio Feigner was basically an honest loyalist. He guaranteed, "I'll share the cost of any ad or blurb you need to get the word out that we'll honor the tickets. Here's 200 bucks, buy some posters for the next date. But get the big stadium."

With that, Feigner ordered another Manhattan. His players proceeded to get a little noisy and slightly looped on beer. Regan confided to Tierney, "I have the feeling a wonderful relationship has begun. If this wild gorilla doesn't have so many drinks some night that he drives off the highway into a tree."

"I believe if he did that he'd survive and go on to hit another hundred trees down the line just for the publicity," Tierney laughed.

The next morning at seven, Tierney roused the Midway Stadium manager out of bed with a phone call to nail down the next date. "It will happen," he said joyfully over the phone to Race a few minutes later.

Regan went back to bed and told Dots, "Honey, I've got another great one coming up."

"Good," Dots smiled. "I think the girls need some high-priced dental work. Hear that?"

Regan was in another world, wondering if Feigner could use some promotional help in this part of the country, whether he and Mark could land him for 20 or 30 games a year. The man was a machine—as long as the Manhattans didn't rust him out.

Race had just finished dinner with the great running back Ollie Matson who would face the Vikings the next day. He was gathering information on the record-setting professional football runner for a column. As they neared the door of Gallivan's Regan was accosted by a freckle-faced, balding man of enormous girth.

Matson thought for a moment that he was caught in an unpleasant encounter, until the man put his face close to Regan's and almost growled, 'You are the best damn sports writer around! How about doing a book on my life?"

Regan managed to delay Matson and push back from the threatening hulk.

"A book? God, I'm still trying to collect royalties for the book I did on young Gallivan."

"I know but this is a real best seller. I can see it getting on television shows and maybe a movie. Nobody's lived my life."

Race asked Ollie to wait a minute and moved to a corner with the intruder.

"Oh, I suppose I should apologize," the overbearing figure said, suddenly softening his tone to a near whisper. "My name's Red Rudensky, the greatest safe-cracker of all time! Have you heard of me?"

Indeed Regan had. Rudensky had gained notoriety from serving over 25 years in Leavenworth and finally, upon his release, becoming a body guard and confidant of Charlie Ward, the president of Brown and Bigelow. This was the world's largest calendar company, which was based in St. Paul's Midway area. He had never, however, met Red before. And at that moment he wasn't so sure that he actually wanted the confrontation. This man, indeed, had an ominous, almost over-powering bearing.

He had been one of over a hundred former convicts employed by Ward, who once served a brief stint in the federal penitentiary for smuggling. Red apparently had befriended Ward, who in turn promised to help him out if Red would join his staff.

Within two years, the swaggering, confident con became a fairly gifted writer, too. And before anyone could actually assess his moral rejuvenation, Rudensky had become the religious editor at B and B and even written beautiful greetings on Christmas calendars.

It was to become a close relationship between the safe-cracker and Race and in two sentences the former convict had Regan's attention.

"Listen, Regan, I was a cellmate of Al Capone's in Atlanta and a friend of Margaret Mitchell, who wrote 'Gone With the Wind.' And I was the guy who organized prisoners all over the country in the war effort to make parachutes and I've got letters from Eleanor Roosevelt to prove it. Not bad for a starving Jewish punk from New York's lower East Side."

Sold. Race excused himself to escort Matson to his car and agreed to meet Rudensky in Regan's home the following week. Matson shook his head, "Who is that rough-house guy?"

"Well, I never met him before but he has lived a helluva life. Can you imagine, Ollie, he was Capone's cellmate one time and I've heard he was the best safe-cracker in the country."

"What's he do now?"

"Writes religious poetry."

"Can't believe it."

"Would you buy a book about such a guy?"

"Sure would."

Regan wished Ollie well against the Vikings the next day and told him, "You're the best who ever carried the ball in a broken field."

"Hope I can show you something," the cat-like and humble Matson said as they drifted apart on Wabasha Street.

An apparently restabilized Jesse met with the Longshots at Gallivan's to announce that his divorce was nearing finality. "Too much heat, too much pressure. She's got her good points but God, I can't seem to hack it at home. So now I'm just going to concentrate on insurance and a few promotions. Okay gang?"

"What the hell," Van shrugged his shoulders. "Everyone's getting divorced these days. My oldest daughter might be splitting up. Nothing to be ashamed of. Abraham Lincoln split with his girlfriend and had a nervous breakdown. They say he was hen-pecked all his life. Imagine, his wife was even pulling for the South in the Civil War."

"Yeah, divorce is not a big deal," agreed Larsen. "I've got three friends who went through it. Only problem is the Goddamned lawyers took most of what both of them owned."

"I've got a good lawyer," Jesse interrupted. "But I think it's worth whatever. It's killing my health."

"Well, Jesse, it just might be a little of that booze, too," Digger added, puffing on a tantalizingly loose cigarette.

At this point, Race swaggered in, his Irish eyes bright with another story from the streets.

"Know who called me last night? He asked, sitting down with the delicacy of a water buffalo.

"Damn, you're rude," Larsen observed.

"Well, listen, men, would you believe Rocky Marciano?"

"The Rock? In town, just to see you?" Van asked incredulously.

"Not really. But he called and we met for dinner at McGuire's. He was with a bunch of big hitters and tough guys from Cleveland. Seems they're here to buy some insurance company that's got problems."

"Allied?" Larsen volunteered.

"I guess so. But anyway, Rocky was in for a little public relations work and told me he's getting 500 bucks a day and expenses. We talked until midnight. He's losing big on some ventures and he's thinking about pulling out of all of them.

"Nicest damn athletic hero I ever met. Would you believe he gave me a hundred dollar bill to buy a friend of mine a drink at the bar and he wouldn't take a penny change. But at times he seems to be really worried about his money and an orchard he owns in Florida."

At this point, Van asked a question for which few had the answer: "What the dickens is a demolition derby? My youngest said she was going to one and I wasn't going to embarrass myself by asking."

Jesse looked at Van as if he was completely demented. "Who gives a damn?"

Regan made a guess, "I think a bunch of cars keep running into each other. That is, until there's only one left running. Gruesome thought, eh?"

A few minutes later, Frenchy arrived. He was pretending to be angry at Race, waving a finger in his face. "Next time you come in my joint I'm going to run out the back door."

"Yeah?"

"Yeah," Landreville explained. "Six weeks ago you told me that Metro Meats would be a hot issue, right? I bought $3,000 worth, right?

"Listen guys," Landreville addressed the group. "You haven't heard this but it's another Regan story. Race came in one day after being out to Hugo to a game farm with George Heimel. He's the guy who's always into meats and fish. Regan tells me that in four hours, from noon to four, Heimel makes $500,000 on his stock because everyone's talking about his plans for a big new fish restaurant down by the airport.

"Know what happens?" the emotionally distraught Frenchy asks. "Well, I run out and buy what I can and Regan says I'll be rich in a year. But I must have been the only fool to buy. Metro Meats has been going steadily down from eight bucks a share to four. I've lost $1,500 and haven't heard another word about the fish restaurant."

Race rubbed his forehead and tried to soothe Vern. "But didn't I bring you half a barrel of fresh fish the guy gave me?"

"But what do I want with friggin' fresh fish? My kids hate fish."

"They'd make a nice gift."

"Regan, are you looney? Those fish cost me about 500 bucks a pound. I don't think the crazy stock will ever come back. Please, you rascal, no more hot ideas."

"You little frog, you didn't complain when I got you that breast cancer detection stock. You told me you made a couple of grand in a month."

"Okay, Race, I'm only kidding. You gave me some thrills with the Foreman fight, too."

Van tried to lighten the proceedings. "Race, you remind me of a guy with the greatest imagination in the world. It enables you to enjoy the good times that never happen."

Race shot back at Van, "You remind me of the typical car salesman. You go on retreat at DeMontreville monastery and the day you come back you're trying to screw some old retired couple."

"That wasn't nice," Van feigned hurt.

As the group dispersed, Van approached Race about a car he had that anyone in their right mind would want for their daughter in college. "Would you believe a four-year-old Victoria with only 7,000 miles."

"No, I wouldn't believe that, Van. What happened, did the 80-year-old retired school teacher die in the back seat and they just found her?"

"You know how to hurt a guy."

Outside the bright summer sun was shining down. Jesse and Race lingered.

"I still don't know what the hell a demolition derby is but do you want to try it?" Jesse asked, adjusting his sunglasses.

Race paused, kicked a loose stone into the gutter, looked down the street and replied matter-of-factly, "Of course."

As if his talk show and highly-read column and his promo-for-the-month wasn't enough, Race managed to get involved in a strictly hype feud with Minneapolis columnist Sid Hartman.

Despite the fact they had once been roomies on University of Minnesota sports trips and even double-dated, Race and Sid managed to convey grim animosity through column needling and vague references to each other's writing skills, all to the amusement of sports aficionados who followed both columnists.

"Regan works behind an iron curtain," Sid once jabbed. "I never see him at a game. He must get his news from the Pony Express."

Race took to referring to Hartman as "Simple Sid."

"He never sees me because he never gets out of the press box or the locker rooms. He thinks race fans and fight fans and hockey fans are aliens. I heard him ask how to endorse a body check during a hockey game."

Hartman claimed St. Paul was 40 years behind the times and over-rated as a sports hotbed. Regan claimed, "The difference between us is simple: he writes what he hears. I write what I think."

Both had once worked for the *Minneapolis Times*, Race as the copyboy and Hartman as a distributor, before spinning his column. Regan would heckle, "I once fixed Sid up with a blind date and she never spoke to me again."

Hartman countered, "Regan writes good fiction."

Legendary U of M hockey coach John Mariucci once explained how to handle a ticklish situation, "I give Sid a scoop in the morning and I give Race a scoop in the afternoon."

Ironically, when Race covered the Laker's cage champs, Hartman was doing promotions for the team which meant that, technically, they were working together. But don't even suggest such an obscenity to either.

Regan was also trying to sell a nationally syndicated men's column called "Ask Charlie" with a profiled sketch of himself done by well known cartoonist George Karn. Race had sent a dozen copies to various syndicate outlets and two of them replied, calling it "the funniest columns we've reviewed in years."

Typical of the column was a question of this sort, "I am nearly two feet shorter than a girl I dearly love. It gets difficult telling her how I feel when I am staring at her belt-line on the dance floor." Charlie's reply: "Keep looking up."

As the syndicators told him, the trouble with his column was that the humor was about 10 years ahead of its time.

"They blew millions," a semi-bitter Race confided to Frenchy.

To keep the action lively, Frenchy and Race diligently pursued a court case in which they demanded an $850 payment from a prominent St. Paul doctor who held up his check for another Super Bowl trip they promoted to New Orleans. He claimed a snow storm, which forced the customers to look for their own return flight venues, broke the trip's pledge of a complete travel package.

They discovered he had traveled with a girlfriend rather than his society oriented wife, which meant, they believed, that he was not only on the defensive but certainly a stupid individual who needed a dose of good morals. One call to the wife would have been a simple operation to thump the doc, Frenchy pointed out.

Instead, they elected to secure the services of attorney Wayne Belisle. However, on the trial date in a suburban court, Wayne was in Chicago on more serious business.

Vern quickly countered with another plan. "I was telling Jeff Mikko, the super shoplifter, about our little problem and he says he'll be our attorney. He knows all the court room gab. He's been up before the court lots of times on charges. He says to just get a witness or two and he'll do the job for nothing. Just for laughs."

On the appointed day, Jeff appeared in a three-piece suit, horn rimmed glasses, toting a heavy briefcase. He opened the case to disclose three thick telephone books. "I'm so good I don't need to even look at my briefs. That'll impress the judge."

Chief witness for the prosecution was Jimmy O'Hara, an ex-state boxing champ, close associate of most of the Longshots and the man Regan was promoting to succeed an aging boxing commission secretary.

"Best trip I was ever on," the husky, good-natured O'Hara swore. "Never saw so much of the French Quarter. Hotels were fabulous. Good seats for the game. Yes, it was worth every penny. And we all realized that we had to shift for ourselves after the big storm. Most flights back to the Twin cities were fouled up. Nothing unusual. I never heard a complaint from anyone on the trip."

Indeed, he hadn't. Meanwhile, the doctor was so shook up over the possibility that his love-affair might be discovered that he answered Mikko's questions almost inaudibly and finally admitted, "Yes, I had a good time. I, uh, probably made a mistake."

Case closed. Mission accomplished. The doc wrote out a check and before dismissing the parties the judge scrutinized Mikko and observed dryly, "You look familiar. I must have heard a couple of your cases."

Without twitching so much as an eyebrow, Jeff looked straight into the judge's eyes and said politely, "Yes, sir. Two or three, I think."

Later, over a steak dinner at the Parker House honoring the winning barrister, a wailing police siren speeding past prompted Jeff to stand and bow his head in mock solemnity: "They're playing my song."

Chapter Sixteen

Call the Tow Trucks . . . Pleasssse!

The King, softball phenomenon Eddie Feigner, was back. Mark Tierney and Race were treating him like royalty. This time it was Regan who suggested a couple of dry Manhattans might interest Feigner and they toasted a successful game. Not only one game, really but two. The scribes had lined up both Bloomington's Met Stadium, home of the Vikings and Midway Stadium in St. Paul, the minor league ballpark.

"To the biggest softball games in history," Regan held his martini glass high in the small, snug, mirrored bar of the old Commodore Hotel. This is where Race liked to go for very intimate special events, away from prying eyes; the spot where it was rumored F. Scott Fitzgerald got drunk after his baby's christening up the street at the Cathedral.

"Fitzgerald would have loved this," Race winked at Feigner.

"Fitz who?" the muscular pitcher interrupted.

"A great writer—the guy who wrote *The Great Gatsby*, Ed. He was from this neighborhood. In fact, he lived in five or six houses within walking distance from here."

Feigner feigned knowledge of the name and then got very serious. "You say you got a labor guy sponsoring the game at Bloomington. I'm suspicious of these guys. Who counts the money?"

"Don't worry, Ed," Tierney said solemnly. "The guy's a union boss. Big, tough operator named Tony Felicetta. He's walked with a limp ever since somebody tried to wipe him out years ago. But they say he's a man of his word. And he's got contacts all over Minneapolis. I wouldn't be surprised if he put 5,000 fannies in the seats. He gets a buck off each $3 ticket but nothing for his amateur team's beer party. And Felicetta got us a great break on the rent."

"Great, if you say so. But remember, men, I can take a look at the stands in a minute and tell you within a handful how many people are in the park. If the guy plays cute, he'll have a 40 ounce bat up his rear."

At this point, the highly imaginative Regan envisioned gang war behind first base, with Felicetta's henchmen throwing grenades at Feigner's four-man troupe, while they charged the stands, bats swinging.

This time, it was a clear, calm Saturday night at Met stadium with only a few fleecy clouds flirting with the diamond. An hour before the game, the turnstiles were spinning a delicious tune and it was agreed by all that Felicetta had done his job well.

When Feigner arrived and got out of his van, he said, "Who's paying for all this security? Cripes! Do they expect the Commies to invade? There's uniformed jerks all over the place!"

After the fourth inning, as Feigner mowed down a team of patchwork players from the Minneapolis Municipal league, Felicetta met with Tierney and Regan.

"Good turnout, eh? Must have 4,000 in here."

Tierney was shocked by Felicetta's estimate. "Only 4,000? God, I figure there must be over 5,000. Pretty solid in the sections behind home plate."

"Naw, Tierney. Crowds always look bigger than they are. And the expenses ran a little higher than we thought. Had to put on four telephone operators just to handle calls. And we added about 10 guys in security so there'd be no traffic snarls."

Traffic snarls? Regan eyeballed Tierney. They knew instantly there would be trouble ahead. Feigner would engage a Marine battalion to get his share and Felicetta always moved with momentum; a good guy but nobody to cross, particularly on his turf, where he had large friends in every shadow.

After posting his 18th strikeout and winning comfortably, Feigner met Felicetta, Tierney and Regan in the hall leading to his locker room. "Just over 5,000 in the stands, Felicetta," Feigner snapped.

"Bull crap!" the union boss snarled back, spitting out half of a black cigar. "I got the count, about 3,900."

"Your head's up your fat fanny!" Feigner roared. "I never miss by more than 50 and nobody jerks me around."

For the moment calm was restored and they agreed to meet at the Lion's Inn coffee shop after Feigner showered. A flush-faced Feigner turned to Regan and said quietly, "That bastard gives us a crooked count and it'll be the last promotion he ever gets involved with."

Tierney had a brilliant idea. "Fitz, the guy we got handling the manifest from Midway stadium, has a key that pops the turnstiles here and in St. Paul. The same builder installed them both. I'll have him give these babies a check. He's here. I just saw him."

Fitz, the laconic ticket manager for the minor league St. Paul Saints, came through in the clutch. He proved through the turnstile count that 5,122 bodies had passed through the gates and that Feigner was right on target. Even after hyping the expenses, Feigner and company should walk away with close to seven grand.

The chunky, dark-browed Felicetta was smart enough to request that his two "partners" escort him to the inn. Race was smart enough to intercept Felicetta in the parking lot of the stadium to let him know that the turnstile's official count put him on the defensive. After all, Race had to live in the Twin Cities and he didn't need the union's ire. He belonged to the Newspaper Guild and most of his friends were avowed unionists.

"That big pig pile is wrong! But I'll see what he has to say," the profane Felicetta told Race.

The meeting took place with amicable salutations—at first. And speaking of smarts, Feigner was bright enough to bring along his players, including a reserve catcher who stood 6'4", weighed 280 pounds and had tried out with three NFL teams.

"I say we've got about seven grand coming," Feigner ventured quietly from a large table in the far corner of the restaurant.

"Closer to five grand," Felicetta argued. "Lot of kids in the stands at a buck." He tapped his heavy cane ominously against the leg of a chair.

"Bull!" Feigner barked, getting louder. His cold blue eyes x-rayed Felicetta's scalp. "About 400 kids. Rest regulars. Here's the turnstile count. Now give in or I'll kick the hell out of you and your friggin' old lady bodyguards right now! And before I leave town, every union member in Minneapolis will know you're a lying, stinking thief!"

Felicetta tried to hold his ground, spitting back, "You're a two-bit carnie outsider, so don't try loud talk." But the threats obviously took the rough-hewed Felicetta off guard. He put his black briefcase on the table, unloaded wads of cash and a crumpled slip listing his expenses, including $322 in phone bills.

"Phone bills!" Feigner roared. "Christ, all you had to do was call the Minneapolis paper and tell them I was in town. You've got to be looney nuts!"

Regan was amazed when Felicetta backed down. "Here's your dough. But no more than sixty-five hundred. I've got security guards up the wazoo who want to be paid. Damn, Feigner, you're the thief, not me!"

Race now prayed the association would end without violence. Felicetta shoved the mound of cash toward Feigner and the pitcher threw the financial manifest back at him. Not a word was uttered by any of the seven onlookers.

"There's the facts, Felicetta. And never try to screw around with somebody who counts people for a living."

The group broke up wordlessly. You could feel the tension all the way to Eden Prairie.

That night, Regan and Tierney took Feigner out on the town, introducing him to just about everyone on Rice Street as they toured the joints. All agreed it was good public relations for the next night's game at Midway. They must have coaxed Feigner into shaking hands with 300 admirers before the night was over. Most of them had never heard of Feigner but when Regan introduced him as the world's greatest athlete everyone from the Stahl House to Allen's, on the edge of town, were duly impressed.

The next morning, Tierney was on the phone at 7:30 a.m. "Look at the sky! Look at the sky!"

It was another beautiful day and forecasters were spouting off that it was due to hold through Tuesday.

This time, Regan arranged for the opposition to be a bit more competitive. Well, actually to be better in one position—the pitcher. For a 50 buck guarantee, Race got Dud Matthews, one of his old-time drinking buddies, to agree to duel Feigner. And what a character Matts was! Matts would give the finger to 500 rival fans when he took the mound. He'd won a couple of state championships in his best days and his rise-ball could probably equal Feigner's for sheer velocity and intimidation.

But Matts was a strange one. He could be polite to a fault and three drinks later he could break his hand smashing it against the wall. Or bump heads with some 250-pound animal on the street. Or leap over fire hydrants on a walk in the loop.

At one time, he also owned a bar and hotel in Brainerd, a thriving resort community to the north. But he went broke because, it was said, he had insulted every citizen of the town within his first six months in operation. Once, after a squabble, he locked out his bar manager in the midst of a Saturday night throng. Then he bought a round of drinks for the house. And ten minutes later, he ordered everyone to leave!

Wiry, almost frail looking, he had an enormous right arm. And he was feisty enough to challenge a wild beast in a shower stall.

"No offense if I beat this big turd?" Matts queried Race.

"Hell no! He'd be your number one rooter. But don't try to bump heads with him, Dud. He'll throw you into the river. This guy is terribly mean and he's the strongest athlete I've ever seen."

The morning of the game, Matts laughed and ordered, "Get me a bottle of Johnny Walker Red for the dugout and you'll see the damnedest duel you've ever watched. I take no prisoners!"

Race actually enjoyed Matts. Many times he'd take him along as a bodyguard figure when he spoke at Wisconsin's Packer-backer dinners. The speaking fees were good but Regan really never knew if the cheeseheads would nail him in the parking lot just for laughs. With the scowling Matts along, Regan felt as safe as a mouse at a ladies' sewing club.

"Hey, this crowd's as big as last night's—with half the expenses!" Tierney joyfully appraised, while sitting in the last row atop Midway Stadium, where Regan and he could check the parking lot and the stands merely by swiveling their heads.

"Well, Ed gave us $1,500 last night and he could cut a bigger piece of pie tonight," Regan announced quickly. "Might hit over two grand for our share. I think the guy's honest to a fault."

"Right," Tierney agreed. "If you don't crowd him, he's great. I Just hope that Felicetta doesn't come across the river with a dozen goons and try to destroy us."

Race pointed out, "We've got four off-duty cops right where everybody can see them. They're worth the hundred bucks."

It was halfway through the first inning when Tierney and Race noticed the ominous procession—six big men walking at a pallbearer's pace down the first base aisle, moving into some empty seats directly behind Feigner's dugout. Felicetta's stocky, rumpled body led the group. His limp made him appear even more threatening.

"God!" Race almost shouted in Tierney's ear. "How could there be those empty seats so close to the field? I hope they don't shoot Feigner!"

What happened next curled the hair on Tierney and Race. Feigner saw the intimidating crowd and grabbed a bat. He hammered it with brutal force on the top of the dugout, leaned up and over and yelled with such volume that many of the fans could hear, "Get your cheap, filthy asses out of here or I'm coming up with my men and we're going to beat your brains out! You've got a minute to be out of the park! No two-bit union bastards are going to scare me, but if you want trouble you'll get more than you can handle!"

"We want a grand back!" Felicetta shouted back but he was up from his seat and beginning to move. "You screwed us last night and you owe us. And I don't forget. You don't give me the green and you'll never pitch in my town again! And that's a given!"

"Get moving," Feigner ordered, almost coolly, staring directly at the group, which was now moving slowly up the steps. "Just keep the Hell moving and keep going if you don't want to spend the night in the hospital!"

Amid a few more curses and threats, Felicetta gave Feigner the finger and disappeared through the exit.

"Oh, man," Race whispered to Tierney. "I hope they don't torch his van when they get outside."

"I don't think Felicetta could stand the bad publicity," Mark suggested. "After all, he's kind of a public figure in Minneapolis. He pulls a lot of political strings. He couldn't stand an arson charge when he's working with all the charities and stuff."

"I hope he doesn't get sore at me. You know, I really kind of like the guy," Race offered. "I roomed with him in Boston during a Celtics-Lakers playoff game. He's kind of a sweet guy under all that crocodile skin. And if he thinks he's right, he'll not back down. I figured he'd blow up more than he did at Feigner. But then he's about 55 years old and he's got to protect his reputation. You know, union pensions and crap like that. But isn't that Feigner a stud? I'd hock my house right now and sign him to any kind of contract he wants. We gotta get him for at least 20, maybe 25 games, a year. I'd give my right arm for a pup out of the guy."

Tierney sighed. "Maybe he wouldn't be so tough without the bat. But who's got the guts to find out?"

True to his word, the eccentric Matts dueled The King to the finish, losing a 3-1 thriller, after which Feigner shook hands with Matts and complimented him. "You're a tough hombre fella. If you were 10 years younger I'd sign you up as a reliever."

And again, true to his macho nature, Matts answered, only half jokingly, "You big pile of dung, I'd love to face you seven times a week!"

They both sauntered off, chuckling to each other. Matts was delighted when Regan fished him an extra 50 bucks at the Stahl House and slid him another pair of Johnny Walker Red bottles in a shopping bag. Race knew Matts would make a good show out of it and, of course, there was next year. Maybe 10 more years.

Flushed with the success of a couple of its members, a few of the Longshots were meeting with renewed spirit and boundless anticipation.

Jesse was clearing up the mess left in the wake of his sour divorce proceedings but his insurance office looked worse than ever. He explained to his buddies that he had hired a new office manager named Jane who he hoped would straighten out the problems in his accounting, not to mention the piles of papers on the floor. "But I just found out she's got nine kids. How in blazes can she straighten out anything? Can't be very smart. In fact, guys, she may have more problems than the United Nations. I'm ready for anything to make a buck."

"Things that bad?" Race inquired.

"Bad? Jeez, my divorce is cleaning me like a cheap car wash. My insurance company is so screwed up I pray every night that none of my clients even stubs a toe! I've got a kid in trouble. The booze is beginning to taste better every day. It's a good thing I can't find a needle or I'd be in the drug market."

Race was delighted to hear that Jesse was anxious for new fields. "Have I got the beauty of all time . . . I've got a beauty for my buddy, Jesse!" Race almost shouted.

They were sitting in the bar of the Holiday Supper club in White Bear, where Jesse would often meet his north suburban customers after work when he got tired of bumping into his peers, pals and his big squadron of relatives on loop sidewalks. Egan, the always impeccably groomed and versatile contact man of varied and oblique interests, was also on hand.

"Beautiful? What the hell have you got on your mind this time, Race? Not beautiful as in a teen-age beauty contest that just bankrupted a pal of mine in Minneapolis. You know the guy, Darrell what's-his-name. Promised first class accommodations for the teen beauties and then put six to a room at a sleazy motel on the highway and fed them at truck stops. Well, spit it out."

"At times your attitude disturbs me, Jesse. But anyway, we talked about it before and nobody seemed to know anything about the subject. I'm telling you again, the killer of all is here—the demolition derby!

"You laughed the last time but I've done my investigating with Head-on-Flint, the guy who's president of the Bash and Crash Club down in southern Minnesota. Those crazy, wild devils actually pay big entry fees to blast their own cars into pieces!"

Jesse's hooded eyes were at half mast no longer. "For nothing?"

Egan even seemed astounded. "For nothing they actually mangle each other?"

"When did you ever see anything for nothing? No, we put up a prize to the last one running. Maybe a grand. But if we get 50 entrants, they pay 10 bucks a piece. That's half the prize money. The rest goes for the posters and junk like that. Oh, yeah, the officials who run it get $200. I tell you, these guys work for almost zilch."

"What's it draw?"

"More than the hill climb and we had a big mob for that one. At three bucks a head we should do over seven grand. The expenses? Practically nothing. Maybe two grand at most."

"But where," Jesse demanded to know, "are we going to stage this thing? The rent is usually the big bite."

"Forget it. Rauchnot's JR Ranch in Hudson is the site, the same as for the suicide hill climb. You admit, he's got the parking and the great location. He keeps all the concessions and if we make more than five or six grand, I told him he could have 10 percent of the profits. Fair enough?"

"I'll say! Nobody's giving away free rent these days."

"And the good part, Jesse, these crazies have an underground that shoots around the information to every two-bit service station and garage in the state. They drew nearly 3,000 at some little farm town near Worthington a couple of weeks ago. They just keep buying 50-buck junkers and patching up the wrecks that aren't real bad and coming back for more. They're some kind of masochists who love to run into themselves. We've been looking for suckers like this for years! We simply supply the location and desire to batter their machinery apart."

Egan loved the sound of this. "I've got first claim when we franchise. In fact, I'll enter my 10-year-old Pontiac."

"Too nice. We want character," Race chided.

Jesse had a question. "I imagine the insurance could sting a little. I've got an angle on a new company trying to push it this direction. I'll get it for a hundred bucks or so. Nobody gets killed do they?"

"Not that I've heard of," Race assured Jesse. "But I suppose a wheel could fly off."

"But guarantee me, no cliffs like the hill climb!"

"No cliffs. This is all in John's natural amphitheater. You know,

Jesse, lots of green grass and the mobs can sit on the hillside away from the crashes. I've got a date in mind. How about three weeks from Sunday?"

"We're on. I'll call the printers and start the ad bills going when you give me the details."

"I'll drink to that," smiled Race, ordering a gin with a splash. Pat picked up the check, while reminding them, "'Demolition Derby' is what we called last year's Saints when John Bailey was on the ice. He's wrecked more people than bad booze!"

The demolition derby appeared to be a remarkable success. Entries totaled 42. The six heats leading to the final round found the 2,800 patrons cheering and clapping and spilling beer in the warm sun.

Best of all, the finals brought together a 22-year-old Mercedes that looked strong enough to waylay a tiger tank, and a strange Ford/Chevy hybrid, which must have been assembled during a Le Sueur corn festival orgy.

They fumed and sputtered and growled and groaned and smoked for nearly six minutes before the Mercedes' shattered hood produced a geyser of searing steam that threatened to disrupt the ecology of the St. Croix River for years. Still it hung in there, carrying on gamely in a junkyard dealer's delight, to back its way into a final, gasping effort of scorched and crying transmissions and tires that sounded like pigs squealing in a packing plant. The Mercedes died of many causes. The Ford/Chevy, to the hard-hat crowd's delight, sputtered away, the winner; a hybrid hero.

The driver was a stubble-faced kid of maybe 19, who obviously was the fan favorite. He came from some dinky village in Wisconsin, so he had the home-state support. He gave the trophy to his mother, who said she always knew her son would be a success in life. He tucked $750 into his greasy jeans and thanked his supporters for sticking with a winner.

It was a pleasant night in the JR Ranch's restaurant. Owner John Rauchnot happily reported that he'd done nearly three grand in drinks and food. He chewed on a Havana cigar and told Regan he'd consider two or three of these destruction derbies next year on the same terms.

Regan and Jesse eventually finished their steaks and moved on to the Hudson Harbor bar parking lot. They had slipped Rauchnot $300 as his share of the profits and the entrepreneurs counted out nearly $1,500 in profits.

"What are you going to do with your cut, Race?" Jesse asked politely.

"Take Dots and the kids up to the North Shore for the weekend. The way they put up with me is amazing. And I'm thinking about getting Dots a car. I think she gets tired of having her mother tote her around. I can squeeze a down payment out of this slice. Maybe another Dodge Dart. Who'd ever think we'd have two Darts in the family?"

"Admirable," Jesse said, without a caustic note in his voice. "It makes the emotional stress of this crap worthwhile to hear you talk like that. Imagine, two Dodge Darts! Your ambition continues to amaze me."

The hours of bliss and self-adulation were shattered with the force of a wrecking ball by 10 the next morning. Rauchnot was on the phone to Race at the paper. "We didn't account for all the chickens, Race."

"What chickens?"

"Well, you know I have my annual rodeo coming up Sunday and it just can't work out with those wrecks all over the field."

Regan was incredulous. "You mean those guys didn't haul them away?"

"A few, pal. But 90 percent didn't. In fact, a couple of those guys, who were hanging around drinking until we closed, said it's the promoters who are responsible for getting rid of the cars. Looks like a World War battleground. I'll bet those ball-bearing plants in Germany didn't look any worse after we got through blasting them."

"I imagine not. Well, do you know anybody who can get them out of there for a decent price?"

"Already checked, Race. "I've got four tow trucks coming in this afternoon. The whole thing may cost around a grand, maybe more. You know, it's going to be a bitch getting those heaps up the hills and out on the highway. It'll take more than an hour per car the hauler thinks. Some are so badly smashed they'll have to pry the fenders and bodies away from the tires just to get the wheels moving. I don't want to be the guy in the black hat but it could run as high as $1,500!"

"Oh, my God! John, there goes all the profit. And none of us even thought about it. I figured those apes wanted their wrecks for another show."

"A few did. Most figure it's cheaper to leave 'em than repair 'em. They tell me they can pick up the crap they drive for forty or fifty bucks.

"You see my point, Race," John said, trying to pacify Regan. "I've got a mountain of junk in my yard and my biggest day of the year is coming up. I think I've been fair about the rental."

"Yeah, yeah, I'm not sore about it, John, just so damn disgusted."

Race called Jesse with the bad news.

"Damn, I was going to get a better sailboat and get back on the lake," Jesse said disconsolately.

"I guess Dots can wait for the car," Regan said. "But worse, I had plans for a demolition league—with franchises."

"Don't forget the tow trucks," Jesse needled.

"Don't even try to be funny. I could throw up."

Chapter Seventeen

Bronk Fumbles, Cowboys Sink

Peripheral events were beginning to take a toll on the Longshots. For instance, Jesse was flinging wild accusations at his wife in the post-divorce proceedings and she was launching a counter-attack, aimed at proving he was more than just a little nuts. He was juggling his insurance agency's books to keep abreast of spending sprees from Chicago to Monte Carlo and the desperation in his hooded eyes on drinking nights belied his usually quiet demeanor.

Billy Larsen's dealings with his family were getting so acrimonious that he confided to Race that his usually placid Swedish genes at times erupted in such unexpected fury that he was tempted to find "a good, honest Mexican hit man on the West Side to cream somebody." How desperate he became after his father died was reflected when he actually showed up for a job interview at a wholesale liquor company.

On the surface, Frenchy would seem to have the specifications of life under solid design, except for the fact that his wife, Cindy, and he were stretching their work habits to the limit. The flashy new Chain Link supper club out on the eastern interstate was a thriving acquisition and Landreville was planning on expanding his operations in the near future to four or five establishments. This meant new relatives' names on liquor licenses and more paperwork by the ton. When he slept was a question nobody seemed able to answer, including Cindy.

Van Avery had sobered up after years of imbibing but it did little to detract from his hilariously complex outlook on life. Except that now, along with hustling cars and attending any function which remotely resembled a new promotional gamut, he also set out to salvage shaky marriages in which either partner was an alcoholic. As Judge Archie Gingold pointed out, Van was doing more good than the AA Blue Book.

The tall, pale-faced Digger O'Halloran, the undertaker, was frustrated in his search for new ventures and his family wasn't too happy when Regan referred to him in his column as "The Happy Digger," linking him to everything from dance clubs to roller derbies.

Pat Egan, whom Regan now called, "The James Bond of Fourth Street," couldn't seem to find the exact pieces of a solid venture, while stubbornly chasing a dream of riches and trying to keep food on the table for a large and growing clan. At the moment, Egan was still president of the Fighting Saints hockey team which, he pointed out, was a "non-profit organization of which my sole reward seems to be only the victory party at the end of the season."

Paige Donnelly, the stout young attorney, had run into a roadblock in the presence of an arrogant new stock commissioner, which delayed his mounting drive to corner all new local over-the-counter issues.

Bob Gallivan, the successful bar proprietor, still had bad luck with hunting dogs, losing another pair to speeding autos. Apparently, his expensive hounds could track down a piece of lint in a snowstorm but couldn't find their way across the street.

And Regan, whom everyone assumed to be in solid command of his career because he had won a first and third place in the most recent AP annual awards, was in a deadly duel with Cabin Still. Determining that martinis were a shade too sedate, he was opting for doubles of the toe-twitching whiskey, which he called "Stab and Kill."

Even Regan's daughters were giving him lectures about his unpredictable behavior and the youngsters were referring to him as

"Quick Shot," after they discovered him pouring down liquid fire at the Breezy Point Resort bar on Sunday morning enroute to Mass.

But Race continued to argue that an alcoholic could not perform his job duties every day and would certainly have been picked up for dangerous driving before now if he were truly an inebriate. The fact that he had bought his way out of DWIs at least a half dozen times with free tickets or crisp twenties seemed to escape him completely.

"And I've got other problems besides the divorce," Jesse was confiding to Regan. "My damn business is kind of haywire. Sounds strange, Race, but it's the oldest family-owned insurance company in St. Paul and it's all screwed up. I can't seem to get the right help. That Jane's no help. Always picking up or dropping off some of those nine kids."

"Bad help, eh?"

"Now don't breathe a word of this but things are so bad I'm using premiums just to keep things together."

Regan was astounded. "You mean some of those high priced clients that insure their restaurants and bars with you are not covered?"

"Kind of like that," admitted Jesse, who was slowly picking apart an orange peel decorating his drink at Gallivan's.

"Well, almost. I'm going to borrow ten grand and pay most of it up and I know the companies. My friend Ozzie Goody has inherited another chunk. Maybe he'll help an old buddy. But it just shows how tough things can be. Got to keep paying the divorce attorney. And I've got to pay the rent and the kids' bills. And I have to act like I'm successful. So I'm throwing another $1,000 birthday party at the White Bear Yacht Club just so my clients think everything is going great."

"You know how to do that, Jesse."

"Hell, I think before Christmas I'll take another trip to Europe. This time, maybe buy some horses in Ireland. At five percent interest I can have more fun with the loan money than the banks can."

"Do you really need horses?"

"Oh, they've got great ones in Ireland! I saw rich sheiks buying 'em like they were going out of style at a farm outside Dublin on the last trip. And Pat Butler, the millionaire up on Summit, says he's got maybe 40 of them. Rents a chartered ship each year to take a bunch of them to the Dublin horse show. But I'm thinking more about runners."

"Jeez, Jesse! How can you talk about the insurance company going haywire and your divorce and then about buying race horses?"

"Just strong-willed, I guess," he winked and chuckled to himself. The whole orange peel disappeared into his mouth and he sucked on a swizzle stick.

"What we need is a really heavy promotional kill. We've been close on a lot of them. What would have happened if we'd won the Indy 500 and some of that state fair stuff made it? Hell, we've been close. Even the demolition derby was within a few moves of being a national enterprise."

Race bit his lip, savoring the bittersweet after-taste of strong whiskey. "I've got some ideas. But I think we've got to go a little bigger, start taking bigger chances."

"Bigger than the Indy car?"

"Now you're being funny, Jesse. By the way, am I covered by my insurance policy? I mean is my auto and home safe?"

"Safe as a baby's crib."

"Yeah, and this time I think we'll use a local publisher who claims he can get Red Rudensky on talk and TV shows all over the country." Race sounded fresh and aggressive.

"I'm proud of you, Hon," Dots smiled, placing a hand over his.

"I'm a little proud of myself, too. How many guys write columns, have a radio show, make speeches, write for magazines and try those crazy promotions? And I think the Sports Hot Seat show could get back on television again."

"I wish you'd give up the promotions and concentrate on the rest."

Regan went back to his home-based typewriter and pretended he had not heard her advice.

It was nearly midnight when Regan's phone rang. Larsen was calling from the bowling establishment. The sound of falling pins made it difficult to hear but Larsen was obviously excited.

"Race, we've got that super big one if we want it!" he said loudly into the phone, holding one ear with the other hand to shut out the tumult of the alleys.

"What's up?" Regan answered.

"Ever heard of the Spirit of America?"

"The one you and Jesse were telling me about months ago, right? Some kind of car."

"Some kind of car? That's the understatement of the year," Swede said with a trace of sarcasm.

"The Spirit of America happens to be the fastest land speed machine in the world. Clocked at 612 miles an hour by Craig Breedlove on Salt Lake! Listen, it's the same car that's on the television show introduction where the guy, I can't think of his name—oh, yeah, Jansen—is always on the run from the police. You know, the hot show, 'The Fugitive.'"

"I heard all that."

"The point is, this car is dynamite and this ex-race driver I know in Indiana, a friend of my wife, well, he can get this car for us for as long as six or seven weeks. Remember Jim McWhithey, from the fair?"

"Ouch, six weeks? What are we going to do, stuff it and show it at Irish wakes?"

"Don't be a wise guy. You always want something different. Well, this has never been around these parts. We've got a couple of months to get a place at the state fair. In a good location. Every kid who goes to the fair will want to see this baby. In fact, it's got a 10-foot tail."

"A what?"

"A 10-foot tail and fins and it's nearly 40 feet long! Damndest thing you'll ever see. My friend, Jim, I think you've met him, well, he can make a deal and even tow it up for us from some place in Michigan."

"There's got to be a catch," Race insisted.

"None at all. We can get it for $2,500 a week, plus insurance. Otherwise, it just sits around some garage. But the pictures, Race! It's large and flashy and they send a lot of huge still photos along with it. Call Jesse. I'll bet he'll love it! McWhithey will supervise the whole operation."

Of course Jesse did. He badly needed an emotional and cash lift.

A quiet meeting with state fair officials produced an attractive location, right off the exit ramp from the grandstand, where the race track lured over 200,000 spectators for musical productions and the sprint and late model features.

Better yet, the officials considered it a hot attraction and agreed to promote it in a good share of publicity releases and radio blurbs.

And best yet, the cost wasn't that bad, about $500 a day for the state fair site. Plus percentages, of course.

So with about the same amount going to the car's promoters and for help and lights and set up, the 10-day package amounted to about $12,000. That was a risk of four grand each from the entrepreneurs. And Jesse got the insurance on customers and the car for just $60 a day. "A steal," he called it.

Huddled the next morning over spiked coffee at Toppy's saloon, the three musketeers could no longer contain their elation.

"Know how really big this can be?' Race asked.

Jesse had a quick estimate. "Well, if we draw 10 percent of the 900,000 they expect at the fair and we charge a buck for adults and 50 cents for kids. We've got to grab about 90,000 people at an average of say 70 cents a head. That's 63 Gs and, frankly, I can't see how we can miss."

Larsen maintained his optimism but his more conservative

Scandinavian nature caused him to lower all estimates. "Well, a lot of people don't know or don't care about fast cars. But let's just take the nuts like us and their kids. I'd say we do 50,000 customers at 60 cents each. That's thirty grand. Take out 12 Gs for expenses and we net 18 happy ones.

"Not exactly a kick in the teeth," Race agreed.

"But I have another idea and I've gone to work on it already," Larsen interjected. "What if I told you we can get a spot for nine days at the Wisconsin state fair in West Allis—the next largest state fair in the midwest!"

"Hey, Billy, you're thinking like Barnum and Bailey!" Race laughed, pumping a clenched fist in the air. "That's what I call ingenious; planning ahead. Hell, that's been our problem. We don't plan out the details far enough ahead."

Larsen was all business. "I've checked and it'll cost a little more than the Minnesota fair's prices, but we can get a corner spot on the same street that leads to the main entrance of their mile track. They draw enormous crowds for their first class racing events. If we get 20 percent of the race fans that come down the street from the track we'll outdo the Minnesota figures."

"God, fellows. This finally sounds like the sure-fire we've needed," Jesse beamed. "Wonder if there's any more fairs we can get into."

"Glad you mentioned it," Larsen grinned. "In Oklahoma and at the big Texas bash that goes for two weeks. They fall right into place on the calendar. They want deposits in advance to hold choice spots. So if we want to ante up a thousand in advance for Milwaukee and $750 up front for Texas and Oklahoma, we can grab 'em all! But the deadline's in 10 days."

"A moot point," Jesse smiled. "Who's going to staff this stuff? Won't we be spread out all over the country?"

"I can get six or seven days vacation and handle the Milwaukee spot," Race volunteered. "But I don't know what we'll do in Oklahoma and Texas."

"I can get a few days off for Milwaukee and maybe three or four for the other spots if it's really gung-ho," Jesse added. The fever was contagious.

Larsen's Scandy cool began to agitate Jesse and Race into visions of grandeur.

"Well, McWhithey, the ex-driver, says he'll run the show for us wherever we want him to go. He'll even drag the Spirit all around and hire the help and patrol the whole works for $150 a day plus expenses. And he's honest as a monk. I've known him for 10 years and my wife's family has been friends of his for nearly 30 years."

"Let's have another Irish coffee and think about it," Race suggested. "We could be shooting for the stars. This is what I call the big time!"

Thoughts of palm-studded beaches and soft surf were reflected in the eyes of the threesome all afternoon. Regan believed each of them could make at least $35,000. Jesse thought it might go to $30,000 and Larsen predicted at least $25,000, depending on the heat in Texas.

At noon the next day, Regan called Jesse and then Swede. "It's on," he said, with all the deliberation and calculated assurance of a dictator starting a war.

Regan started work on his book about Red Rudensky, the ex-con with the feverish determination to make himself a national celebrity. The more material Red gave him the more excited he became. Each Monday, on his day off, he would take a bottle of Cabin Still into the rec room of his house and hammer out two or three chapters. He did it in the profane adult language of the true con. With Rudensky, he needed little imagination.

But what enthralled Race was the enormous amount of detailed information Rudensky gave him. There were over 40 letters from wardens, from Earl Browder, Eleanor Roosevelt, Margaret Mitchell and the head of the calendar company for which Rudensky now worked, Charlie Ward.

One day, race shouted up to Dots, unable to contain his enthusiasm, "God, Dots, this is going to make us a million bucks!"

The even-keeled Dots, who had been through more than a hundred entrepreneurial thrills during the Regan roller-coaster ride, merely shouted back, "That's nice, dear!" And then added politely, "How's the Gallivan book on sales doing? Any royalties still coming in?"

Brought back to reality like a man falling over a balcony, Regan thought a moment before replying. "Well, best as I can figure, we've sold maybe 75,000 books but the royalties keep getting smaller. The latest check was for just $900. Prentice Hall claims it's mostly discount and special sales now. But we had a pretty good run. I think I've collected over $3,500 as my share. Not bad for a first-timer."

That's nice, dear. By the way, what are you going to call the new book?"

"The Gonif."

"The what?"

"The Gonif. That's Jewish slang for a thief."

"Catchy."

Strange things were happening to Regan these days. One was destined to make him a legend in the "Insensitive Husband" club. A blunder that for years to come would be fodder for radio shows, columnists and frustrated wives in counseling groups.

Race's mishap happened on the homeward leg of an auto trip he and Dots made to relatives in Chicago. It was her birthday and she had curled up in the back with a book and blankets.

Race pulled into a service station/restaurant/cheese shop in Wisconsin, exactly 97 miles from home. He rushed inside to pay his bill and, glancing at the pile of blankets in the rear seat, took off, telling Dots' form, "I'll keep the radio down so you get a good sleep."

At decent intervals, he glanced over his shoulder, amused at her steady, silent sleep, knowing she was tired from a hectic weekend of partying.

Pulling into the driveway at home, the couple's daughters raced out of the house shouting, "Happy birthday, Mommie!"

Opening the car door the flabbergasted girls chorused, "Where's Mommie?"

Race untangled the blankets, exposing the greatest disappearance act since Evil Eye Finkle hid under the ring during a boxing riot on Long Island. The answer was abundantly clear: Dots had slipped out of the car and into the cheese shop for a quick look when Race pulled out. Naturally, he had assumed she was asleep under the heap of wool.

The phone rang five minutes later. Not wanting to upset the girls, Dots waited until she thought Race would get home before she called.

When Race pulled into the service station/restaurant/cheese shop, he was greeted with loud boos, chorused by four truck drivers who had taken up the vigil of caring for the stranded Dots, lending her a couple of bucks to buy a hamburger and fries and surprising her with a candle-topped cupcake for her birthday.

It was hilarious to everyone but Race. He never lived it down.

Then Race forecast that Eddie Stanky, the fireball manager of the Chicago White Sox, would be fired in six weeks. Stanky insulted Regan in the Minneapolis paper. Regan accepted Hal Scott's invitation to reply to Stanky via Scott's WCCO television sportscast, where Race challenged Stanky to meet him in a fistic duel after the game. The site: in front of the station.

Stanky replied that Regan needed a keeper.

Regan laughed the loudest when Stanky got the ax—five weeks later.

With momentum that would blow down a lighthouse, Gallivan's

Longshots hurled themselves into a series of promotions that would have left a Spartan crying in his saddle.

Oh yes, the Kiddie Karnival went through as scheduled with a gala Fourth of July celebration in Midway stadium that boggled the imagination and shredded the investors' wallets.

Over one hundred clowns, radio celebrities, dancing bears, seven animal acts, trickster poodles and more balloons that an anti-aircraft battery could shoot down in a telephone booth were at hand. And, of course, a fireworks display that would rival the battle of Gettysburg for noise and flashing explosives.

Only one problem:

Ninety percent of the potential customers stayed in their cars in the parking lot! For fifty cents change they bought reserve seat privileges. Since it was a municipal lot they were breaking no laws—only the promoters' hearts. They gleefully admired the free fireworks which boomed and zoomed over the stadium's ramparts.

While nearly three thousand car-sitters gloried in their cunning, the measley four hundred honest customers inside the ball park couldn't complain about dropping four bucks apiece on a fun show, but ironically the fireworks display was what the kids really wanted to see. And those rotten, cheating grease balls in the parking lot's cheap seats had won the day.

Since Larsen and Reagan had to clean up the party remains before an amateur baseball tourney was to open the next day, they spent five frantic hours after the show in the clubhouse rooms pulling, leaping for, and throwing a variety of obstacles in an effort to bring down the 700 helium balloons which now swayed in colorful profusion from the ceilings. Curses, hysteric laughter and dispair turned the Swede and Race into bedraggled, exhausted losers once more.

Before leaving for home, Dots tossed a smile and provocative remark their way: "For $3,000 or so a ticket that it cost us, you should have sat down and enjoyed the show. It was a good one!"

Finally Regan gasped a hoarse hope as they cleaned up the mess at three a.m.:

"Swede, we've still got 500 new balloons in the boxes. We should be heroes with every kid on our block who throws a birthday party in the next ten years. You *were* planning on giving them away, weren't you?"

Another sure-fire money maker went down the tube when famed football and wrestling hero Bronko Nagurski asked of Race and publisher Bernie Ridder, "Will you be serving liquor?"

This heart-stopping query came after Race and Ridder had proposed a plan for a new sports-celeb restaurant in downtown St. Paul near the old Auditorium. Bronk was to become a greeter, a host with the most. For that chore he'd have the dinner club carry his name, and share in the profits.

Regan could see himself cooking up enlightened promotional schemes and sitting in the rear of the spa in a white jacket chewing lightly on a quality cigar.

After Bronk had consumed a fourteen-once steak in the Lowry dining room and listened patiently to how much this would do for his waning mat career, the gentle giant asked about the liquor. When told that the nectar of the gods was where the profit floated he shook his head. Solemnly, he explained:

"Oh, my little wife would never let me get involved with anything that liquor was a part of. I could never do that. But I certainly appreciate you asking and the steak was wonderful."

The deflated Race found himself wondering how such a sweet guy could ever have thrown Abe Kashey, the villain, into the St. Paul Auditorium theater's orchestra pit or go 60 steaming minutes against Cliff Gustafson under the hot Fargo sky. Not to mention steamrolling Chicago Bears' foes for over a decade.

Bleeding but still game after the fireworks flop, Regan teamed up with Jesse and the first major soccer event in St. Paul history.

Councilman, Sev Mortinson was ecstatic over an idea he concocted with the inspiration of an Austrian jewler who operated his small shop next to the Faust Theater. The group spawned a promising but screwy game plan. Mortinson proposed a two night semi-round robin at Midway Stadium. Four teams, two games each. Irish verses English and Swedes verses Germans would be the opening matchups. The Irish would wear green, the Swedes would be in orange, the Germans in blue and the English in bulldog red.

The jeweler named Franz, an avid expert of the soccer society, pointed out that most of the amateurs in the Twin Cities were Swedes. So, half of the Irish team would consist of Swedes and they would also make up half the English roster. Germans abounded. The proposal looked plausible as long as the media didn't interview the players.

The event proved the worst flop in Midway Stadium history. Exactly 122 fans showed up the first night and less than half that jiggled around the stands for the second performance. Even with the councilman's influence and discounted rent, the trophies, jersies and clean-up charges sent this Longshot promo down the drain to the tune of $1,500. Fortunately, the players did it for laughs.

A ray of hope appeared briefly for Regan when the famed pugilistic promoter and manager Jack Hurley appeared in town. This was the amazing resin intellectual who promoted his own amateur, Pete Rademacher, into a world title fight with champion Floyd Patterson which drew forty thousand fans in Seattle.

Over midnight gin at the Blue Horse, Hurley proposed that Regan write a book about Vince Foster, the ill-begotten torso of tragedy who Jack claimed would have become the greatest middle weight money maker in boxing history. Rape charges, a nervous breakdown and eventual death on a dark Minnesota road claimed its toll.

After hours with Hurley, Regan could even envision the title of the book, "The Rapist Sold Bibles".

Actually the combination of ranch/restauranteur/promoter John Rauchnot of the J.R. Ranch in Hudson and Race was the most unlikely of the impresario tandems. John was all facts and figures; Race all fury and fantasies.

But in their second large winter rodeo stint in the St. Paul Auditorium, it was John who let numbers get in the way of facts. A year earlier the initial cowboy competition they put on was primarily to make a buck for the police band. This time the firemen were to make a few grand.

Neither John nor Regan cared that much about making a kill since John was a nut on broncos and bulls and Race thought Larry Mahan, the world champion cowboy, was so wonderful that he talked Dick Long into handing the bull-blaster a green Cadillac convertible for his stay.

But John could clench a silver dollar the way a dying man grasps his preacher's hand.

"I found some cheap dirt," he explained to Race. "It'll save us $1,500. and maybe buy the firemen a good sized tuba."

"What in blazes is 'cheap dirt'?" Race wondered.

They found out the morning of the opening three-day stand. Forty truckloads from up north dropped tons of dirt on the Auditorium floor. Within two hours of leveling off the rodeo surface the dirt grew mushy. Unseen ice, in frozen streaks, began to melt. An hour after that, it was a quagmire. By six p.m., two courageous steer wrestlers were gasping for air as nearly two feet of mud threatened to engulf their lungs. A Florida swamp in dead of night was safer. Quicksand would have been a treat compared to this lake of grit and gumbo.

"No way! This show's off!" an angry Mahan shouted.

The first two performances were cancelled before the promoters furiously rounded up a dozen truckloads of sand from the St. Paul Public Works.

The rodeo managed to get in a pair of performances after the sand somewhat solidified the field of action, but some of the cowboys refused to take any more chances. Auditorium officials threatened law suits after the black gravy choked the plumbing system.

Rauchnot vowed never again to trust guys selling cheap dirt from up in the frozen north. The show dropped $5,800 and Race again was heading for the loan counters.

Regan and Frenchy almost stumbled into what would have become, they claimed, "The winner of all time." At the urging of Dave Brooks, brother of hockey hero Herb, they tried to make and market the "Super Seed Sucker", aimed at pulling the seeds out of watermelons without damaging the inner fibres.

"Ten million people eat watermelons," Race would observe, "but with no seeds . . . wham! That figure skyrockets to 50 million!"

Out in a run down warehouse which Barney Gardner steered them into, a dozen would-be investors listened to the warm-up tune of the little engine as it hummed, hissed, and hiccuped a bit. It was shut off and the slim nossle was inserted into a whopping green melon and in words that would make the Indy 500 starter wince in jealousy, Regan proclaimed:

"Gentlemen, start the super seed sucker!"

You've heard of crap hitting the fan. Nothing you can visualize matched the eruption of this mess. While investors and inventors ducked for cover, the watermelon blew up, throwing its innards as far as ten feet against walls, shirts, suits, ties and angry faces. The cleanup took nearly two hours.

Through it all, the hail of melon sinews and rines and slop, Brooks could be heard shouting, "Gentlemen! Gentlemen! . . . Please remain calm. We're just a little ahead of our time!"

This night Race awoke form his nightmare vividly recalling that he was screaming for help as he tip-toed through broken glass with a state fair deputy sheriff chasing him down while waving a badge in one hand and a Billy club in the other.

Just another horrifying replay of his disaster five years previously with the infamous putting contest at the fair, a flat-out bust that cost him and Jesse four grand.

They had fastened 500 cuddly stuffed brown Teddy Bears to the framework. Naturally, they figured only a handful of participants would win. I mean when Snead and Jimmy Demaret and that young hot-shot, Arnold Palmer, could miss them from three and four feet who among the masses could make any of those 10-footers on the outdoor carpet plateau; three shots for 50 cents—the odds all in favor of the promoters. Right?

Dead wrong.

As the construction man who built the raise platform, Pat Conroy, explained after 1,800 of the two-buck prizes had been claimed, "You should have given them something tough like throwing darts at spiders."

The first night, Regan's oldest daughter, all of ten years, drilled in two of three, jumped up with glee, proclaiming, "It's really easy, Daddy. I want two bears!"

Regan shrugged off the sordid dream with the explanation to himself: 'must be anticipating the Spirit of America extravaganza.'

Chapter Eighteen

Father Groppi and Sitting Bull

It was the evening before the Minnesota state fair opened. The sun was setting just over the 10-foot tail of the mighty Spirit of America. By Minnesota's late August standards this was a beautiful night; clear, temperatures in the high 60s and official forecasts for a first-day attendance of nearly 100,000 filled the vast 300-acre tract with anticipation.

The Spirit's corner was a natural, next to the giant ramp carrying thousands to daily grandstand attractions, which included everything from dog and pony shows to square dancing, country music stars and entertainment legends like Al Hirt and Liza Minelli—and, of course, the 10 days of auto racing.

The Spirit was enclosed in a seven-foot high red, white and blue canvas in a thousand-square foot pen, with spotlights focused on the giant tail so that as night fell the scene actually became eerie, albeit spectacular. A tape with background music from "The Fugitive" television series, plus an announcer broadcasting the specifications and speed records of the machine rolled continuously.

"I want to revise my estimates," Race murmured to Jesse. "Bet you a hun we clear close to 40 Gs. It's a natural."

"Well, that's a little high but could be," Jesse agreed. "That spotlight on the tail sure shows up. You can see it like a beacon for two blocks in all directions."

Larsen and McWithey were busy hosing down the huge speedster and polishing the blue and white body and red tail with a diligence that would have suggested this giant belonged in their own private collection.

"Lars, this car doesn't have an engine," McWhithey observed almost casually.

"Damn, if it doesn't," Swede agreed. Neither seemed too taken aback by the fact. "But then it's the flashy car people want to see. Why bore them with an engine? They all look alike."

When they brought it to Regan's attention, Race shrugged his shoulders and gave the reply that he would dole out so many times over the years, "Fake it."

Jesse was nearly convulsed in laughter and had to spit out a mouthful of gin and 7-Up. "Fake it! You know, Regan, you are a work of art! That should be our slogan: 'Fake it!' We should have a crest made with just the ring around it, only the words 'Fake it!'"

"Well, who gives a hoot about a lousy, greasy engine?" Race snapped. "The chassis is the thing. Who'd pay just to see an engine that went 612 miles an hour? That'd be a bore. Jets are mostly empty space anyway. It's the car, this big friggin' piece of iron and color that people want to see. I'll wager another fiver that not one person even notices the engine chamber doesn't have anything."

"Hope you're right," cautioned Swede. "I don't want to throw any water on this party but I think the fair contract calls for delivering an engine before a car can be considered whole."

"Screw 'em," Jesse argued. "We're making the fair, the fair's not making us. Let's just not mention it again. Let's just praise the car."

The group seemed vindicated the next morning when a racing columnist from the Minneapolis paper did an inventory of the machine, never mentioned the vacuum in the speedster's innards and informed all that his paper would have a big Sunday spread with color pictures—the works—on the giant machine.

This, Regan knew, would force his own paper into another display and along with TV news clips would certainly assure the machine of becoming a colossal attraction. But, of course, it was foot and mouth exposure that the Longshots were counting on to bring in the moola; farmers from Wadena talking to farmers from Paynesville.

By 4 p.m., Swede received the call for which he was waiting at his bowling emporium.

"It's me, Regan. And we're knocking 'em dead!"

"God, how many?"

"Well, I haven't the exact figured but we hit 1,000 bodies by noon! That's in just two hours. And they've been steady. In fact, there's been at least seven or eight customers around the car right up until now—and they move through pretty fast. Like six or seven minutes. One time I counted nearly 30 inside the walls. They're nuts about the Spirit!"

"Really? Hey, if this keeps up how many will we hit by closing tonight?"

"I figure close to 4,000 and about 75 percent are adults, which means over three grand. That's $30,000 if we keep it up and, of course, we've got the two big Sundays left. We could double it by tons those big days."

"So maybe we go to $40,000."

"Yeah and who said that was the magic figure—who?"

"Right on, Race. First prediction you've had on the nose since Willie Pep knocked out Jackie Graves."

"Don't get cute. Remember, you could be out of work or peddling booze from your car if they keep tearing down the West Side!"

"Hey, I'm so happy I think I'll pour myself a straight gin. But re-member, we could still get bad weather and some jerk could still sue us because we don't have an engine."

"Swede, you're a helluva guy but don't bring a casket to the party. This is a steady winner, baby, and I think word of mouth will hype this thing a good 20 percent a day. Would you believe a 50 grand take?"

"And don't forget Wisconsin, Texas and Oklahoma!" Swede actually shouted.

"Hey, we could hit nearly $200,000 if those fairs are as good as you say."

"Good? Well, Wisconsin's got twice the hot racing fans that this state has. And everything in Oklahoma and Texas is into speed. And oh, yes, we've got all our spots confirmed at those locations. And I figure if we give McWhithey a two or three grand bonus he'll handle all the hauling and locate any extra help we need. You know, he's set a sprint speed record at the Minnesota state fair four years ago. He's got guts but he's kinda between jobs."

The idea of expanding to three more fairs raised such wondrous implications that Regan twisted and turned in his sleep. Jesse actually fantasized that he'd have such a luxurious trip abroad with his earnings that he'd finally meet the Irish colleen he so dearly yearned for—after the memory of his bitter divorce dimmed, of course. Larsen, naturally, was more practical with his fantasies. He assessed what kind of attorney the profits would permit him to hire in what had become a bloody legal mess with his family.

And the money kept rolling in—Sunday, Monday, Tuesday—Imelda Marcos would have left the Philippines for this action.

A brief shower on Wednesday stalled profits only slightly. More than 6,000 stood in awe of the Spirit on the first Sunday and the second Sunday should have proved equally successful. Halfway through the fair's run, the Spirit had lured in close to 25 Gs and would gain the admiration of the old carnies who had been around big tent action for years hustling everything from frozen Big Foot to the Snake Lady.

"Damn, who would have thought you could build such a machine and that so many would pay just to look at a car standing still?" one Midway admirer told Larsen.

"It isn't exactly your run of the mill street machine," the Swede reminded the old-timer.

"Yeah, but it proves there is a sucker born every minute."

It was on the eighth day that the roof of the dream began to leak a little.

The 10-year-old boy looked innocent enough but when he yelled across the machine to his dad, "Hey, Dad, this thing ain't got no engine!" a trio of blood pressures began to rise like the head of an angered cobra.

It happened that the whole collection of Longshots in this venture were on hand at the time. Regan quickly put his arm around the shoulders of little Tony, while almost instantaneously holding out his other hand to the lumbering, somber farmer father.

"Hey, this little guy of yours has good eyes! And he's got a good question. The engine's being reconditioned in Akron for another run next year. But most people don't care about that. They only want to see the big daddy's chassis."

"Not me, paw," contradicted the kid. "I think it's a gyp if we don't see no engine. That's what I like, the engine."

"Right, Tony," the man from the soil agreed sternly. "These people took our buck fifty and never said nothin' about no engine being here. What the hell, that's like selling an ice cream cone without the ice cream."

By now, Jesse was in the picture.

"Absolutely right, kid, you're absolutely right! Tell you what. Here's five bucks. You go out and take your Dad for a nice hot dog and some pop. This car should have an engine and we hope to have it back in the next day or two. You come back maybe Monday and we'll have it for you and you can see it for free."

"If it's reconditioned by then," Regan said, glaring at Jesse.

Larsen had a better plan. "Tell you what, are you fellows from around here?"

"No, we're from Fairmont but we're staying at my sister's up on Snelling."

"Well, I run the Mohawk bowling alley and restaurant. You know it's just six miles away from here. Here's our card. You come over any time you're here and bring your sister. You can bowl and have a nice dinner on us. You like to bowl?"

"Never did it," the dad said without a trace of gratitude.

"Well, try it, you'll love it. And Tony, here, you keep right on being investigative. And you should be proud of your son, sir. Not one other person from the 25,000 who've seen this machine even noticed it had no engine. My, my . . ."

"Well, I think it's still kind of a gyp. I should go to the head people around here and give a holler. Hell, you should advertise it's only half a car. You wouldn't get half the people."

"You're right," Jesse tried to placate the farmer. "You're absolutely right. But the big shots who own this car fooled us, too. They didn't tell us they didn't have an engine. Left us out on the limb."

The long and short of it dispersed through the crowds.

"Think they'll cause trouble?" Race asked Swede.

"Well, if they don't show up at the bowling lanes, I wouldn't bet one way or another."

Two evenings later, the farmer, his son and six relatives showed up at the Mohawk. Larsen proceeded to get the adults slightly looped and kept the kids happy on the lanes. When the party was over, the farmer invited Swede and his family down to their Fairmont farm.

"I can hardly wait," Swede managed with a straight face.

As the Longshots prepared to make their stand with the Spirit in West Allis, a suburb of Milwaukee, they met with exuberance in Larsen's office at the Mohawk. After the hugs and salutations, Swede went to his adding machine and jabbed out the happy figures: The Spirit had taken in $38,744, expenses had run just over $11,500. The healthy profit of over $27,000 bolstered the entrepreneurs' spirits as much as Jack Dempsey's slugfest over Angel Firpo did for promotional genius Mike Jacobs or the Two-headed Lady did for P.T. Barnum.

Regan finally had a winner. "When we're through with the rest of these fairs, we'll be wallowing in greenbacks. Oh, yes, don't forget to report the profits to Uncle Sam."

"Uncle who?" Jesse grinned. "I haven't paid him anything for two years. They only check about one out of five thousand."

"If they check me, I'll wind up in Alcatraz," Larsen said solemnly. "Think I'm going to report all my vending machines? They keep me in socks."

Regan grew very serious as he toyed with a double martini, a drink he returned to only in times of crisis or joy. "Well, lemme give you guys a little story before you get cocky. You can take those statistics, Jesse and stick 'em where the buggers grow. Do you have any idea who came to my house the other evening, right at dinner time?"

"The Good fairy?" Jesse joked.

"Laugh, you wise guy. No, but two well-dressed, sharp young guys from the government. One was from the IRS, the other from the FBI. Don't ask me how they teamed up but they had all the credentials."

"They think you were a syndicate boss? Maybe you should junk that black fur coat."

"Hey, this is serious. Anyway, they're investigating my friend, Rauchnot and the JR Ranch, where we've had a few events. Right, Jesse? Mainly they were into the rodeo I put on with John in St. Paul."

"Seems they don't think John is reporting all his income and it's big numbers. But anyway, they find a check I wrote him for $900 after the last rodeo, the one in the mud that nearly suffocated all the cowboys. I explained we had a loss and they were very polite. But don't tell me, Rogers, that they don't investigate.

"Something else, too. I called Rauchnot and he's going crazy. Says he's as clean as a baby in a new diaper and that they're using him for a test case. But his lawyers alone are going to cost him over 50 grand just for openers. He's taking the case to Chicago, where his accusers have to charge him in person on neutral ground."

"Yeah, but that's something special," Jesse insisted.

"Tell it to me when you're bringing John and me chocolates in the can."

Flushed with success, the Longshots were generally ecstatic as they headed for Milwaukee and the Wisconsin state fair. They had no reason to even remotely consider that they might be retracing the footsteps of General George Custer on his way to the Little Big Horn.

As Jesse pointed out on the drive to Sudsville, they were afloat with coin and had knocked 'em dead at the big Minnesota extravaganza. They had a proven attraction and Wisconsin's bash was known for its vast numbers of speed nuts. It was only a question of how much the Spirit of America machine could draw.

The Spirit still had no engine but since only a handful of complaints surfaced in St. Paul few if any could be expected in the new arena. As Regan pointed out many times, "Wisconsin people are not as smart as Minnesotans. You need only look at Green Bay's cheeseheads in the football stands. They're about two pounds of hair removed from gorillas."

Operating this venture again gave everyone an added sense of security. The fact that Larsen had taken five days off to join Jesse and Regan turned this into a team effort—one for all and all for one.

The first inkling that something might be amiss surfaced when the group checked into the hotel, some six miles from the fairgrounds. "What do you think of all the marches?" the lady behind the registration desk asked the group.

"What marches?" Swede inquired.

"The ones that are getting all the headlines in the papers and are all over TV," the lady answered. "You know, the ones that priest, Father Groppi, has started for those freedom nuts, the ones who want all the racial equality. That can be really a red-hot issue in a Polish town."

"Father Groppi?"

"Yeah, he's one of those weird kind of religious freaks who's going to straighten out the world. You know, everyone equal. He's had a couple of marches and they're getting bigger every night. He's aiming them, I think, right at the Wisconsin state fair to get all the attention when visitors are in town."

"Trying to hit the fair?" Jesse asked incredulously.

"Sure. The fair's in for real problems as I see it. They're talking about added police because there might be racial tension. Maybe even riots."

"Shitttt . . ." Regan whispered under his breath to no one in particular. Instead of submerging themselves in the newest problem, the Longshots retreated to the Spirit's new concession. There they picked up the *Milwaukee Sentinel* and quickly flushed out the four-day weather prospect. "Rains, chills could dampen the fair."

"Dammit, guys. Maybe this Milwaukee stop isn't what we dreamed about—like a forecast for rain and riots," Race pondered.

"That's nothing," Larsen added. "A security guard claims they're going to put on an 8 p.m. curfew throughout the fair's dates just to keep people off the streets."

"A curfew?" Race shook his head in disbelief. "A curfew, rain and freedom marches? Who is this crazy priest anyhow, another Father Coughlin, who blamed Hitler on the gold standard?"

"I need a drink," Jesse stated, hoping the suggestion would ignite the spirit of adventure and success which filled the little group on the trip into Wisconsin.

After the second round of drinks from their private jar of martinis, Regan began to rekindle the fire of optimism. "Well, the curfew could mean more people in the daytime looking for something to get the freedom marchers off their minds. Right? And the rains could simply freshen the place and keep the dust down, right? And the next round of marches may never even begin or they could be centralized downtown, right?"

A duet of "Rights!" greeted the question. The Longshots were due to meet McWhithey's moving team at the fairgrounds the next morning for the setup. Tonight they would coat themselves in gin and vermouth and sleep the sleep of angels. Rich angels.

Just as General Custer had underestimated the strength of his foe, the Longshots had no idea of the strength of the subversive forces which lay ahead the next nine days.

On day one, fair attendance was down nearly 25 percent because of gloom, mist, chilly temperatures and an obvious uneasiness about the possibility of racial unrest. Threatening headlines and newscasts added to the bleak atmosphere and the Spirit lured in fewer than 600 customers, despite its attractive location on a main walkway just two blocks from the prime entrance to the racetrack. Because of the lack of action, Larsen opted to fly back to his bowling establishment and Regan threatened to fire the shaggy looking barker who had replaced the tape recording on the public address system.

On day two, the sun shone for five hours before clouds enshrouded the premises. Attendance dwindled to only 455. Regan fired the announcer and journeyed into the loop to purchase a blond wig and threatened to do the hawking himself.

On day three, the crowds were still well below average and the nightly curfew killed the fair's customers after 6 p.m. Jesse proceeded to get drunk on Wisconsin ale after consuming eight bratwurst sausages in one sitting. He also proceeded to vomit on and off for nearly four hours. Race went back to the hotel to count the day's receipts, which lay strewn on the bedspread. A total of $306, which he promptly threw in a paper bag and lugged to the hotel's front desk, where he cashed it in for three $100 bills. From there he went to the motel's restaurant and ordered a 16-ounce sirloin and said to Jesse when he arrived, "You puked away today's profits."

On day four, Regan assumed the blond wig and dark glasses, although there was no sign of rain. "Step up and see the world's greatest and fastest machine!" he shouted to race goers strolling past after the matinee sprint race.

"Never take a child past this amazing machine without showing it to him or he'll never let you forget it! You owe it to your children to show them a stupendous, amazing, gigantic car—the world's fastest! Imagine, it goes 620 miles an hour! That's 6-2-0. You've seen it on TV, you've seen it in the movies, you've seen it in magazines! This is your last chance to see the blazing Spirit in person before it goes into the big museum in Washingtonnnnnnnn, Deeeeee Ceeeeee!"

Back at the hotel, Swede had returned with good news. Regan could call Morrie Steinman, the PR specialist from St. Paul, who once rode a horse up the Capitol's steps to hype a Buck Rogers movie. He'd agree to come down and help and even hawk the Spirit because he knew Milwaukee crowds. He also new a hot-shot car dealer in Sudsville, named Selig, who had bought the Brewers baseball team and might be interested in a huge promotion for his large auto franchise.

The desperate Regan called and got Morrie for $200 a day and a hotel room. The fiery little huckster arrived the next afternoon.

By the time he got there, the Longshots were groggy from drinking and in despair. They had already cancelled out of the Oklahoma and Texas fairs and were seriously considering blowing up the Spirit of America.

Morrie had an infectious aggressiveness and humor that could turn a funeral into a Bugs Bunny short. His brother had started the famous Dancing Waters of Florida fame and Morrie believed he could sell a pig farm to a rabbi. He was short, bushy-haired and wore enormous dark-rimmed glasses to match his full scale nose. He also had a giggle that could turn into a boiler-maker's roar in a matter of seconds.

Morrie was like a Boy Scout stepping into the breach between Sitting Bull and George. Receipts did move up 20 percent but barely enough to cover his expenses.

Rain continued to fall. The papers continued to warn of imminent violence in the wake of the Freedom Marchers. Father Groppi continued to lead the oppressed. The small crowds at the fairgrounds continued to ignore the Spirit of America. The Longshots continued to drink and curse the fates.

As Regan put it, "There's a giant hand up there somewhere in the sky that wants to see the Crucifixion again. And it's selected us to land on the crosses!" A little dramatic, but in the eyes of these born losers, certainly a theory to consider.

Race and Jesse did get to meet Mr. Selig, who said it was a little late to get involved in a state fair promotion, but he took Morrie and the Longshots out to lunch. Regan would always remember that Selig forecast that the day would come when he couldn't afford to own a baseball team because the expenses were beginning to "kill me." Selig also pointed out Milwaukee was a toddler in the television revenue business compared to New York and Chicago.

Selig introduced them to his thin son. "If Buddy here amounts to something, maybe he can straighten out baseball."

The Spirit's crowds pulled in less than $5,500 and with Morrie's salary and hotel expenses, electrical connections and rent their expenses soared to nearly $20,000. That did not include the 14 bottles of whiskey and gin the braintrust had consumed. The loss was a solid $18,000 and if you added the money owed Jim McWithey and his moving team, the ads and radio blurbs, the expenses wiped out any profit from the Minnesota concession plus another $850. Adding up-front dough forfeited to the Texas and Oklahoma fairs and the red ink mounted.

There was one last way out, Jesse concluded. "Maybe we'll just haul her out during the break-down time tomorrow morning, forget paying the last rent installment and plead temporary insanity if we're caught."

In anticipation of such a fun event, Race suggested that at midnight they take Jesse's Ford sedan and see just what it could do on the fairground's fabled one-mile oval, which had hosted the likes of speed legends from Barney Oldfield to Foyt.

So it was in the dead of night, with the mist falling, that Jesse and Regan cracked through a chainlink fence, denting the Ford but gaining access to the hallowed oval. Jesse actually managed two laps at "A solid 98.5 miles per hour," as Race described it, before the fair's security people hauled them in. It was the first time in Milwaukee track history that a driver had been nailed for going too fast in search of the greasy Golden Grail of speedom—at midnight, in the rain, without a fan in sight.

Accepting their humble apologies and apparently unaware of the cracked chain, the officers charged the culprits a mere $50, since they were leaving town the next day.

As they left, one security guard asked, "Were you guys drinking?" To which Regan replied with feigned indignation, "You don't think we'd drive like that if we were sober, do you?"

The guards even laughed. And Jesse predicted, "Those SOBs will try to test their own cars on the track as soon as we get out of sight."

But getting the Spirit out of sight the next morning wasn't so easy. Much more tenacious than the Longshots had anticipated, the security check and management were over them like a cave-in. When Larsen handed over the cashier's check for nearly $8,000 it was like giving a gallon of blood to save the life of your absentee landlord. McWhithey settled for half what the Longshots owed him and proceeded to hook up the Spirit for its trip back to Michigan and owner Craig Breedlove.

The long drive back to St. Paul was a trek of misery and mostly aching silence for the little group.

"Life is friggin' strange," Jesse mused. "Here we've got our sharp brains, strong imaginations and it all goes down the drain in Milwaukee rain."

"And don't forget that screwy priest," Race emphasized. "He's enough to make me join the Mormons."

Naturally, they called off their appearances in Oklahoma and Texas, explaining after forfeiting their deposits, "The wheels came off the Spirit."

Chapter Nineteen

How About A Green Beer, Sister?

"You're really saying we need a miracle to get even, aren't you?" Jesse asked, only half-joking. He and Race were pondering the complexities of show biz over a late snack at Gallivan's following a hockey game.

"I'm saying we're all in a bad bio-rhythm slump. We could use a mild success to get on track. I've got Feigner, the softball ego. He's booked for about 20 games this coming year. Nothing really big but the guy averages 966 fans wherever he plays in Minnesota, Iowa, or Wisconsin. And if it doesn't rain it's a nice little profit. He really slays 'em in St. Paul. You know that."

Jesse burst into rare unfettered laughter, "Nine hundred fans per game outside of St. Paul?" he sputtered as he spilled half of his martini on the floor. "Regan, I can't believe you! You mean you're going to be satisfied the rest of your pathetic existence to beat your brains out on promos for 966 bodies? Hey, I could do that well with a miniature pony race in Rice Park."

"You miss the whole point, wise guy. That 966 equates to about $2,500 each time out. A nice, steady grind, I'd say. Just for booking that baby it's a clear $350 bucks per and all I have to worry about is an accurate count. And one thing for Fast Eddie, he's honest. He might pitch while he's juiced, but he's honest."

"Okay, Eddie the Softball King, is honest. But what have you got in mind?"

"Something solid, not big, just enough to show we can still produce." Nobody spoke for a moment and then Rogers' eyes lit up under a rare lid elevation. "Hey! Let's tie in something to the St. Patrick's Day parade. You and Bob Gallivan started the crazy damn celebration and it does bring 100,000 people to downtown for five or six hours. Why not something to draw them in, besides booze and broads."

"Okay. I've got it," Race's hands went up in the air like a referee signaling a touchdown. "Irish wolfhounds! A special display of Irish wolfhounds, telling the world they are the biggest, most honored dogs on the planet, capable of killing a wild wolf in 30 seconds, 175 pounds of mayhem. They are the most powerful, meanest hounds in captivity."

"Wolfhounds? Where are you going to get them? Where are you going to keep them? Who's going to clean up the tons of crap they'll drop?" Jesse railed.

"Yeah, I suppose it's a little nuts. And all us silly Irish'll want to see them for nothing in the parade. Know something else, Jesse? I did a story on two of those big beasts for Northwest Airlines' in-flight magazine. They got more mail than they have for any piece in years."

Silence engulfed the pair but only for 30 seconds or so.

"Hey," Jesse beamed, "what about a boxing match? We used to have them every St. Pat's day for years but nothing lately. I don't mean a big match. Let's rent Stem Hall at the Auditorium. Seats about 1,500 and we'll serve corned beef sandwiches at the concession stand."

Race was warming to the idea. "We can push that green beer, too! How about beef and green beer? We can charge five bucks to get in and five bucks for corned beef sandwiches and a couple of bottles of green beer. So we've got a couple of fights and a real party with maybe a couple of Irish crooners."

Rogers' imagination was flowing like the Johnstown flood. "And I know a bagpipe guy who will blow his brains out for ten bucks and a freebie to the fights. God, Regan, we might be on to something that could grow into an annual party! Maybe so big that next year we can stage it in the Auditorium and draw thousands. Hey, waitress, how about another drink?"

Race was unloading ideas like a county truck spreading salt on an icy highway. "I know we can do over $5,000, that's just under four bucks a head, with 1,500 people. Presume the fighters on a four-bout card cost a couple of hundred a piece. Hell, we can make a couple of grand. But that won't be the important thing. The big deal is that we'll be using this show like the Commies and Nazis did in Spain—a warm-up for the big kill."

"Now you're bringing history to the table," Rogers laughed. "But that's right. We just haven't had tune-ups in any of our big ones. If this goes on a small scale it goes through the roof on a big scale. We just need cheap fighters, cheap workers, a real cheap rental deal with the city and about 10,000 cheap handbills downtown. We'll float them at 10 o'clock in the morning the day of the fight, right during the build-up for the parade so the crowds can jabber about it for a few hours and decide that it's the best deal in town."

The two walked into the brisk night air. "You know, St. Paul is a real sleeper," Race pointed out, wrapping his arm around Jesse. "If we make it big someday, I'd like to put up a quarter-mile asphalt auto racing track around here that we could use for rodeos, fights, tug o' wars, concerts, cycle shows and classic car meets."

"That's what I like about you, Regan. One minute you're talking about a nice cheap little promo to get a few bucks out of the red and the next you want to rebuild the city. You are from Mars."

St. Pat's day turned out to be ideal for the fight promotion—from the standpoint of weather. It was brisk, a bit on the chilly side and there was a 50/50 chance of rain forecast for the early evening. Just the kind of messy stuff to drive the celebrants inside. The whole package, with bagpipers, three fights, corned beef sandwiches and green beer, boxing ring and help shouldn't come to more than $6,500. That means just 1,200 fans would crack the nut. The rest would be gravy—or green beer, if you like.

To cap off the proceedings was an ten-round main event, much better than anyone had anticipated. In one corner was Jumbo Jim Beattie, pride of the Irish working man. The towering 6'7", 220-pound former amateur champ was making a bid to become a professional challenger in the heavyweight ranks.

"His only problem," Race was saying, "is the fact he's a bigger target than Hiroshima." But Beattie could jab, move pretty well and claimed he had hooked up with a New York promoter with "good connections." Naturally, for only $500, Beattie wasn't going to fight Omar the Mad Bomber.

But Rogers had talked Freddie Askew, a lanky black apprentice sparring partner, called for this occasion The Dark Destroyer, into a little workout for $200. Askew could wing a few from the county line but, as Beattie guaranteed, "I can stretch this guy with the back of my gloves," totally disregarding the fact that Askew was a splendid athlete and in good shape.

Beattie always figured to draw a few of his neighborhood school chums. And he could also recite poetry. Jesse promised the big boy that sometime during the evening he would get the chance to regale his Irish followers with tales of Brian Boru, legendary Gaelic king. Beattie owned a wide vocabulary, was an amateur actor of sorts but had been handicapped by the words of a medical specialist who claimed he was allergic to boxing gloves—not the punches but the horse-hair stuffing.

Jesse and Regan, always early starters on St. Pat's day, went right into the tumult at Gallivan's. Proprietor Bob kept the round table available to the Longshots and their wives and children during the hectic celebration. The previous year, half a dozen fisticuffs broke out in front of the Wabasha thirst emporium and this time Bob was prepared with two off-duty cops at the front door. Only recognizable drunks and acquaintances would be permitted in.

Even under such demanding security the place was mobbed by 10 a.m. and the hospitality was such that as Bob proudly proclaimed, "We treat 'em so nice that only 10 percent ever go out to watch the parade."

Sheriff Kermit Hedman fired his pistol at exactly noon, when 4,000 marchers began the trek from Rice Park to the train station. It was truly a sea of green.

Professional Irishman Charlie O'Leary was talking up a storm when Race confronted him in Gallivan's.

"Am I going to the fight tonight?" Charlie replied. "God, I hear they're pouring green beer. That's enough to turn me away. They'll be puking lumpy green stuff all over town. Hope you've got nothing to do with this one, Regan!"

The astonished Race, who had kept a very low profile on this score, shrugged his shoulders. "Nope, just some amateurs running it, I guess."

His stomach began to quiver. He shouted out to Jesse, who was wearing a green derby, "Listen, Jesse. O'Leary claims green beer turns him off."

"Forget him," Jesse replied emotionless. "That guy's the number one knocker in town. He hasn't been right since he guessed the sun would show up in the east. I'll tell you something about Charlie, he bought an Edsel. That about says it all."

Of course, Charlie had an opinion about Rogers, too. "He'd screw up DiMaggio's swing. They tell me he left half the tickets for Gallivan's party in his office drawer."

Regan always said the Irish would never get Alzheimer's disease because they never forgot their feuds. The Rogers-O'Leary one was a classic. Secretly, however, Race figured they loved to torment each other and would be lost without an adversary.

Box company mogul Len Halper always liked fights. Race crawled up to Len at the bar and inquired, "Going to the fight card tonight?"

"And see Beattie wallop some poor kid half his size? When are they going to get him someone to fight? He's been hitting on midgets and cripples."

"Not exactly," Regan contradicted. "Beattie's being taken along at just the right pace."

"Yeah, slow and slower," Halper laughed.

Race and Jesse inched toward Jack McLaughlin, a guy who would support a Protestant for mayor if you got him in the right mood. "Going to the fight tonight?" Race repeated.

"I might if I can quit drinking," Jack replied. "Hey, this is a celebration! And you can see enough fights in the street. Who has to pay to see another one?"

Race confided to Jesse as the tumult grew, "These are basically drinking types. Anyone with common sense wouldn't be in here."

"Is that why we're here?" Jesse ribbed.

"I'll drink to that," Race agreed.

Stem Hall couldn't have been much more devoid of bodies had an IRA bomb rumor permeated the premises. By 9 p.m., about 200 stragglers appeared, plopping down their five bucks and expecting to see a recreation of the Dempsey-Tunney fight.

After hours of preparatory imbibing, some were in a happy mood and willing to try green beer or arsenic lemonade. Others wanted only a chance to sit down and inventory the co-customers. A few old-timers actually were enjoying the nostalgia of past recollections of St. Pat fight days, like the time Del Flanagan dismantled ex-champion Johnny Bratton after being floored early on.

But there was a paucity of action around the concession stands, where the green beer option was a part of the fight ticket. And only a handful had taken their bites out of corned beef sandwiches. This could be a problem, since the green beer was arrayed in a dozen 20-gallon kegs and a flat payment from the promoters had been demanded. No consignment on this special. And 500 corned beef sandwiches had been catered, all encased in little green bags.

Regan was so distraught before the first fight that he could only recall the day when he pumped gin into his Moonburgers at the state fair. "Might work now but most of these guys are so whacked already they'd never notice the booze in the beef."

The preliminary fighters stumbled through their paces as Jesse retreated to the toilet to throw up. A day of intermittent drinking, an attack of nerves and the sight of empty seats had finally done in the usually callused promoter. Race agreed with Jesse that he probably had an ulcer.

Another 50 customers or so showed up by the time of the main event but there were still four chairs to every citizen's Fanny. Public address announcer Van Avery, no amateur at igniting boxing throngs, was also having a difficult time getting excited about the proceedings. When he announced that a preliminary fighter with a 3-11 record was "A serious contender for the world title honors," an obvious used car follower of Van's shouted back, "For God's sake, Van, that guy's got less of a future than the '57 Pontiac you sold me!"

The atmosphere in the hall was dismal and the bagpipes sounded like tortured pigs squealing before the kill. However, the main event, which was signed to be a laugher, turned into a near classic, and caused a debate that rocked the state's resin commission.

In the first round, the impossible happened. Askew, the Black Destroyer, acted like one. With a fierce attack, he toppled the towering Beattie with a resounding crash, which shook the very foundations of the ring. The stunning double left hook, right cross combination was completely unexpected.

At that point, however, Askew made a bad mistake: standing over the fallen Beattie, Askew tried to decapitate him as Jack Dempsey had done to his foes in the days before the neutral corner rule was enforced.

Referee Denny Nelson, who was to gain international fame, tried to usher Askew away from Beattie so he could rise from the floor. For his efforts, Nelson was promptly thrown halfway across the ring by the enraged Askew. And while the Black Destroyer continued to rant that he had been cheated out of a knockout, Beattie regained his senses and came back to be awarded a stirringly close decision.

Calling it the "Irish Robbery," Askew's supporters turned radio talk shows and the state boxing commission meeting into pulpits in their drive to overturn the decision.

Regan, trying to placate the loser, made the mistake of offering him a corned beef sandwich and mug of green beer. Askew promptly told Race where he could insert them.

No hearse was ever quieter than the mud-splattered van traveling into the dark night, a machine which Jesse had borrowed from the card's timekeeper in a desperate effort to get rid of the green beer and beef sandwiches. It was midnight before everyone, who had volunteered, could load the kegs and food into every square inch of the van. It was decided to deliver the load to the Little Sisters of the Poor, gratis.

"We need prayers," Race told Rogers.

"We need a friggin' shrink," Jesse answered.

By 12:30 a.m., the Little Sisters had said, "Thanks but no thanks." They didn't take in food but promised to pray for the deliverants. They suggested their second cousins, The Poor Clares. "They could probably use it."

Neither Regan nor Jesse really knew what they meant by that. Were they hungry themselves? Would they distribute it? Would they give it to their watch dog?

Anyway, it was nearly another hour later on this dreary night that the Poor Clares were recipients of the prize. Their convent house was on the other side of Minneapolis. They were happy to take the sandwiches but politely turned down the suds.

Again it was a deadly silence that enveloped the van as Rogers and Regan drove through the early morning fog back to Stem Hall.

Finally Jesse broke the silence. "What now, Race? Something bigger or smaller? You know we lost close to five Gs or more. And I've got to return these friggin' full barrels. Imagine, those brewery creeps wanting the kegs back. I have a good notion to hammer them full of holes."

"Hey, not a bad thought; a keg-hole popping contest at the state fair. Wonder what they do with their old kegs," Race asked innocently.

"You've got to get help, Regan."

Just a couple of months later, another cinch retirement deposit cropped up with a conclushion that completely rattled the composure of Regan.

Fairgrounds racing promoter Frank Winkley had secured the rights to televise the Indy race directly from the track. He had rented the fairground's Coliseum and would install four 12-foot by 18-foot screens. It was the first time in history Indy officials had agreed to let the vast nationwide racing crowd in on the instantaneous action.

Regan leapt at the chance to invest with Winkley, particularly when Frank made this point, "Must be at least 10,000 Twin Citians who want to see the big race but can't get away for a trip. We'll sell them five-buck tickets and they'll be right on top of the action. I'd like to get the concessions, since the race takes over three hours and we can sell a mountain of hot dogs, but the fair biggies want those. We can get the building for a couple of grand and set the screen up for another couple of Gs. Oh, yes, we give the track five grand for the rights."

Race was so eager to get in he knocked his gin on the floor, prompting the waitress at Gallivans to grouse half-kiddingly, "We are getting the real riff-raff these days when they let in sports writers and racing nuts!"

"You mean for around ten grand we get the whole package? Man, it sounds like a steal!" Regan enthused. "I'll bet we can get in 7,000 bodies at five per. We make a killing!"

Winkley was way ahead of him, but what did you expect from a racing promoter who could recite over a hundred of Shakespeare's sonnets and still be tough enough to threaten to knock race driver Bill Schindler's block off if he kept cutting off rivals.

"I've got another angle on the seats, Race. The Boy Scouts will do the set up with all the benches around the fairgrounds and then tear down after the show for a little contribution. I know they won't charge much. That clean-up can be a brute. The benches will be our seats, all on the ground floor."

Race was in seventh heaven. No worries about piling a bunch of loonies into a tour bus. No worries about getting through traffic to the track or getting lost. He'd be able to bring Dots and the girls out for a holiday dinner. In fact, they'd probably love the race on the big movie screens—and four screens! Not a bad seat in the house!

Well, it turned out that there really wasn't a good seat in the house. While nearly 2,700 racing fans watched in horror on the Coliseum's screens, one of the few early lap disasters unfolded at the old Indianapolis brickyard. Caught right in the middle of the explosions, fires and flying, jagged steel coming into the homestretch, was Regan's close buddy and speed idol, Eddie Sachs.

The holocaust took nearly two hours to untangle but only a few minutes for Sachs to die, his machine a burned out shell of smelted iron and torn, gutted entrails.

The somber Coliseum crowd sat at a funeral pyre. Virtually nobody wanted to eat or drink. Dads had to explain to children the enormous loss. Even the glib Winkley and always talkative Regan had trouble looking at the screen.

"From the looks of the customers I don't think any of them will want to come back next time," the promoter muttered to Race. "There are idiots who say people go to races only to see somebody get hurt. They are nitwits. Concession stands die when serious accidents happen at a race and somebody gets hurt or killed. Particularly a guy like Sachs. The whole racing fraternity loved his wit and spirit."

Nearly a third of the Coliseum customers left before they re-, started the race.

Race didn't even feel like taking the family out. Fortunately, they had not attended the screening. The next day, when he met Winkley to appraise the financial details, he was glad he didn't have a hangover. It seemed the Boy Scouts had submitted their bill for cleanup and it came to over $1,200, a figure about six times higher than either of the backers had anticipated.

Winkley was still in shock. "Somebody's behind these little creeps! Aside from that bill, we made about a grand. With that bill, we drop a couple of hundred. Can you imagine—and it sounded so good."

"And the scouts looked so nice in their uniforms," Regan offered.

Then he perked up with that irrepressible will taking over his common sense organs. "Hey, Frank, I was thinking, maybe next year they'll screen it in Technicolor. Wouldn't that be something?"

Chapter Twenty

A Hair Raising Spectacle

Even the loquacious Regan could not explain how Dr. Nicholas Smith came into his life. Perhaps it was in Johnny's Bar in the Midway. The little joint was in the middle of St. Paul's thriving truck neighborhood, where six major overland transportation companies coexisted amid a steady rumble of 32-wheelers. Sometimes Regan liked to get away from the Longshots and sports crowd to meet, as he put it, "men of a different ilk."

But it wasn't the beefy and drawling truckers from all over the country in whom he was interested on this rainy spring afternoon. It was an impeccably dressed man in his fifties, with snowy white hair, a strong chin and rather prominent nose. His impressive form demanded attention.

On this day, the well-conditioned, smartly attired stranger was wearing a very expensive black and white checked sports coat, grey slacks and what Regan guessed to be 200-buck alligator shoes. The whole package exuded success.

Unlike the loud truckers and florid-faced executives from the nearby transportation companies, Smith had the gracious, eloquent appearance of a man who had been there and back; a solid citizen who had made his fortune and was now more concerned with investing it.

"So, you're Regan, the writer," Smith acknowledged after a brief exchange of words about the weather and Harmon Killebrew and

St. Paul Mayor Charlie McCarty's big new Lincoln with the police siren and toys. "I'm Doctor Nicholas Smith."

"What kind of doctor?" Regan asked quickly.

"Well, if I tell you, you'd probably make jokes about it," Smith replied, nursing a particularly heavy mixture of Scotch and soda.

"Try me."

"Well, as a writer, you might appreciate this. You see, I can grow hair on bald heads."

"Hold on, Doctor Smith!" Regan interrupted. "You say you can grow hair on bald heads? I mean, nobody, absolutely nobody, including Einstein or Bell or Edison, has ever made that breakthrough. You've got to be insulting my intelligence."

Dr. Smith tipped back his head and let out a very large laugh, which seemed to be emanating from the round of his heels.

"That's what they all say. The skeptics. But I had hoped a man with your obvious scent for the facts would listen. I can indeed grow hair where hair has never grown or where it once grew and has disappeared. I have done it hundreds of times and I am in the process of opening an office right across the street. In just a matter of time, perhaps a few months, my hair-growing system will be the talk of the town."

"Hey, wait a minute, Doc. If this is true, why not Chicago or New York or even Minneapolis? There are far bigger markets than St. Paul and why would you want to open a potentially big kill in a place where you might have to grind it out? There are more skeptics in this area than in Manhattan, you know."

"Don, may I call you Don?"

"Of course."

"Well, the patents are pending on my machines. I don't want a lot of notoriety until the ground work has been laid out. That's why I picked a rather obscure, provincial midwestern town. I'm from Cincinnati. But I wanted someplace with no pressure, where word of mouth can carry the advertising load. That is until I'm ready to pour in the millions it takes to get the big newspaper ads, television and radio."

"Well, let's say you're on the right track. What about this machine?"

"Ahh, the real meat of the matter. It is a tremendous machine. We use electrodes, mild shocks, scalp stimulation, subtle impulses and even massage to generate growth. But it is a magic combination. All, of course, to energize growth. I have 'Dr. Smith's Original Hair Growth Formula,' which will sell for $2.95. It also is being processed in the halls of political power and the patent offices.

"I'll tell you, Don, this remarkable combination already has helped over 400 people to happier, healthier lives. These are people who have been ruined by bald pates. It has brought renewed life to even some children who have been deprived of natural hair growth through illness or accidents. It is truly amazing. Praise God that he has designated me to master the wondrous breakthrough!"

"If this is true, you and your partners—now there is a real question, how many partners are in on this?"

"Oh, the beauty of it, Don! Only my nurse and assistant, Miss Evo. She is a darling and has been with me through thick and thin. She was the one who pointed out that not only did the machine and formula seem to be working wonders on hair but dozens of patients said the treatments actually cured their sinus problems!"

"Hold it!" Regan commanded. "Damn, Doc, you are beginning to sound like a medicine man or a carnie. You sure you didn't park a tinker's wagon out in the lot?"

Again Doctor Smith howled in glee and finished off his scotch and soda. He ordered another double dose. "They all say that in the beginning, Don. Then a couple of weeks later, when the hair begins to sprout, they want to buy shares of franchises. You see, it will be the most successful health aid in history. Nearly 25 percent of grown men are worrying about hair loss or ensuing baldness. That's about 40 million in this country alone. If just half of them buy into my system of restoration and transformation, I will sell well over two billion dollars a year worth of treatments. There will be need for 5,000 centers around the country!

"If you get in on the ground floor, you'll be able to buy the newspaper and hire 50 sports writers. In fact, I get so excited about my ideas that I have trouble sleeping at night. If it weren't for nurse Evo soothing my emotions, I'd be rattling around without sleep for months. You may say I'm crazy but the proof is in the results. Let me show you."

Dr. Smith opened a bulging billfold. Pinching inside one of the small flaps, he dug out a palmful of photos. "Just look at these. See this boy of 14 with no hair? Absolutely none. Now look at this picture; same boy, just six months later!"

Race's eyes opened like a vulture spotting a head-on. The teenager indeed appeared to have hair all the way down his back and to his beltline.

"Name's Tommy Woodrow, lives in Paducah, Kentucky. Lost his hair in a childhood malady. His family had given up. But I restored his hair in a matter of weeks. The young man now plays a saxophone and can hardly wait to be seen in public."

"That's amazing," Race breathed heavily.

"Here's one of Claudie Cladder. She's a stenographer in Bowling Green. She lost her hair through bad dye in a beauty shop. She got a respectable settlement but what is that to a bald woman? I heard of her through friends, looked her up and offered my services without charge. Within three months, look at what my treatment did for her." And with that, he produced a picture of a ravishing redhead, with locks that seemed to plead for Sampson's caresses.

"Impressed?"

"They could be phony pictures."

"Not if you read the letters I have. Over 200 letters, stating my machine and formula have proven results. Some of these people are ready to nominate me for sainthood. Nurse Evo says I'll eventually be nominated for president. Just kidding, Don."

Regan knew he was on to something; either a bonafide schizo con man, whose backseat was covered with snake oil—or the improbable of improbables: a screwy genius who indeed had found the elixir of root restoration!

"Drink up, Don and we'll go down the street. I'll give you a free treatment. I can see a trace of thinning in your fine pompadour. I want you to meet Nurse Evo and I can show you my office, which will be open for business by next week."

They crossed through heavy University Avenue traffic to the southwest corner of Raymond and University avenues. Regan felt a surge of elation. After all, when Louis Pasteur said he had cleaned milk how many lined up for a gallon? When Joe Namath shouted a couple of years back that he would lead the Jets over the Colts, who gave him a chance?

Dr. Smith opened a door to a small office, which was brightened by a dozen wall pictures, all pouring their glow of Mother Nature's wonder over what looked like a weather-worn barber's chair. Dr. Smith ordered Race to sit in the chair and he ushered Nurse Evo in. She was a striking blonde encased in a white uniform, which would have been too small for somebody only half as large as the buxom assistant. She wore a smile on heavily purpled lips that might have been stamped out in a ball-bearing factory. Her fingernails looked long enough to dice a truckload of watermelons before breakfast.

"Howdy, Mr. Regan," she said amicably, with a trace of Rebel drawl. "Here for a treatment, sir?"

Race felt uncomfortable. For a moment he pondered what kind of treatment she meant. He hoped these weren't zanies straight out of the Happy House, who would torture and impale him in broad daylight on a street with hundreds within ear shot. Stranger things had happened.

"I hope what Dr. Smith says is true."

"He's an absolute genius, Mr. Regan," Evo gushed. "His machine can do just about anything. Do you have any cows, Mr. Regan?"

"Cows?"

"Yes, you know, moo—moo—moo."

"No, sorry, I don't."

"Too bad. Dr. Smith's machine also cures mastitis in cows. We tried it out at a farm show in Lincoln and the cows really loved it."

"Miss Evo's too kind," the smiling Dr. Smith interjected. He then parted gray drapes at one end of the office. "But now, here is 'Dr. Wonderful.' That's what I call my machine."

Regan gulped when he saw what Smith had wheeled alongside his chair. His first thought was that H.G. Wells would have loved it!

"You see, there are just six attachments, each coming back to the main source of power," Dr. Smith pointed out, caressing the metal and posing like a lover.

"They work electronically. These little suction cups fit over the head, the sinuses, or wherever the patient wants them. I'm very meticulous. The six are put over the scalp and rotated every two minutes and 23 seconds. This must be precise. If it's on a shade over that specified time the treatment must be renewed from the start.

"Rarely does this happen. Besides, Nurse Evo has a very scientific mind and her brain is like a Swiss watch. Of course, the timer helps, too. After the treatment and gentle massage, the patient must sit in a dark spot and relax for at least 15 minutes. I ask them to think of forests and over-hanging vines and sea weed, like the artwork on the walls. Oh, yes and layers of strawberry shortcake."

"Strawberry shortcake?"

"Yes. Most of this is mental. A happy outlook is so important But the machine has already done the work. The images make the patient more emotionally open, like a mother opening her arms to a lost child.

"My patients are saying, 'I'm open for my hair's return. Return to me, beautiful hair.' The restored roots seem to vibrate with anticipation. See my long, white hair? I lost it all when I was forced out of my job as a landscaper. That's why I devoted six years of my life to my machine. I got my medical degree in Scalpathology in Dayton. That's my degree on the wall."

By now, Dr. Smith was fastening the small rubber cups and wires to Regan's scalp. For a moment, Regan had images of Dr. Frankenstein creating his monster. What if he showed up at the office with fangs and scales growing out of his arms? Jeez, this was eerie.

"Ready, Nurse Evo? At the count of three, I will put on the switch."

'God,' thought Regan, 'what if I'm electrocuted while the world walks by without a clue?'

The machine suddenly took on a life of its own. At least three lights were blinking. Strange sounds, like beeps and the groaning of a sick dog, filled the room. Race felt small shocks permeate his scalp, none intense enough to bring pain but still interesting little jabs that felt like prods from a sharp shower spray. Strong tingles was the best way to describe the sensation.

After what seemed like eternity but actually was less than three minutes, Dr. Smith shut off the machine, moved the rubber clamp to a new position and again pulled the switch.

After this had been repeated three times, the anxious Regan inquired, "Just about through, Doc?"

"Just about. Your scalp is vibrating quite nicely. Do you want to give your sinuses a shot, too?"

"Maybe the next time. I've really got another appointment."

After disengaging the mechanism, Nurse Evo asked, "Feels good, I'll wager."

"See you later, Mr. Regan," Doctor Smith smiled. "You were a good patient. Bring us some customers next week for the gala opening."

Better yet, Regan thought, I'll bring you a TV show! Sports Hot Seat was going back on the air Sunday mornings and this would be a helluva sponsor. And maybe, just maybe if this thing worked, Dr. Smith would like a partner.

Didn't they laugh at the Wright brothers?

"Of course, we need a sponsor," Sports Hot Seat moderator Jimmy DelMonte was saying. Cupcake, as he was called by his friends, was a rotund man with a classical cherub face, huge dimple in his chin and a reputation for being a shade zealous in his regular stint as the host disc jockey for his "Tuesday Mom's special."

The syrupy show was dedicated to all those lovely and romantic young housewives for whom Cupcake's soft, soapy voice was their conduit for surreptitious fantasies of love and adventure. Jimmy was rumored to have lost a few jobs by actually entertaining his more ardent fans with drinks and words of romance in the studios of various midwest stations.

He was the ideal host, however, for the Hot Seat. A former St. Thomas College and semi-professional baseballer, he knew athletics as well as music.

He had worked the Hot Seat television slot before, being remembered best for volunteering to let one of the world professional wrestling champs, Verne Gagne, apply a sleeper hold on him in the mat man's attempt to prove that the lard larrupers actually jousted in earnest.

The fact that Jimmy collapsed completely into unconsciousness was the talk of the town. He was out for nearly three minutes while Gagne frantically slapped his face, explaining, "He should wake up any second . . . any second . . . any second!" Regan had to do the last commercial to get the panel off the air.

The next day, a sore-necked DelMonte sued Gagne, his wrestling promoters and the station for $10,000. He settled three weeks later for two new suits and a steak dinner for two at Murray's.

Jimmy was exuberant at the prospect of getting a sponsor like

Smith. "Hell, if he can grow one hair a week on a customer, the guy's going to make a mint. You know, Race, I think the only problem we'll have is if I break out laughing in the middle of a commercial. You know this is ridiculous. Beautiful—but ridiculous. I just hope the Attorney General's office doesn't come down on us. I don't know if they'll appreciate a hair grower. They were upset three years ago over our jock strap commercials. They were really ticked off when we said our jocks were the best protection for the family jewels outside of an armored truck."

The first patient Race brought to Dr. Smith and Nurse Evo was Bert Sandberg, an egotistical but somewhat charming foreman of his father's thriving construction business. He had been a former prep star and college athlete who could remember every time of every track race he'd ever run. But he had trouble accepting his baldness, which struck at the tender age of 28.

"God, Race, I can hardly wait!" the muscular Bert whispered in Race's ear as they parked behind the small office. "I want the whole treatment. I'll pay up front. You know, Race, if what you say is true, I'll take you to Vegas for a week!"

"Hey, I'm not that sure. It's just that this could be the real thing. You judge for yourself. But don't blame me if it doesn't work."

Sandberg got nearly an hour of electrodes, massages, lights, heat and the whole bleeping noise procedure and then thought about lettuce and strawberry shortcake for another ten minutes, while reposing in a darkened corner.

"What payment plan would you like?" Nurse Evo smiled, while hovering over Bert, her mammoth breasts like two billowing clouds almost blotting out the remaining light.

Taken aback by the sudden show of such voluptuousness, Sandberg's usually trip-hammer reactions were mired momentarily before he answered, "What kind of plans do you have?"

"Oh, oodles!" Evo cooed. "The master plan is for $1,000, including 45 treatments. But we have a smaller plan for $500. That would give you 20 treatments, once a week or until your hair is restored in full. Your scalp is so healthy looking. I'm betting the $500 plan will do the job."

Bert could hardly wait to get out his checkbook and write the full amount.

Regan stood fitfully by. This Sandberg could be one nasty antagonist in the street with his fists. Regan hoped he'd be happy—please, God, just one little hair.

Smith went for the Sports Hot Seat show in Sunday mornings like a tiger cub going for a leg of lamb. "We're made for each other—the show and me," he beamed. "Regan, you've got the sports crowd and they're all a little vain. I bet we have them lining up down the block to get treatments. We'll dive from this into Dr. Smith's milk-pill supplements to groom those gigantic thatches of hair our machine will produce."

That night, Race broke the news of his new discovery to Dots. Once again, she deliciously cut through to the bottom line with winsome humor and thorough appreciation for Race's wild get-rich schemes.

"If it works, bring it over to clean the kitchen floor. If it grows hair, cures sinuses, knocks out mastitis in cows, it must have qualities to cut the buildup on linoleum, right?"

"Golly, Dots, you sure know how to hurt a guy."

Race, however, dreamed that night of a mansion overlooking the Barcelona Bay, with a huge 40-foot masted sailing ship not far out on the water and its name embossed in green and gold on the white hulk: "Dottie's Dream."

A couple of weeks before the first Hot Seat show, backed by Smith, was to go before the cameras, Race watched as Bert leapt toward a window in the doc's office, waving a hand mirror. "It's there, right there! A hair right in the middle of my bald head. A hair, break-ing through!"

Sandberg was giddy with joy and began a small dance around the office. Nurse Evo grabbed his hand and spun him as Regan sang out lustily, "My wild Irish hair!"

Dr. Smith just shook his head, "To even think there are doubters."

Race embraced Bert. "See, I told you this guy was onto some-thing!"

"I'll never forget you." Bert looked Race in the eye and solemnly held Regan's hand in both of his. "You don't know what this means to me."

Again, Race was dreaming dreams of fortunes. He was pondering whether to keep his future yacht in Barcelona or dock it in Naples. Dr. Smith's hair-raising machine certainly could bring great wealth to those in on the ground floor. Imagine what a spectacular over-the-counter stock issue this baby would become. He already had a call in for barrister/stock expert Paige Donnelly.

Sunday's Sports Hot Seat television show, with Race, Mark Tierney and Jimmy DelMonte on the panel, was not only a lively dis-cussion of whether hunters in general were obnoxious, drunken slobs, or just plain idiots, but also the hair-growing commercials were the talk of the Monday morning coffee crowd.

Race's phone was ringing of the hook from friends, acquaintances and the general public asking, "Is that hair-growing thing for real?"

It put Regan in a rather tenuous situation; he couldn't really declare Dr. Smith's break-through device a sure winner and he didn't want to turn off the enormous interest the commercials had generated. Regan couldn't blame bald-headed men for becoming excited. Smith had blown up to life size half a dozen pictures of his supposed patients who had restored hair growth through diligent use of his machine.

For Regan, this was a day replete with visions of gold cascading down from the heavens and deep concern over how he could really get into Smith's operation—provided the resourceful doc had indeed perfected a cure for baldness, the plight destroying the social and mental well being of so many Americans.

His euphoric fantasy was to be short-lived. Tuesday, the phone was alive with ominous warnings from the Attorney General's office. Basically, the officials from above had ordered the advertising agency to quietly desist from the hair-growing claims. In other words, get another sponsor to replace Smith or take the show off the air.

"What do you think, Regan," Jerry Fishbein, owner of the advertising agency they were using, asked in a voice quavering with no small amount of terror. "We sure don't want the Attorney General closing us down. The publicity could be a killer and all our integrity—yours and mine—will go down the tubes."

"Know what you mean," Race agreed matter-of-factly. "I suppose it's just too damn good to be true. But what makes those stupid asses at the capitol think they know if Smith's machine is phony? Are they experts on hair growing or what?"

"Well, the guy who called me explained that in 3,000 years nobody ever perfected such a machine and that all the people who have claimed to have such treatments are either in the can or the mental wards. It's never been done. And technical experts claim it's impossible."

"Hell, Jerry, I saw a hair pop through Berg Sandberg's bald pate and where did Smith get all those satisfied customers?"

"Hey, Race, I love the thought. I could see a little fuzz myself. But apparently they did some quick checking on this guy Smith and he's no more a doctor than Jack Benny. In fact, they rate him a little nuts. I think they're more angry about the guy than his product. Apparently he's been pulling scams all over the country. They claim they got nearly a hundred complaints from people who claim the guy's a fraud."

"Well, there goes $20 million up in flames!" Race blurted. "If some jerk from New York came in here with a bunch of degrees, the creeps up in the capitol would welcome him with open arms. If he opened a plush office in the First National Bank instead of a cave on University Avenue, they'd be lining up to throw him cocktail parties. I still think he's got something. If not for growing hair, for helping cows and sinuses."

"Hey, Race," Jerry laughed, "you sound a little strange from just hanging around with the guy for a month. Take it easy. I'll grab us another sponsor. I think Hamm's Beer might be ready for another shot. Or maybe the clothier, Danny Howard. He really likes you."

"Thanks, Jerry. You take millions of bucks out of my hands with one call and expect me to welcome a haberdasher. Oh Lord! What a lousy day."

Following that debacle, Race and his friends were viewed with growing skepticism by their peers in the city's better bistros.

Race became involved with Vikings coach Norm Van Brocklin in a shadow-boxing melee in Van Brocklin's office after hours. They agreed to slap to the face and punch with closed fists to the body. Regan, to his surprise, hammered Van Brocklin into a large wastebasket. "That was as hard as you can hit?" the incredulous Regan asked the vocal football coach.

"Yes, dammit! That's why I did all my fighting with my mouth," Van Brocklin explained, while trying to extricate his gangling frame from the wastebasket.

Later that night, after several drinks at the Rand restaurant, Van Brocklin insulted Gallivan when Bob requested that the coach open one of the Vikings' St. Paul luncheons with Mike Rabold as key speaker. Rabold was Gallivan's favorite lineman. Van Brocklin leapt to his feet in the crowded dining room and shouted, "No goddammed Irish saloon owner is going to tell me what to do!"

The aging but fearless Gallivan leapt to his feet too and threatened to punch the coach into the street, and turn his square Dutch head into a something resembling a rotting pumpkin.

With the help of 300-pound line coach Stan West, Race separated the two. West then hustled Van Brocklin down West Seventh to a coffee shop.

Later, Race explained to the Longshots, "Van Brocklin's a little un-predictable, just like his quarterback, Fran Tarkenton. But after knocking around in his office, I'm convinced Gallivan would be a 5-to-1 favorite in a brawl. Van Brocklin fights like a girl."

Perhaps others could see that Race was becoming entwined with too much too often. Whether he felt the questionable glances of his friends and partners is debatable. His consumption of martinis and Cabin Still was rising but he still sculpted a column which drew over 60 percent of the male readers and surprisingly nearly 25 percent of the female subscribers. His mail was volumes higher than even the love-lorn columns and he was winning writing awards.

Frankly, who cared if he drank? Apparently nobody—if you didn't talk to his wife.

Chapter Twenty-one

Only Fear: Rain, Riots or Fire

Van Avery tried to cheer up Race as the Longshots filed toward Gallivan's round table. "You know, Race, if I had realized you really wanted to grow hair on heads I'd have loaned you my two teenage daughters. They're keeping me broke going to the hairdresser's. Girls' hair must grow like mushrooms on Sucker Lake."

"You tell me now."

"I heard about the low-lifes punishing your splendid image. How can the attorney general worry about hair-growers when the Capitol's offices are filled with cons?"

"You got it, Van."

Jesse appeared on the scene and somebody asked, "What's up?" Haven't seen you for a few days."

"Lousy," explained Jesse, his brooding lids dropping to quarter mast. "I'm going nuts. My office is a shambles. Another gal, the one I hired three weeks ago, quit. She wants another baby. Damn, she's like a sow. Her husbands just a janitor. They must live in a cave. God, my office is so messed up I'd rather visit a dump every morning. I hope I can keep the damn business going. I've got just one gal trying to handle 800 policies."

Embalming specialist, Digger O'Halloran, was aghast at that statement. "You mean you enjoy your playboy life style with just 800 policyholders? I thought you had 8,000!"

"Well, I've got rid of a lot of car junk and term crap. I've been going for the bigger things. Do you guys realize I carry extensive policies on over 25 restaurants in the Twin Cities? If any of them have a big flare, I'm responsible. One of them's insured for over a million!"

Digger almost let his drooping cigarette slip into his coffee. "A million! Who's got that kind of place?"

Vern Landreville stuck his chin out in mock defiance, "Places. They're mine. Jesse knows I need big coverage for the Stage Door and Chain Link. They have very costly paintings and a bar that was hacked out of a tree during the New Deal."

Digger was amazed. "Jeez, Frenchy, I didn't realize the magnitude of your operation. I had no idea of what an elegant, impressive group our Longshots are. I suppose I should import a Parisian hairdresser for my corpses. The new slogan could be 'You look better after death at O'Halloran's mortuary.'"

"How'd the latest old-time fight film draw at the Prom?" Larsen inquired of Van.

"Hey, Race, what was the take on the old fights?"

"Pennies. Oh, what the hell, we had 400 fans but the film with Jack Johnson taking the dive against Jesse Willard in Cuba split right at the vital part. Nobody still knows if Johnson winked at the press row while shielding his eyes from the sun. Remember last time? A fire nearly burned us out. That little old movie collector, Barney Gardner, is a glutton for punishment. Fires, celluloid cracks, he'll probably have a heart attack some night during the Pep-Saddler brawl."

"Did we make any money?" Van asked innocently.

"Probably two hundred and you can keep it. That ice cream parlor that bought a hundred tickets for promotion was all yours. Take the green and go hear Woody Woodbury. I hear he's coming to Nick Mancini's steak house." Regan knew full well Van would not take his wife out in public for fear of ruining his image as a late night loner, but Van thanked him profusely.

"Any more reports on the midget football league, Race?" asked Jesse facetiously.

"Yeah, we're dealing with two prospective franchises: The Georgia Germs and the Memphis Mites. Not to mention the Toledo Thimbles."

The gang roared. Race could always handle his own in the needling department. His proposed midget football league always drew laughs and he was beginning to brighten up after the disaster with his hair-growing commercial.

Thunder Klunder, the motorcycle fanatic, arrived and whispered in Race's ear that he wanted to see him at the Schmidt Brewery. "Got a date for us with Bobby McElvane. Call me tonight."

Regan knew what it was about. He and Thunder had informally discussed what could be the Longshots' largest promo of the decade; a multi-day international cycle reunion at the fairgrounds. Nobody in this area ever dared to bring together thousands of cyclists for a three-day bash that'd include bands, displays and constant partying. Regan feared that if you even mentioned that sort of outing to the uninitiated it would prompt a response such as, "You've gotta be crazy! Those cyclists will tear up the fairgrounds and kill each other!"

Anyway, Regan forgot everything as he fantasized about what could be a giant production—if the state fair board of directors went along and if the sheriff went along and if the brewery went along. He scarcely heard another word during the morning. This would be an adventure, pure and simple. Guys daring to do what nobody else would even consider—living on the edge, going for broke. God how he hated that phrase!

Race thought he could get Van to head sales. Thunder would handle the raw cycling details. And he would be in charge of publicity across the nation. The budget would be big but he was in good shape with at least three banks that were fairly itching to give him more loans. If the brewery invested in publicity and promotion, this could be a mammoth success.

The conversation had turned to politicians trying to build a new indoor sports stadium in downtown Minneapolis.

Van, who started every day by looking at the signatures in his autograph book of the 1927 Yankees, was adamant that this would be the ultimate failure.

"Baseball, indoors? Absolutely never go. I'll stake my life on it. If the politicians ever try to force that down our throats, I'll move to Overshoe Gulch. Baseball's great because it's outdoors. What's greater than watching a close game out under the stars and moon at the Met? Or sitting there with the hot sun burning through you and a nice breeze on your neck behind third base? Put the same game indoors and it becomes a pinball machine—no class, no color, no atmosphere."

"But it's coming," Digger emphasized. "Minneapolis downtowners are pulling strings like puppet shows. I'll bet that they've got it iced."

"No way," Race interjected. "The people won't stand for it. Only the Vikes and the Minneapolis loop investors want it. They're still sick because they backed the Met out in Bloomington. Hell, I don't think they've sent a special bus from the loop out there in 10 years. Know what? Mill City bigshots used to tell me Bloomington would die because it had no hotels or booze licenses. In five years they've put up six hotels and a dozen joints. Minneapolis has hated Bloomington ever since."

"But it's coming, Race," Jesse volunteered. "A friend of mine is a detective up stream and he says strange people are always moving around that area over there by Fourth Avenue South and Fifth Street. He keeps hearing talk about a new stadium."

Ironically, just four days later, scrap iron mogul Lou Kaplan threw a lovely buffet out at the Criterion restaurant, with an assemblage of politicians and city and county officials. Regan was delighted to be listening to attractive and perceptive Joan Smith, the Criterion's pianist, who was playing, "It Was Just A Neighborhood Dance." She remembered, as she always did, that it was his favorite.

Kaplan unveiled a beauteous $10,000 architect's model of a new sports stadium to be located just north of University Avenue, virtually on the border of the two cities.

"We can get the land from the railroads. We'll have huge parking and both cities would benefit equally," Kaplan explained, rising to the top of his 5'4" frame to emphasize the vast potential of his plan. "I've got substantial pledges from heavy hitters on both sides of the river. Remember how St. Paul lost the Met Stadium to Bloomington because 50 frightened Minnesota professors living in St. Anthony Park thought it would be too noisy."

Minutes later, Kaplan was approached by a state legislator who whispered in his small ear, "It's a great plan, Lou, but you've got electrical problems."

"Electrical problems?"

"It's already wired for the Minneapolis loop. In two years it'll be signed, sealed and delivered!"

Lou didn't want to believe that nonsense. But Race saw him reach for a table edge for support.

Enroute to the brewery, Thunder, Van, Race and part-time promotional sideliner Bunny Bilini were thrashing over the elements of the International Cycle Reunion.

Race, as usual, was the conversational spearhead. "We can get lovely June dates from the fairgrounds, so it won't be too hot. We can get Sheriff Kermit Hedman's support but we've got to hire 30 deputies per day and pay them scale. McElvane thinks he can get at least $10,000 worth of printing and brochures and pamphlets and posters out of his brewery. We should take care of him real well."

Thunder was in complete agreement. "Yeah, and give him a piece of the action. But this should be great for his suds business. Those bikers could drink $10,000 worth of cool beer in one day if the weather's warm."

Van pushed his grey hat back on his head and wrung his hands in mock excitement. "I can see no reason I can't sell 50 booths at $300 apiece and a few at $500 for displays. I've got feelers out already. That means bike shops, all bike equipment and anything that's remotely connected to cycles. And hey, I checked with the highway department. Know how many bonafide licensed cyclists there are in this state?"

Thunder was quick to answer, "Over 40,000. And another 100,000 in Wisconsin, Iowa and the Dakotas."

"And another 300,000 bikes within a 500-mile range and that distance is nothing for these callous bun busters," Van enthused.

Regan pondered specific figures. "Let's just say five percent of 700,000 and we've got 35,000. Half of them will bring pals and lovers. That's over 52,000. They pay an average of $8 per head. That adds up to—$256,000! Throw in another 15 grand for booth space and we've got a winner that's hard to comprehend. It could net 200 grand!"

"That's not all," Bilini interjected. "I've got enough concession people lined up to handle any crowd we get. I'll put up at least a dozen stands. Figure $3 a head profit on beer and food. If we draw 50,000, that's $150,000. I think we can make over $300,000 total!"

They agreed it would be a five-way split. There wasn't a shadow of a doubt that the group would pocket at least 60,000 simoleons each.

"And, of course," Race grinned, "it becomes an annual event, maybe even a winter deal indoors at the Auditorium."

"You mean Civic Center, don't you?" Thunder corrected.

"I keep forgetting the fancy new place. I shouldn't, not after the way the dykes chopped it up during the World Broomball meet. Promoter Fred Macalus was a wild man!"

"Going back to that one, Race?" Van wanted to know.

"Only if they outlaw the brooms. Rubber mops maybe. But who needs to risk somebody getting killed with a broom and their whole friggin' family laying lawsuits on you?"

"Let's just hope," Bilini said, as they pulled into the brewery parking lot, "that we've counted all the nuts and bolts. Let's hope the bikers think this party is worth traveling across the country to see."

"Have no fear," Van piped up. "Beer, heat, loud music—that's what these creeps live for. Oh, excuse me, Thunder. You are a gentleman and a scholar and a biker."

Thunder laughed. "Ninety percent of us are decent guys. Even the speedrome nuts like myself. I broke a lot of my bones but I never broke anyone else's."

A few minutes later they had the good news: the barons at Schmidt Beer would do virtually all the printing, put their logo on all the publicity and give McElvane as much time on the project as he needed. And they'd supply all the beer barrels and keep them rolling. As McElvane said, "These are tough competitive days and every brewery's trying to zoom in on the drinking crowd. Nobody's come up with a more likely bunch of heavy drinkers than the bikers."

And when McElvane's boss heard the projected figures, he told Mac there might be a nice little bonus in it for him. And to think he had a piece of the action, too!

McElvane offered them all free beers. Van had officially dried up a year ago but he nibbled at the foam.

By nightfall, Race had contacted three national motorcycle magazines about special feature stories, ad space and the sale of booths. From the tone of it, they were intrigued and agreed that, being centrally located, this could turn into an annual colossus.

One magazine magnate opined, "This can be the spring-summer event of the year." And when he heard that the fairgrounds had over 200 acres to offer, he said quite sincerely, "With that space, I think you might be underestimating the crowd."

When Regan told Dots about the next main event, she sounded impressed, too. "Honey, I've always liked the bikers we've met. I just read where they have doctors and attorneys and teachers in their clubs now and the Hell's Outcasts are even trying to turn it around."

"Listen, sweety," Race beamed, "this is the one that can't go wrong. It's long enough, the price is right, we've got a good team and the fairgrounds is big enough to hold an army. And we've got the concessions and exhibition space. With this one, we retire!"

"What's it going to cost?"

Her practicality sometimes cut Race to the quick, particularly when he was fantasizing about the many trips to the bank the armored car service would be making from the cycle bash. "Oh, we'll budget it at around $50,000 but we figure each of us can make at least that."

"Any worries?"

"Hey, hon, nothing can stop this one. Nothing short of a flood, fire, or riot!"

They both laughed and hugged. "You do have some pretty wonderful ideas," Dots whispered in his ear.

Chapter Twenty-two

Pardon Me But Aren't Those Attack Dogs?

A devilish sleet storm hit the Twin Cities the first week in March. Race was cooped up in Gallivan's friendly tavern with four of the Harlem Globetrotters and for the first time in six years, weather had forced postponement of their exhibition against their resident punching bag, the Washington Generals.

At night, Gallivan's catered to a family-style sports crowd, all of whom seemed to know each other and spoke with some authority on everything from darts to roller derbies.

The Trotters on hand seemed to welcome the night off. "It's a damn grind this time of year," one of them explained.

Race had always done laudatory columns on the genuinely clean entertainment qualities of the Trotters and had recently penned a piece on Trotters superstar Goose Tatum for the Northwest Airlines in-flight slick.

The players regaled with Race and he got a napkin full of filler notes from them during this little sojourn in a sanctuary of goodwill. They talked about the Lakers and expansion news and college star Elgin Baylor's driving ability down the lane and what Jackie Robinson meant to players of color.

One of the older team members even remembered earlier appearances of the Trotters in St. Paul, when they had to stay in private homes or college dormitories instead of first class hotels.

The conversation was interrupted when Race was called to the phone. The voice of attorney Smitty Eggleston was on the other end of the line. "Know that goofy, drunken priest we befriended a week ago at Connor's saloon?" Smitty asked.

"Yeah. I thought the guy was heading back to his flock at the reservation."

"Well, he's still here, in my apartment! I can't get rid of him. In fact, that old sports coat you gave him—the funny red one with the big plaid—well, he's wearing it all the time. Dammit, he refuses to put his Roman collar back on. He called his mother in North Dakota and told her he's breaking away and she accused him of falling in with bad friends. That's you and me."

"Can't we just throw a few bucks in his pocket and take him to the bus depot?"

"Not unless you can lift 250 very muscular pounds with a strong attitude," Smitty answered.

Smitty and Race had met this very mellow and strange priest over drinks and had become enthralled with him and his story of having spent seven years at his calling on a Godforsaken Indian reservation near the Canadian border. He had told them, between gulping down three stingers, that he had just worn out mentally with the tough life and all the violence amongst his flock.

"I had to get away. But my superiors and my mother are going crazy. I just took a bus and got off in St. Paul," explained Father Charlie.

"Praise be to God," said Smitty solemnly. He was genuinely concerned, as he was over anything that gave off even the slightest hint of sorrow or social injustice. Just a year before, Smitty, who was separated from his wife and two children, had taken in an alcoholic lawyer. His guest continued to get inebriated, although Smitty confiscated his bottles and told him no drinking would be tolerated inside the small apartment.

It was weeks before Smitty discovered that the clear glass goblets in the top of the cupboard were filled to the brim with gin. Not even Smitty's sharp eyes could detect that there was anything of a liquid nature in the gleaming glasses, until, that is, he inadvertently reached up and knocked a vessel to the floor while searching out a box of swizzle sticks for guests.

But reclamation projects did bring joy to Smitty's life and Race agreed that Father Charlie was a worthwhile piece of humanity, certainly an object to be saved, refurbished and sent back hale and vibrant into his nest of feathers in the wild north.

Except that, as Smitty pointed out, they couldn't get rid of him.

"Think of something," Race advised. "Meanwhile, the Trotters are going to replay their game here in a couple of nights and I'll get him a ticket. Maybe we can lose him in the crowd."

"Are you kidding? He'll stick to us like a leech."

"I was hoping that he'd look at that red sports coat of mine when he sobered up and realize that we're a little crazy."

When Race returned to the table and the Trotters, he told them about plans for the super cycle extravaganza. The little Trotter, named Ozzie, summed it all up. "Weather. That's the whole thing. In Minnesota, the weather dictates everything you do in your life. Look at us tonight, with the wind howlin' and my poor body shakin' from knuckles to knees."

"If you think the weather is bad tonight, let me tell you about the big one." And Regan told them the story of white death. That's what they called that Armistice Day blizzard in 1941. The Trotters listened intently.

Regan's small group made intent listeners as he unraveled the tale with just the right touch of urgency and terror in his voice. "I remember it well because my school football team was to play in the Twin Cities title game.

"It started with 60 degree temps in the morning—a Saturday morning. It was the duck hunting season and thousands headed out to the marshes. It was so nice and the forecast was not that bad. A lot of them only wore their hunting shirts or took light jackets. A lot of them took their kids.

"Well, by two o'clock the temperatures started to dip and an hour later, out of nowhere, the damnedest storm hit that you could ever believe. You couldn't see across the street. It really slammed into the area about 90 miles south of here, along the river, where all those little islands provide such great duck hunting.

"Nothing the hunters could do. It hit too hard and fast, with the temperatures dropping to freezing in less than three hours. The hunters caught out in the reeds and woods couldn't even see well enough to get back to their boats. It was horrible.

"Nearly two dozen people lost their lives. We had pictures at the paper with fathers, their arms around their sons and their guns just laying by their sides. A friend of mine, Ted Strasser, got to his boat and just aimed it at where he thought the shore might be. He made it, but three or four other boats near him got lost.

"You're right, Ozzie, Minnesota weather can be a blast. Look outside. Would you want to be wandering in the woods at 12 degrees with that crap coming down from the skies?"

Ozzie assessed the facts, "Man, the sky wins around here."

Preparations for the International Motorcycle show went swimmingly. Van took enough time out from selling cars to peddle two dozen exhibitor booths. Concession stands were built. The brewery came through with 20,000 spectacular multi-colored brochures. Sharp ads in six national cycle slicks hyped interest. Enough television and radio blurbs as could be afforded whetted local interest.

Reservations for campsites from 22 states were in the files. A contingent from Mexico promised 50 visitors. The local press did a huge color picture and feature on the high caliber of wheelers, like doctors, old ladies, lawyers and school teachers. Race's buddies with the Hell's Outcasts offered to do any kind of patrolling for free but Sheriff

Hedman wasn't interested. Five months of tough work would pay off with "gigantic returns" in Race's words. Another cinch yacht down-payment fund, he guaranteed his partners.

With a scheduled start for the third week in June, Thunder Klunder, Regan and Van were confident they had picked the right time and place for their colossus. For five previous Junes this week had been virtually free of any heavy rain. A few damp summers, perhaps, but nothing that could threaten an extravaganza of such genuine national proportions.

It was just eight days before the event when the first ominous distractions surfaced. Heavy rains were sweeping the Plains states, moving up from Kansas and Missouri against a low pressure area. They would be coming through the Dakotas and Iowa and Minnesota, depending on wind shifts. Long-range forecasters were predicting six to seven days of dampness over a 10-state area.

"Nuts! Would you believe this?" Klunder asked over a beer at the Manor. "Hell, it's been a near-perfect June—until now. And would you believe I thought those cycle pals of mine were tough. But all we're getting on phones the past couple of days are cancellations. One guy from Nebraska told me that a bridge was washed out. I told the sissy to put his wheels on his back and swim over. In my younger days we'd have laughed at such crap."

"Well, if it doesn't hit southern Wisconsin and northern Illinois we're still in this thing big," Race said hopefully. The double gin and splash of lemon had fueled his spirits.

Van put in an optimistic vote. "And our concession people will all be on hand. They come in any weather. You know how tough they are at the fair. They're used to anything from above. We've got one guy coming in from Sioux Falls to peddle chocolate candy miniature motorcycles."

"Well," Thunder surmised, while jotting figures on his paper napkin, "so we lose 20 percent. We still could do 30,000 bikers. And that's a wad of green."

"That's if the rain doesn't hit here the next couple of days," Race almost whispered to himself.

It could and it did. The Minnesota skies opened up with downpours, threats of tornadoes, interspersed with maddening drizzle. On the morning of the eve of the opening, the three-day classic was in danger of being washed out itself. The campgrounds on Machinery Hill were mud sloughs. There wasn't a dry spot on the fairgrounds, except under cover or in the few bleak buildings, which were being opened for exhibitors.

Regan poured himself a triple shot while huddling under the grandstand with Thunder. Bunny was off trying to help the drenched workmen complete the concession stands. A few of the distributors were trying to make the best of the situation, cursing to themselves or mumbling that the Hell's Outcasts must have put a curse on the proceedings. Even the 200-buck per day "Cyclemania" band wondered if it could keep its horns from rusting out.

"Damn! Feigner and his softballers must be in the state," Regan managed to croak to Thunder. "I swear, that character is the best rainmaker since medicine men danced on corn cobs. He's usually rained out about 10 of ever 25 dates we book him. Maybe not that many but it always seems we're worried. God, if it doesn't stop we won't sell enough tickets to pay for a pizza."

"Worse, Race. We'll owe so much at the bank they'll be coming after our houses," Thunder groaned. "I'll lose mine before I get it built!"

"That's a great picture, Thunder. Can you see us handcuffed on the front page of my paper with the headline, 'Cycle promoters refuse to pay bill.' End of a nice sports-writing career."

Despair moderated to discomfort on Friday's opening. The skies broke slightly by noon on Friday. By nightfall, a bedraggled crowd of 2,000 was stomping and dancing and boozing to a four-piece polka band, one of three silly musical acts on display. Cancellations were enormous. But there was still the weekend to go and the fairgrounds could hold any amount they could try to jam in. Maybe, just maybe, the biking stampede would overwhelm the turnstiles the last two days. If the rain quit.

By noon on Saturday, the dampness dissolved to hazy skies that finally welcomed a warming sun. By nightfall, another 3,000 were on hand, pulling wheelies and shouting and huddling in the renewal of road kinships. Race took nearly $7,500 to the bank at 7 p.m., total gate receipts for the first two days. With a break, even the disappointed Klunder could see the chance of a $60,000 day on Sunday, when prices went up to $10 per head.

In a moment of unwarranted optimism, Race invited a neighbor couple to join he and Dots for a late Italian dinner at a small restaurant at the corner of Snelling and Larpenteur Avenues. The sun had just set as they picked at their spaghetti and Dots asked, "How's it going, Don?"

He looked her straight in the eye and said with a strain of defiance, "Couldn't be much better. If we do a little business tonight and get a break in the weather Sunday, we'll come out of it smelling like Chanel No. 5." He put his arm around Dot's shoulder, ignoring the friends and whispered, "You're my good luck charm. I love you, honey."

Dots grinned that magnificent smile and whispered back, "As long as you're smiling, I'm happy."

Bill Wesa, Regan's guest, was peering out the window at the restaurant. "What are all those squad cars doing in the parking lot? There must be six or seven of them!"

Regan put down a huge wad of spaghetti embedded between his fork and spoon and stared in disbelief. "Jeez, they've got attack dogs! Must be something really big in the neighborhood."

"Or at your show," Bill reminded.

"Oh, God, I hope not!" Race was up from the table and pushing out the door in a matter of seconds. "Officer! What's going on? I'm Race Regan from the paper."

A large, red-faced cop looked agitated as he tried to calm his dog. "Yeah, Race. Oh, there's some kind of big riot at the fairgrounds with those leather-brained bikers. We're bringing out some firepower before it gets too far out of hand. Apparently all those young sheriffs' deputies are scared to death! Whoever promoted this insanity has got the wrong people trying to control it."

Race's heart was pounding with such force he thought it would erupt through his shirt. "But I thought all those deputies could handle it. Er, the promoters told me how well policed it was."

"Yeah, but who's got experience against 40 or 50 drunken cyclists? Those guys are nuts and I guess they've taken over one building and are claiming hostages!"

"Ohmigod!" Regan muttered to himself. He rushed inside, threw a $20 on the table and told Dots there were problems. "See you at midnight!"

At the fairgrounds' entrance, another half-dozen squad cars could be seen. It was utter chaos. Dogs were barking and growling. A spotlight was honed in on the agricultural building. Regan asked another cop what was going on.

"These sons of bitches got drunk, tore up the streets with their cycles and when we ordered them to stop about a dozen went into that building and they've barricaded the doors. There must be another hundred or so people in there with them. I just hope nobody gets injured."

Regan pushed on and encountered the head of the young deputies. "Why can't your dozen deputies do anything? You're empowered to arrest the bad guys."

"Do anything?" the thin, gaunt task force head repeated. "Hey, fella, that's Pork Chop Hill! There's 20 or more nuts threatening everybody, people screaming they're going to take over the world. This is madness! Our guys wouldn't go near them without machine guns."

"Hey, I thought you were paid to do this."

"We're paid to keep things quiet. Not risk our lives against a crazy bunch of cycling wild men!"

Race rushed to the fairgrounds office where Klunder, Bunnie, Van, two fair officials and Sheriff Hedmen were congregated.

The Sheriff was the first to greet Regan. Hedman's usual affability had turned to icy concern.

"Race, I had a feeling this might happen. Remember, I told you some of these guys are nuts. Just a few of them can ruin it for 5,000 decent people. I don't think there's more than maybe a dozen in all involved. But they've scared the bejesus out of everybody around here. They've smashed a couple of concession stands and ripped up a couple of snow fences. As far as I can tell, one or two have shotguns but I haven't heard any shooting. I've got four squads of county sheriffs and St. Paul police are helping. With the dogs and manpower, we'll root them out in a half hour or so."

Regan simply bit his fingernails to the quick and seemed stunned.

Klunder said quietly, "Everything's gone wrong—friggin' weather and floods and now a riot."

Van pushed his tweed hat back jauntily, clamped his hands together, then put a fist in the air and almost shouted, "It's the greatest publicity in the world guys! Tomorrow you won't be able to handle the crowds!"

Hedman had known Van for years and pointed a firm but friendly finger in his face. "Sorry, Van, ain't going to be no tomorrow! This one's gotta end tonight. I just can't take a chance. I stuck my neck out even cooperating with it. You guys have to close right now and cancel out tomorrow."

"Oh, please, common, Kermit," Regan pleaded. "If we clean the mess up fast how about giving us just a few hours tomorrow. It's a make or break day for us!"

"Race, we don't need any Sunday riots in St. Paul."

"But this is Falcon Heights. Really, it's not St. Paul."

"It's my territory. And we don't police it any more or permit any of our deputies. You can't open without protection. Look what happens at circuses like this. Those young deputies aren't up to this kind of confrontation."

Race looked at Thunder and swept a legal pad off the desk. "Well, if we don't open tomorrow, we wind up losing a ton."

"You can't fight the Sheriff," Thunder said objectively.

At 1 a.m., Race managed to call Hedman from home, hopeful of pleading his case one more time. He also hoped Kermit remembered that he'd made a speech for the Norske Torski club last year, not to mention the crippled but game horse he donated to the boy's ranch.

"Everything at the fairgrounds okay?" Race asked tentatively.

"Well, if you can say getting a riot under control is okay, yeah, we corralled three or four and put the cuffs on them. Most of them got away. One guy smashed his leg running into a post on Como. The whole damn affair was a mess and it really frightened all the good cyclists. We're not going to run the sleeping bag crowd on the hill by the barn out until daylight. We don't need any more trouble tonight."

"One more shot, Kerm. God, we've got a lot stuck into this thing. Please, I beg you! Just give us one more shot for Sunday."

"Well, Race, you've always been good to me and I appreciate that three-legged horse you gave us for the Boys Ranch kids—it can't run, but it limps pretty well. So okay. I'll give you guys from 8 a.m. until 2 p.m. Take in what you can. But if there's one rumble we close the gates, pronto!"

Regan was profuse in his thanks, promising the sheriff everything from free boxing tickets to a couple on the 40-yard line for the Vikings.

Race slept only four hours that night, stopped at an all night doughnut shop at dawn and met Klunder and fairgrounds director Mike Heffron at the fairgrounds entrance. Heffron had the city edition of Race's paper with the page one headliner: "Police, Dogs Quell Cycle Riot."

"Finally, a break in the papers," Race grinned. And not a word about a shortened Sunday schedule.

Heffron summed it up. "My heart goes out to you guys. You had a helluva plan. But who can't figure on floods and riots."

He had no more uttered these words of empathy when sirens began wailing from the south on Snelling Avenue. Within seconds, while the trio watched speechlessly, three giant fire-righting rigs wheeled through the large entrance gates and rumbled toward machinery hill. Toward the north, puffs of black smoke curled skyward.

"God! The barn's on fire!" Heffron shouted. "Those crazies set fire to the barn! Sorry guys but these nitwits are out of here. We're closing the gates!" Minutes later, the sheriff arrived back on the scene.

Kermit was adamant. "No more! It's off. Sorry Regan, Klunder but these idiots don't know when to quit."

Thunder climbed into Race's car. His dark glasses were covered with steam from his moist face. Maybe a tear or two was buried beneath the lenses. It was enough to make even a cool, pragmatic man like Thunder question his fate.

"How can this be?" he asked Race. "We'll never get this close to the big one again. Know what the odds are that you could wipe out a cinch success with a flood, fire and riot?"

"Yeah. About ten million to one."

"Maybe more."

They parked in the lot where the cops and attack dogs had gathered 12 hours before. "You know, Thunder, I wonder if God hates what we're doing," Regan pondered, staring straight ahead and looking at nothing.

"Damn, sometimes I wonder. I just got through telling my wife we'd add another couple of fireplaces in this big ark we're building in Cottage Grove. You know, she's nuts about fireplaces. And now I have to tell her I don't know if we can afford a second bath."

Thunder shook his head and looked down at his hands, folded neatly in his lap. "Maybe we're greedy. Maybe we should all be happy to just have a roof over our heads and windows that close."

Thunder took off his dark glasses and wiped his brow with his forearm. He put on a faint grin and philosophized for a moment. "Best damn times I ever had in my life were when I was cycling around perpendicular walls, racing against hell in the speedromes. Shit, I cracked up bones every few months and never had more than 40 bucks in my jeans, but Lord I was happy. And free and without a care.

"Now I'm overhauling cycles, running swap meets, hustling cycle shows out in the Dakotas and doing this promotion crap. I'm building a house I can't afford, trying to keep my wife in a Mercedes convertible and getting my step-daughter a decent education. And you know what? I'm a complete nervous wreck. Some friggin' thing is completely haywire!"

Race suggested therapy.

"Therapy? With what? I can't afford a shrink!"

Regan paused, a little afraid to mention it, but finally grabbed Thunder by his sleeve, turned him around and stared him straight in the eyes and said firmly, "Let's put a wild cycle race on in the Midway baseball park, like we talked about a few months ago! We'll let 'em rip and slide around the base paths and give out half-price coupons all over the cycle shops and up and down Snelling Avenue. You don't sit and ponder this crap. Some shifty-eyed philosopher once said, 'When you lose you don't ponder the wealth you lose. You count your blessings!' We've got our health!

"And know something else? I doubt God really hates us. He wouldn't let us keep doing this crap if it was wrong. We're lucky. Most guys I know who are going nuts are working in stuffy offices."

Thunder scratched his chin, pinched his right ear, cocked his head to one side, grinned and asked, "Cycle races on a ball diamond? Can we think it over for a while?"

The motorcycle debacle or as Race put it, "The friggin triple play of fate—fire, floods and a riot," had just missed breaking even by about eight grand each. A half-dozen shaky concessionaires couldn't come up with their final payments, the insurance premiums were higher than expected and a small group of angry exhibitors from local and regional areas refused to pay for their exposure because the last day was not completed.

Worse, the fair's moguls wanted $85,000 more to replace the aging barn, which was reduced to ashes, along with a new concrete floor. However, barrister Donnelly rode to the fore, pointing out— and quite rightly—that the fair's officials were responsible for damage done in camping areas since it was the fair that charged the bikes for the overnight camping space. Also the fair should reimburse the promoters for an abbreviated show.

Once the disaster was only an angry memory, John Friedmann called Race, offering his new Civic Center for a cycle show the following year. "It's mostly concrete. I'm sure they can't burn it down."

"You rat!" Race fumed, hanging up jarringly in John's ear.

Race dialed Friedmann's number a few minutes later. "What kind of deal?"

Chapter Twenty-Three

The Tropicana Loves Us

Jimmy DelMonte, the wheeler-dealer super spieler radio and TV personality, who was moderator on most of Race's shows, called Regan from Las Vegas.

Now, this was particularly strange since they hadn't been on good terms since Jimmy threatened to sue Race, the station and a PR firm over use of the name "Hot Seat," the title of Race's TV sports panel. Yes, the one on which wrestler Vern Gagne applied his deadly sleeper hold to Jimmy as the show went to a commercial with Race selling fur hats for Danny Howard's clothing store on Wabasha.

"No hard feelings, Race. You were always my idol and you still are," Cupcake pleaded.

Race missed Jimmy. They spoke the same language, carried the same elusive dreams of wealth and posture and succumbed to the same promotional fantasy demons.

"Yeah, Jimmy. What's up? Mainly, what's up in Vegas? You playin' the slots?"

"No, but I've been very busy, my friend. You know how I loved the Hot Seat show. Remember how I used to say that some day I'd take this big time? Well, the time's ripe! I've got a biggie from White Bear who is backing me to the tune of 25 grand just to do a couple of pilot shows. Hart Cardozo is my angel. A great guy. If he likes what he sees, he'll get more backers. They'll pop for a half dozen more shows. I take them to the national networks and get bids on them. From there, we're on easy street!"

"Where do I fit in, Jimmy?"

"Hell, Race, you are THE MAN! You are the moderator. I am the director and producer. Just for these pilots you get $700, plus an all-expense paid two-day jaunt out here to Vegas and a great stay at the Tropicana. Right into the big time.

"You see, Race, I've also got the Tropicana's owner, Deil Gustafson, the banker, behind us all the way.

"That's where the pilots and eventually the national show will originate. We're going to do our pilots in the Blue Room, right where Mel Torme operates. We'll pack the place with 500 hotel guests who, for free, get to see Race Regan perform!"

Race was stunned. He knew that Jimmy always had visions of a national show but he'd screwed up so many minor deals Race didn't believe DelMonte could ever operate on this level.

"How come you're not going to moderate, Jimmy? You know you're one of the best."

"Naw, too old. I want to get behind the camera. You've got the zap and zing. You're after-fight shows were terrific because you can arouse the young guys and the old guys. I need your good looks and fast mouth. And pal, if this goes, you can fly out once or twice a month and make four or five shows that we put in the can. You can do them on your days off. And for that, you'll get at least $1,200 per show. Did you hear me? Twelve hun! And if the show really connects, you could work up to two grand per."

By now, Race was twitching. "Jeez, Jimmy, when do we start? When does all this hotel stuff get going? And who are the guests for the pilot?"

"Great guests. On the first pilot you tangle with Verne Gagne again and comedian Alan Suess. Verne and I patched things up over our little feud. He'll bark and growl and threaten to manhandle the funny little guy who acts like he's gay. You sit in the middle and keep them apart.

"The next show it's Hall of Fame New York Giant tackle Roosevelt Grier and Doctor Julius Jenks. You get into serious stuff about drugs. Rosie says he was once on some high-powered pills and he'll talk for the good of youth. Dr. Jenks will interject high-powered crap about drugs in sports and steroids and what emotions means to teams.

"I'm getting life-sized cutouts of you guys to stick all over the Tropicana's lobby. You'll be famous before you arrive. I've already picked out your picture from some glossies I had of our shows.

"This is it, Race boy, this is the killer! I know you can make this show move like a rat in a storm sewer. And guess what? I think our camera man is a relative of Errol Flynn's. Maybe his kid. The technical guy's got a old letter from Flynn and lots of snapshots. Anyway, can you get off next weekend? You can fly in Saturday night, do the shows Sunday and fly home on Monday."

Race was hardly listening to Jimmy. His mind was wandering to a penthouse suite overlooking the yacht basin in Lauderdale. That would be a great place to own if the show went over. He could edit scripts on his yacht. Closer than Barcelona.

"Yeah, Jimmy. But make sure you send the airline tickets a couple of days early. I don't want to be sitting on the flight deck if this is a silly scam. I've been left holding the bag before."

"You'll have the air ducats in 24 hours and a limousine will pick you up at the airport. I knew you'd love this, baby. It's the big break we've always waited for!"

Race decided not to tell Dots or any of the Longshots until he had the plane tickets in his hand. Imagine! Starring at the Tropicana on national television! He knew those acting genes would pay off sooner or later. And man, $1,200 for a few hours work! It didn't get any better than that. Move over Harry Reasoner!

It was coming off!

Race was in the skies, heading to Vegas! He could smell the riches. Not since he played the violin and sang for Horace Heidt in high school had he felt so fulfilled. Lord, this was actually happening. DelMonte had the plane tickets in Race's hand a week before the flight. His juices were flowing like a spring book. He didn't even need to finish his second martini, which he always looked upon as flight medicine.

Now, he thought, he must play it cool. Not show too much emotion. He'd interviewed the greatest in sports for years. His radio talk show had exploded to a top rating. He had been asked to play Calvin Griffith, owner of the Twins, in the annual baseball writers dinner show. Jeez, of course he was good!

But the Tropicana! That was really the big time. He had stayed there once, while covering a fight. He had heard Mel Torme perform in the Blue Room, right next to the Follies Bergere.

On another trip, he and Dots had been seated in the front row at the Follies and their chicken dinners had been delivered just as the lights went down for the show. When Dots complained of feathers on her chicken, Regan got into a heated but quiet argument with the stuffy waiter and when the lights came back up, they'd discovered that the feathers had fallen off a peacock ensemble worn by one of the statuesque girls in the show. Both had laughed so hard that the bell captain had asked them to control themselves.

Gosh, just below was Vegas! The last time Race and Dots had enjoyed a free week's vacation was at the reopening of the completely refurbished Aladdin Hotel, where Dick Kanellis was the manager. Dick was the husband of singer Connie Francis and he'd treated Regan royally because Race had once secured tickets for him and his family to see his brother play football for Iowa against Minnesota. Not only was Regan treated like a king but four of Dots' California relatives were invited along to share the feast.

On opening night, Dots almost passed out when they were seated at a stage-front table, when Kanellis unveiled the city's first bare-bosomed casino chorus. The dozen maidens jiggled and jounced and would have given a Puritan apoplexy. Dots almost swooned at the plump sight but she hung in there, as did the chorus girls.

Anyway, Vegas, which Regan in his column, had dubbed the city of sun, sin and over-rated sex, threw open its arms at the airport.

Two handsome young guys introduced themselves to Race, got his bag, escorted him to a white limousine and while one drove the other regaled Race with the words he loved to hear, "You must be an important man, Mr. Regan, to have the limo pick you up. I saw the cutout of you in the lobby of the Tropicana. I think they're going to have a very big crowd for your show tomorrow. The whole hotel staff seems excited."

"Oh, baby. Tell me more!" Race almost shouted.

As the big machine dropped them off at the imposing front door, Regan was engulfed in the arms of DelMonte. "Man, we are on our way! We are going to hit it big!" Jimmy gushed, his round, cupid cheeks flushing almost as bright as the neons on the strip.

"Relax tonight. Order big. I've got you a suite and you can just sign your name for everything your little heart desires. If you want to go to a show, just ask."

"Thanks," Race explained. "But I called a second cousin of Dots from the airport. He's the number three security boss on Howard Hughes' staff. He's an ex-juvenile judge from L.A. and was hired by Hughes' crew to help oversee his sprawling Vegas empire. We're going to have a quiet dinner at the Tropicana." Race savored the situation.

That night, over lobster and the best whiskey money could buy, the security boss studied the casino staff carefully. They sat in the lobby and then cruised the casino after dinner while the security man asked Race, "How well do you know the owner from the Twin Cities, this Gustafson?"

"Had a few drinks with him. Why?"

"Well, from what I can tell, he's hired a bunch of bad ones—some of the same people I got rid of from Hughes' places. At least four or five just on this shift. Might have a dozen in all. He'll be skimmed to death."

Regan said he'd pass the word along to the banker. But, then, what the hell, he knew the guy wouldn't listen. Bankers never listened.

At 2 p.m., the Blue Room was jammed with 500 SRO happy-to-get-in-free patrons. Regan figured this crowd would fill the place for a cooking show on how to simmer turnips.

Gagne was all smiles and promised not to mess up the comedian, Suess. The skinny little giggler with the dainty wrists seemed frail enough to blow away but he had a crackling, high-octane voice that could shatter a goblet across the lobby.

The repartee was fast, frenetic and funny. Race hassled Gagne about being in a "phony" sport. Gagne countered that he heard sports writers were the bagmen for every promoter who ever lived. Race said he announced over radio the only two honest wrestling matches in Twin Cities' history. Gagne shot back that with Regan's stature he wouldn't be able to pin the weak sister in a dwarf colony.

The comedian kept asking Vern, "How can anyone be mean to you when you've got such wonderfully blue eyes?"

Finally, Gagne, feigning anger, tried to get around Regan, shaking his large fists at Suess while shouting, "You sickening little twerp, I'll throw a bear hug on you that'll crush your puny body from stem to stern!"

Then Suess turned the crowd into guffaws of laughter when he stage-whispered, "Promises, promises, that's all I ever get from you, Cutie!"

The second show was equally energetic but along different lines. The doctor was amazed to find out Grier had actually tried juicing himself with drugs. Grier confessed to several games where he used various drugs to give him what he thought would be more speed and power and energy. Yet, he pointed out, while the audience looked on in rapt attention, that the drugs failed him miserably.

"In one game against the Eagles, I could hardly drag myself off the field in the second half. Drugs are killers! Kids should never try them thinking they'll help performance."

It was a sound, chilling show with the doc admitting he had years ago supplied certain athletes with addictive medication, hoping to soothe their injuries and pains. But he, too, made an emotional plea for youngsters to repel the advances of those who promised to give them "medicine" to aid their performances—even if they were team trainers or physicians.

And Regan was completely at home in the absorbing discussion, pointing out how a Fort Wayne hockey team he once saw would take "speed" pills in the third period to keep the veterans' legs moving as the game wore on. And how, in a five overtime game against St. Paul, they unraveled in the late stages and were the walking dead at the finish of a losing cause.

DelMonte was ecstatic. After the show he introduced Race to the man who was bank-rolling the pilots and who happened to be flying home on the same plane with Race. Cardozo, a former furniture company executive, now the owner of several small radio and television outlets, seemed as enthusiastic as Jimmy.

"Never saw a pair of better sports shows; one with humor, the other with sound advice. I think some national network will be interested somewhere down the line."

Race collected his fee and spoke of many subjects to Cardozo on the flight back. Cardozo promised to talk to a couple of friends about investing with him in another dozen pilots. But first, he had planned a hunting trip to Alaska. A friend was going to fly four of them into the wilds.

As Hart dozed off on the flight, Regan was on Mars, wondering how he'd say 'goodbye' to the Longshots when he moved to LA or New York.

While Race wasn't paying attention—being caught up almost entirely thinking about Las Vegas and his riches—Jesse got the two of them involved in a recreation and camping show in the old Auditorium.

Jesse had somehow become enamored of rotund Jewish comedian Jackie Vernon. And about all Race could remember about the original proposition was that Jesse said he could get Vernon cheap and that he'd draw thousands with his dry wit and stories about his mother's soup.

Before he knew it, Race found himself owning half of the three-day production.

Over steaks at Mangini's two days before the camper show, Regan inquired of Jesse, "Just what the heck kind of deal is this and how much do we need to break into the clear?"

"About 10 grand. At two bucks a head, that's just a little over 4,500 bodies. Might do that the first day."

"Know something, Jesse?" Race mentioned off-handedly, while picking a hang nail, "I haven't heard a damn thing about this show except in Hank Keyborn's outdoors column. Granted these things can catch on overnight but where are the promos? Where's the advertising, may I ask? And something else, how exactly did I get involved?"

"Relax, Race. We dumped about three grand on radio and a couple grand on newspaper ads in both papers. We've got 30 pieces of equipment and the concession owners paid us about $1,500 to get in. I think we'll do okay."

If a total attendance of 1,855 for three days gooses your psyche, they did okay. Adding to the distress of yet another failed promotion, Vernon and Jesse fought bitterly over the comedian's payoff. Vernon shouted, "You guaranteed me $2,500 and I won't take a penny less!"

Rogers countered brashly, "You guaranteed me you'd draw big crowds and kill 'em with jokes. Hell, you drew nobody and you couldn't have gotten a laugh if you tickled my old grandmother with a feather duster!"

Before they came to blows, Regan steered Jackie out of the way of Rogers' wrath and promised him a grand.

Later that night, while sitting in the Lowry Hotel bar, Vernon told Race he considered Rogers a "Rotten slob; not fit for promoting or any other kind of human endeavor."

Race, a bit shell-shocked from learning earlier the show had cost him close to four grand, partially agreed, "It was a stupid promotion. Yeah, sometimes that Jesse is a dumb dude."

Not so dumb as to fight bad biorhythms. Jesse rushed to a travel office and purchased a $2,500 tour to Greece, explaining to Race, "I always wanted to see Mount Olympus."

The front-page headline hit Race like a thunderbolt through his nine iron: "Five Killed In Alaska Plane Crash."

Race wiped his glasses before he could force himself to read past the first paragraph. It was right there in cold, chilling print. Hart Cardozo and hunting companions were wiped out in the crash of their airplane into a mountain.

Race had sincerely liked Cardozo and admired his business skill. He was the kind of man Race would have followed. The only other time he felt that way was when he'd met Jimmy Hoffa—maybe Branch Rickey. Some people were made to lead.

An hour later, DelMonte was on the phone from Vegas. "We won't give up, Race. Cardozo was a helluva guy and had powerful friends. I've got a lot of connections out here, too. Just met a guy from Albuquerque who builds balloons . . ."

Regan wasn't listening.

Chapter Twenty-four

Lassie Loves the Bridal Suite

It was a period of self-analysis and transition for the Longshots. Regan vowed to Dots to ease up on the gin and promptly switched to double shots of Cabin Still. The whiskey was laced with six drops of water, which he promptly followed with a barbecue beef sandwich at Toppy's saloon.

Recently, Race had switched his loyalty from Gallivan's to the tiny, out-of-the-way Toppy's—for the simple reason that everyone in St. Paul, it seemed, was sticking their chins over the Longshots' shoulders and interrupting their plans of grandeur. Didn't those jerks have a life?

He was also finishing the book on Rudensky and it was quite an experience. Just the night before he'd been reading Margaret Mitchell's letters to Rudensky. He particularly enjoyed the ones in which she thanked the ex-safe-cracker for the gift of a ball-point pen from Brown and Bigelow.

"I was thrilled. With a few of these I could have written 'Gone With the Wind' in a week. As it was, I autographed everything in the apartment but the cat's tail!"

Race had secured local publisher Paul Piperman to get the book in print. Race was sure that it was a good move, except that Piperman, who was also an attorney, had a knack for publishing any event or work he came in contact with. He virtually guaranteed Regan and Rudensky that their book "The Gonif" would earn appearances for Red on the Merv Griffin Show and What's My Line quiz on national television. Larry King's talk show from Miami was a given. After all, Red was a Jewish convict-hero and that had to have dazzling implications.

Race wanted to continue his promotions but wasn't quite sure which direction to take. His motorcycle extravaganza flop had sapped a large chunk of wind out of the Longshots' sails. The Longshots all seemed to be scrambling for new loans from unsuspecting banks.

Nobody was quite as confident, not nearly so hard-edged and feisty about their ideas as previously. All of the Longshots appreciated how long and hard Regan and Thunder and Van had worked on the cycle disaster. If they couldn't make it go, what chance for other operations?

Jesse said it best as he edged up to Race's working elbow at Toppy's long bar. "No more practicing for any of us, Race. The practicing is over."

Race didn't answer. He stared at his drink, slowly turning the chunky glass around in his fingers. "I'm a little shaky from it all. But I've got a thought."

"I'm still standing."

"Well, last night, just when we were getting Erin ready for bed, we talked about her eighth birthday. Comes up in seven weeks. I asked her what she really wanted and she said, "Lassie." I thought she meant a stuffed dog. She loves Collies. Well, she said, "No, I mean the real Lassie! Why can't we bring that doogie in for my birthday party?""

"Easy, Race," Jesse laughed, almost to himself. "I can almost smell something here."

"So I made a couple of calls this morning because I haven't heard much about Lassie lately. Maybe a re-run now and then. Now, don't jump to conclusions. I didn't promise Erin anything but as I was sitting in my chair listening to the 'My Fair Lady' tunes, I got to thinking about Frank Leahy."

"What the hell are you talking about? I thought you said Lassie — not Leahy."

"Well, lemme get to it, Jesse, for God's sake! Remember when I spent nearly four hours with Leahy in the Nicollet Hotel during the ill-fated American Football League meeting?"

"Yeah but what the devil's that got to do with the birthday party?"

"Well, here was a guy that I had covered over a decade before who was the hero of the football world. I was there when he rushed into the Southern Methodist locker room instead of Notre Dame's to congratulate Kyle Rote on his tremendous game that almost knocked the Irish out of the national title. Remember?"

"Who can forget?"

"So this Leahy was at the top of the pyramid. He was eventually crushed by financial losses, lousy health and that day I met him he was trying once more to get it all together, maybe as coach of an AFL team. They offered him big money but we were sitting on his bed in that Nicollet hotel room when it hit me; how fast you can lose it all. You know, your health, fame, money. It can all go down the tube in a couple of years. This guy was a king — now almost a pauper."

"What the hell's that got to do with Lassie?"

"Lord, Rogers, let me finish before I throw this drink in your eye. It's got everything to do with Lassie. Leahy was a big man who saw it go down the tube in a matter of a few short years. How many more years will we even be able to shoot for the stars?"

"Hey, Race, we've done more already than most of the people on the globe. God, how many people dare to feed 40 Indians dry martinis and then run out of food like you did? How many are nuts enough to buy an Indy car and trust a driver who's never been there before? How many are crazy enough to build a motorcycle hill and then see the winner crash over a cliff? How many . . ."

"Forget the horror stories. I'm just telling you that we'd better grab a piece of the damned action before it's too late. Who cares when they bury you if you've blown a few grand on some wild schemes? I admit we've taken some goofy chances. The thing is, we believed in them. We dreamed. Like Larsen says, we've got a thrill of seeing some guy buy tickets for his whole family for something we created out of thin air."

"You made your point."

"Okay. That's why I brought up Leahy, to make a point. And now my thought: if Erin would like to see Lassie in town, how about the other thousands of little kids in the Twin Cities? How about their young parents who were brought up on the dog? I don't care if it's been four or seven years since its last TV regulars. I think Lassie would knock 'em dead. In person. At a big site!"

"Damn," Jesse looked right past Regan. Almost in a trance. "You know, my kids were nuts over that dog. They'd wind up screaming, 'Here comes Lassie!' during all those silly-ass chases. And the parents, too. Sure, they'd like another look at the hound."

Race was beginning to get a buzz, too, as his enthusiasm soared once more.

"So the next morning, I called around, got our movie critic and he says to call the William Morris booking agency in L.A. He thinks they handle the dog. And he thinks Lassie, or whichever one is playing him now, makes public appearances. He gave me the name of the trainer, a guy called Rudd Weatherwax. Give him a call on your toll phone, Jesse. Call this agency, this Morris place. If we don't get Lassie, maybe we can nail Rock Hudson."

"Maybe Liz Taylor!"

Late that afternoon, Rogers contacted the Morris agency and met with some success. He called Regan at the paper about 5 p.m. as Race was getting ready to head to his radio show.

"We can get that hairy beast for around three thousand but we've got to take along a couple of its friends."

Race was shocked by the quick action and wanted to know, "Friends? What's he got, an entourage of turtles or pet mice?"

"No, other dogs. Seems like Weatherwax, the trainer, has a four- or five-dog supporting cast for Lassie. I'm going to talk to Weatherwax in a couple of days and find out the dates and details. The guy at the Morris Agency says they can put on a helluva show. Lassie's been opening a lot of grocery stores and doing other promos. I don't know the details but it sounds like we might have something. Where do you want to have it, Race?"

"Met Stadium, of course. And at least two shows!"

Jesse nearly hung himself on the phone cord.

"Met Stadium? Two shows? Regan, get off that heroin. No more Cabin Stills. What are you talking about? You know the Met holds 15,000. Multiply that by two and you have 30,000 seats. Not in your wildest imagination, Race. You must be going looney!"

"Absolutely not! Know why, Rogers? Because just two days ago I met a publicist for Pure Oil filling stations. Know how many are in this metro area? And the state? About 50. Those blue and white checkered pumps are everywhere. Mostly hot crossings. I've got a plan for Pure Oil. And they're short of hot promotions!"

"Okay. Okay. Maybe you've got something." To tell the truth, Jesse was stunned. He imagined Lassie could draw maybe four or five thousand if everyone got lucky. But 30,000 seats, that was bordering on the improbable.

They agreed to meet at Gallivan's at 7. Meanwhile, Race had a radio show to do with Landreville. It was going to be a hunting and fishing interview and Frenchy was going to portray a Canadian guide passing through the Twin Cities from Montreal. He'd answer in Canadian French and be interpreted by Regan.

The idea was to insult American sportsmen for being crude and unknowing and to slam this country's natural habitat as being over-rated and under-developed.

The show turned into a sizzler with the five-phone intake system lighting up like a birthday cake. "Who is that Canadian bum?" "Get him off the station!" "Regan, you gotta lotta guts listening to that crap!" "All Canadians are squirley!" "Talk English, you French Frog head!"

To Race's mind, this was one of the wildest shows. Frenchy shrugged his shoulders. "Was I all right?"

"Marvelous. The best! And come on over to Casey's Saloon. I've got a proposition for you."

Over drinks, Frenchy heard Regan's dog story—or as Regan broached it, "A real shaggy dog story." Frenchy's wide eyes looked like something spinning out of an H.G. Wells space odyssey.

"Lassie? Really?" Frenchy, too, seemed a little stunned. "Are you sure Lassie's still popular enough? Last time I saw him in a movie had to be 10 years ago and I can't remember if he found his way home."

"Eight years," Race corrected. "Yeah, Lassie got home."

"Well, I hope the kids remember him. I know a nice little gymnasium. Our church needs a charity. Maybe this could be it."

"Are you nuts?" Race was indignant. "Church gymnasium? Jesse and I are shooting for 30,000 people at the Met."

"The Met?" Frenchy was as dumbfounded as Rogers had been originally.

"I just thought you might want in, Vern."

The Frenchman chug-a-lugged his whiskey, got a mischievous grin on his round face and shoved his right hand through the dark hair on his hard head. "How much?"

"Five grand gets you a third and we'll need a little extra help."

"Like what, for instance?"

"Your brother, Blackie. And that old Cadillac limousine of his. We want him to greet Lassie at the airport in a tux with the big car and we'll have a red carpet."

"You've got Blackie and the car and a rented tux. But forget the five grand. What the dickens, Race, Lassie won't know if he's on a carpet or a cloud. Dogs don't know nothin'. Well, hunting dogs do. Want me to imitate a French Canadian hunting dog?"

Race had been a bit tense since Rogers' call but he had to laugh at Frenchy. "You should have imitated the mating call of the French Canadian hunting dog on the show. We might have gotten some input from a few Spaniels and Golden Retrievers."

The air off the Mississippi River felt good on Race's face as he drove down Shepard Road. Maybe it was an omen. Landreville refusing to take part in the dog show; what did he know? This could be an enormous promotion. Even if they filled just half the Met's seats.

Pure Oil's chain co-ops and a PR guy named Felix promised they'd give away 75,000 half-priced tickets and pay for the printing. They'd also flash the news of Lassie's coming for a month on their scoreboard at all Met events. The Met itself would put the show at the top of its coming events board on the freeway corner.

Race and Jesse decided that $3,500 would be the limit of their advertising, a few radio and TV spots and five days of small ads in both newspapers. They were counting on Pure Oil to hand out those coupons steadily for a month before the show. Even by accident, Race felt they were assured of 7,000 to 10,000 bodies in the fold at four bucks per head average.

Rogers lined up four other animal sets. The old safe-cracker, Rudensky, got 104 members of the St. Paul Clown Club to grin their way around the cavernous Met for a small fee and WCCO radio and TV kids personality Captain Klutz agreed to do two shows for $300.

Regan also said he'd take it to the "common man." He gave his barber, milkman and butcher 500 coupons and Rogers did the same thing. "Give 'em away" was the order. Five-buck tickets for $2.50 had to be a wondrous lure.

It was a happy omen when Race's neighbors, the Olsens, asked if they could have their collie, Spencer, photographed with Lassie. Of course. Sid Olsen took off a day from the post office just to groom Spencer, "So he won't be shown up by Lassie."

Regan's daughters invited all their friends to the first performance and at promptly 4:30 p.m. the evening before the big Saturday event, Lassie's Western Airlines flight from Los Angeles arrived at the Minneapolis-St. Paul International Airport. This in itself proved to be almost a climactic event.

Not only were Lassie, Weatherwax and Lassie's "friends" arriving on the plane but Bob Hope was just leaving. He had been appearing at a major charity event before 12,000 at the St. Paul Auditorium the night before. Perhaps 50 onlookers recognized Hope but a rousing mass of 200 men, women and children surrounded Lassie and company when the plane arrived, prompting Hope to muse, "Never expect to draw a bigger crowd than kid stars or dogs."

The plane unloaded its colorful passengers on the tarmac outside the terminal. The first news Regan and Rogers got was congratulations from the trainer who told them they should be proud. "It's the first time a dog has ever flown first class on Western!"

"Add $200 to the budget," Race whispered to Rogers.

Moments later, Weatherwax was angered at the sight of the Olsens and their dog, Spencer. "Get that mangy dog out of here! It might have a disease!" the trainer shouted.

The Olsens were crushed. No pictures, no calls, no letters.

Frenchy's brother, Blackie, was on hand in sparkling tuxedo with a young lady dressed in red ballroom chiffon. Weatherwax's anger soon cooled. He had collected three other dogs in cages, "Suzy couldn't come, she has a cold," he explained.

There was an eye-catching limousine journey to the Thunderbird and the honeymoon suite for Lassie followed by a picture of Lassie, pen in paw, at the guest register. By now, the lobby was full of hangers-on. Little children were squealing.

Race told Rogers, "There might be 50,000 kids here by tomorrow." Rogers just nodded, completely enthralled by the proceedings. He obviously was stunned by his good fortune. Finally, a killing.

The other dogs were put in Regan's car and delivered around the corner to an ordinary hotel room. The trainer explained, "I'll sleep with Lassie and keep a check on the others. Lassie gets lonesome. That's why Lassie loves your idea of the bridal suite. It makes the dog feel special."

Indeed, Lassie looked like a potentate as he lay across the pink silk comforter on the bed. Race could have sworn the dog winked at him.

Over a steak dinner at the hotel that night, Weatherwax explained that Lassie was indeed a male and that he wasn't a pure-bred. "A little German Shepard is in him, so the long nose is not quite so long and a little more photogenic. And this is not the original Lassie. This is the third one. We've always got lots of pups being groomed down the line. Every five or six years we know we'll need another new, fresh Lassie."

Rudd didn't seem like a bad guy once you got to know him, Rogers surmised, as he and Regan sat in Race's car.

"I suppose you get to be a little nuts trying to make a fortune with a pet," Race observed.

"A little nuts or a genius. I hear the dog's made him nearly a million bucks."

Race looked at a few posters he had left over and smiled. "If he makes us 50 grand tomorrow, I'll kiss him and buy that hound a dozen pork chops."

Race didn't really sleep well that night. He dreamed he was being chased by bloodhounds. He awoke just before they caught him. Dots was shaking him, "You were screaming like a banshee!"

Race hoped it wasn't a harbinger of things to come. Of course not. Silly thinking.

The first performance of Lassie was scheduled for 11 a.m., which made it natural that Race and Jesse would meet at Gannon's restaurant. It was just a block or so away from the freeway that carried through the Fort Snelling tunnel and down the way five miles to the Met Stadium.

They agreed to share their mutual anticipation jitters over a couple of quickies and maybe a cup of coffee. Rogers looked dapper in a dark green sport coat and grey slacks. Regan adjusted his good-luck red and black flowered tie.

"The weather's just right—a little dark but perky and cool," Race smiled. "Not the kind of spring day you'll take your kids to the beach but just right for indoor fun. Right, Jesse?"

"Perfect. Not too hot, not too cool. Say, I went over the figures again last night with my accountant and I figure we're right at the $13,000 mark. Four thousand customers, including maybe 50 percent softies on coupons, should put us over the hill. With two shows, we'll easily do that. That many customers should stumble in."

"Sure as hell should. Any word on what Pure Oil is doing? I couldn't get hold of my connection last night."

"My oldest kid says he went to the station out in Highland and nobody offered him anything. But that's not unusual. Those pump jockeys wouldn't know a coupon from a pale of piss."

"Lord, I hope that's not the case all over. My golfing buddy, Billy Kane, had a handful the other day. He claimed his kids brought them home."

"Is he going?"

"Naw. Says he's seen enough Lassie crap over the years. He's taking his kids to a driving range."

Jesse seemed taken aback. "That's not a good omen. But what the heck, didn't we figure there are another 100,000 kids around who should be interested—if they've heard anything about it."

Race ordered another double gin, this time with a little lime. There were only two customers at the bar. Regan stared at the empty piano bar to the side. "Wonder if we should have talked Frenchy in. He was getting hot. But then if we made a ton, we'd be killing ourselves. I was looking at pictures of yachts in Lauderdale by the Sea last night. I'd love to surprise Dots and the kids with a big boat. I might even name it 'Lassie Sweetheart.'"

Jesse walked around the bar to the door and peered intently through the small glass window. "Oh, man! Race, get over here!"

Regan, sprinted to the door. Jesse was already outside, vocalizing in a voice that'd make a choir or angels euphoric, "Look at this! My God! It's a traffic jam. Look! They're locked up for two, three blocks. They've got to be going to see Lassie!" He was pumping his right fist into the air.

Regan put his arm up in the air and juggled his drink. "Hey, if it's this big at 10:15, imagine what a monster it can be a 11! Lordy, we've finally hit! Lauderdale, here we come! Pull up the anchor! What color yacht do you think we should order?"

Jesse squealed. Race raced back inside to the phone just behind the coat room door. Rogers followed, "Going to call Dots?"

"Not just yet, she's on her way, I imagine, with the kids. I'm first going to call Frenchy at his place and tell him he should have forced us to take his five grand."

"You're miserable!" Jesse chuckled.

Regan nearly shouted into the phone. "Guess what, Vern, they're lined up for six miles! We've got the damnedest traffic jam on West Seventh you've ever seen. We're right in front of Gannon's. Must be 300 cars backed up from here. I can't see much toward the Met but you can be sure it must be a terrific crowd or they wouldn't be feeling the impact way back here. And this early!"

"Lemme in! Lemme in!" Vern pleaded. But he was genuinely happy for Jesse and Race. "You finally did it, you rascals. Will you give me a ride on the new yacht?"

"Hell no," Regan gushed. "But we'll buy a six-course meal at your place next week after we pick up some new duds."

Chapter Twenty-five

The Smell at the End of the Tunnel

Back at the bar, Race ordered another double gin. Jesse settled for a cool beer. Traffic was still piled up like a dead snake on West Seventh. The sun was basking brightly where an hour before the sky had been ominous shadows and muggy haze.

Regan glanced at his watch. "Jesse, we better belt these fast. If the traffic doesn't break we'll have to go around the back way and go up Highway 13 and cut over the Cedar bridge. I wonder if the highway patrol knows about this traffic? You know, we may have to get over there and put on more security and maybe a couple more ticket sellers. I've only got six lined up for the first show. And—Oh, God!" Regan looked astounded, "I forgot to call the Met and check out how it's going. I'll be right back."

Rogers had no more than tossed down his foamy beer and wiped his lips when Race returned looking somewhat concerned.

"Couldn't get through to the ticket window but I talked to some jerk in the business office. He seemed surprised there was an event on. Just said, 'Oh, I didn't know we had a rush.' Damn, didn't know! I figure there are cars tumbling all over each other in the parking lot. I suppose he's some buck-an-hour idiot they hired on Saturdays when no one wants to work and they won't pay time and a half."

"You're right. Nobody wants to work on weekends. Didn't he see or hear anything unusual? Like lots of cars and horns?"

"Naw. He didn't know his can from his nose. I told him to go to the ticket office and tell the people there to get more help. The manager wasn't around. But he's kind of a yo-yo, too."

Finishing their drinks, Jesse and Race walked out the door toward their cars. The traffic seemed to be moving. Maybe the Met got more help at the parking lot. Maybe the flow would be steady and strong.

"Imagine, Jesse, if the same snarl is on the other side of the Met. We could do that 30,000!"

"Maybe more," Jesse agreed as he began to sing, "Happy days are here again . . ."

Race climbed into his dented Dart and moved slowly toward the flow of traffic. At that exact moment, a Highway Patrol car rolled up from the other direction and turned into Gannon's parking lot.

Regan thrust his head out the window and hailed down the officer. "How's the traffic up ahead of this back-up, officer?" he shouted.

"Didn't notice much. We just got the oil tanker that tipped over in the Snelling tunnel back on its tires. Should be no problems up ahead."

"You're saying there's not a jam up around the Met?"

"Didn't notice any."

"An oil tanker in the tunnel . . . oh Christ! Oh, nooooo."

Regan pulled into the now smoothly flowing traffic and felt the pit of his belly drop to the floor. He had trouble shifting into drive. His right hand trembled as he put it back on the steering wheel. He gulped. His mouth felt as dry as Desert Gulch and his left eye had a small twitch.

"Oh, God," he pleaded, "don't have this one flop! Oh, God, please . . . how could I face everybody. Oh, God—tanker—crash—tunnel, noooooo."

Maybe the cops weren't paying any attention. Maybe there was a steady throng. Maybe the oil tanker had nothing to do with the huge jam. Maybe . . .

The Smell at the End of the Tunnel

Arriving just 10 minutes before the performance, Regan looked for Jesse's blue Cadillac. It wasn't parked in the reserved spot. The parking lot was as vacant as the Flin Flon tourist center in the dead of winter. Oh, there were a few cars slowly making the exit off the freeway into the Met's gigantic lot but they were coming at a rate of three per minute.

Regan hoped they were piled up five deep on the other side of the Met. Regan prayed to himself—but no such luck, only about 30 or 40 cars were sitting in that area.

He dropped his head to the steering wheel, conceding the inevitable. No Rebel at Gettysburg could have felt more empty.

"Hey, Race, are you all right?" Jesse asked, accompanied by a half-grin.

"Yeah, I haven't had time to connect the hose to the exhaust yet."

"How the shit can this be? An empty parking lot for Lassie?"

"Not easy, but we did it," Race answered, shielding his eyes from the now glaring sun. "And," said Race, as he climbed slowly out of the car, "let's get in there and face the music. I hate to see that cocky trainer. He'll be tearing us apart for a lousy promotion."

"Forget that nitwit," snapped Jesse, in one of the few moments when his built-in cool let his emotions boil to the surface. "I'll bet your neighbor's old beat-up Collie could have drawn as many people."

The two forlorn figures marched into the Met. Six people, including three kids, were in line. Regan stopped behind a ticket booth, knocked on the door and asked one of the sellers, "How many Pure Oil coupons came in?"

The answer nearly paralyzed him. "About 14 or 15."

"Jeez, I could have got more just handing them out in front of my house!"

Jesse remained hopeful but even he now experienced the cold pang of defeat crawling up his spine. Trying to ward off the inevitable capitulation, he said gamely, "Maybe the two o'clock show will knock 'em dead. Lot of dads have chores around the house on Saturday mornings."

'Jesse, I thought I was the incurable optimist. You must be taking cocaine to talk like that."

They walked back toward the nearly empty Met and stood at the top of the main floor stairway, almost in he corner of the building. Clowns were everywhere. Balloons seemed to be everywhere. It was festive. The only paucity of action was in the customer's section. There couldn't have been 75 people in the audience.

Race spotted Dots, her mother and his daughters, who had invited a dozen little girls as Erin's birthday guests. "There's the bad news, Jesse. The good news is they all seem to be having a good time. It's really bad when the crowd's so thin you can easily spot your loved ones. It's okay though when you can see them laughing. Look, Erin's petting Lassie and she's got three clowns all to herself. Know how this performance will go down in theater history, Jesse?"

"No, how?"

"The only one in all the world where every kid had three clowns to himself. That's got to be a Guinness Book of Records event."

⟡ ⟡ ⟡

Regan didn't want to look into Dots' eyes.

"Sorry, honey but I guess we take a bath."

"Could have been worse," she answered sweetly.

"How?"

"Lassie could have bitten a kid."

Race could not believe her. Dots could find a pony in a box of manure. She could get ten to life in the can and ponder how she could decorate the cell. She could have married a serial strangler but say he certainly knew how to snuggle.

Regan put his arm around her and felt some of that infectious good nature flow into him. It seemed in moments to recharge his dying battery. "There's always the afternoon performance," he said quietly, sounding himself like Scarlet O'Hara, sighing, "There's always tomorrow."

His daughters came over and hugged him. "You're the greatest dad!" they chorused, before introducing him to all the little girl friends, who looked upon him as a nice genie who produced this exciting party out of thin air.

Regan walked slowly to the mezzanine, gazing up at the empty turquoise seats, which looked like an uncharted sea of despair.

The old con, Red Rudensky, was garbed in yellow, his face painted in a blue sadness.

"I've seen more people in solitary confinement."

The afternoon session did little better than the morning's fiasco. No wonder the young Pure Oil executive was nowhere to be found. Regan would have gone for his jugular. Pure Oil had flopped dismally on the coupon give-away.

At five o'clock, Race and Jesse were at the Thunderbird paying the $200 bill for Lassie's bridal suite layover. They sat, staring silently at nothing in the darkened bar room.

"What do you think we dropped, Jesse?"

"Maybe ten grand."

"Know something? I'd rather have stacked up the ten grand in a big pile and set a blow torch to it. At least I'd have had the fun of seeing the flames."

Jesse was more upbeat. "Your kids loved it. The neighbors' kids loved it. And once again, you come home with enough balloons for every damn birthday part in the neighborhood for the next 20 years."

Regan tossed down a double gin as if it were soda pop. He reached in his shirt pocket and hauled out the manifest from the Met. "Look, Jesse. Just 140 people for the 30,000 seats. That's almost impossible. We could have saved three grand in advertising and just thrown open the door with half a dozen lawn signs and done as well. I swear Lassie was crying."

"And look at this cleaning bill for over $300! What the hell was there to clean? Three Snicker wrappers! That's a rip off. We were the only things that got cleaned."

It was dark when Jesse and Race wandered out into the Thunderbird parking lot, feeling no pain. They had paid off Lassie and Weatherwax. They would certainly sleep the sleep of the exhausted.

As they parted ways, Race got his usual second wind. "Jesse, you know as I was looking at the empty Met parking lot I was just wondering, maybe down the line—not right now, but in the future, we could stage a road-race around this lot. Never been done before. What do you think?"

"With our luck, they'd run over us. Don't call me, Race. I'll call you."

Rogers stopped before he got in his car. "You know, Regan, you really are a certified friggin' mental case. But I love ya!"

Race didn't hear him. He slumped in the front seat, muttering to himself, "Why do you hate me, God?"

Naturally, with his luck, God didn't answer.

Epilogue

At his wife's insistence, Race Regan checked himself into the Heartview treatment center in Mandan, North Dakota, where he gained sobriety, returning to his job as a sports columnist on the St. Paul papers and winning seven more awards for journalism. He also co-authored a best-selling book on alcoholism with his counselor, Dick Selvig, called "High and Dry." He also wrote a book on legendary football coach John Gagliardi. Of his many promotional defeats, he now says, "The good thing was the fact I wound up with a solid credit record after borrowing from seven banks and a credit union." Oh, yes, he finally had a couple of winners, drawing a record 8,500 fans to an amateur boxing card, the proceeds going to Team House, to help young alcoholics. He also hit on an 80-1 shot at the Hot Springs race track called, "Jose's A Pistol."

Jesse Rogers also checked into an alcoholic treatment center in Minnesota but not before losing most of his worldly possessions. He was forced to serve nine months in prison for a variety of felonious charges related to his insurance business, which closed. This time, he lost two homes, a second wife and two children through accident and disease. He has made public his problems and is now the president of his own High-Tech computer business. He, like Race, works with youth addiction programs.

Frenchy Landreville parlayed his business expertise into a successful string of Twin Cities restaurants and became a millionaire at the age of 50. He is semi-retired and resides between a summer home on a large Minnesota lake and a winter retreat in Naples, Florida. He says of the Longshots, "They taught me how not to do business—the hard way! But nobody in this life ever had more action or fun." Oh yes, he hunts tigers and rhinos in Africa and says, "I always make sure I have a bus driver who doesn't get lost and a gun that works."

Bill (Swede) Larsen lost his bowling alley and liquor sales route and eventually moved to Indiana, where he was last seen tending bar in a small town saloon. According to observers, he still travels to the Indy 500 and dreams of owning a winning car.

Thunder Klunder quit the promotional business and bought a small printing company in the Minneapolis suburbs. He trail rides his motorcycle and is involved in the Black Hills cycle fiestas each summer. He nearly bought a small wooden bicycle track before he discovered insects had corroded many of the boards. He says, looking back, "If it were the time of the Longshots, I'd have bought the layout, staged a big race and seven cyclists would have fallen through the track in the feature race." Oh yes, he finally built the big brick house but cut back the fireplaces from five to three.

Digger O'Halloran sold his funeral parlor and promptly put together a minor hockey league, owning six teams. The far flung league folded with an accumulation of heavy debts. However, he points out that nobody's ever had more hockey passes in one season. "You lose a few and win a few but the laughs are worth the tears." Last seen, he was trying to rehabilitate a former IRA sniper and investing in Florida real estate.

Chuck Van Avery continued to sell automobiles for a variety of dealerships and pursued his hobbies of heckling and doing the PA announcements for amateur and professional boxing and wrestling matches. He lived long enough to crash the gates at the Roberto Duran-Sugar Ray Leonard fight in Montreal, slipping and talking his way through five checkpoints. However, the Twins baseball team ended his professional heckling career when it moved into the Metrodome indoor arena, where Van explained, "My voice could not be heard above the air conditioning machines." He died shortly after while hustling calls in a church boiler operation where he raised money to battle diseases in infants. His only regret: "No film clips of the chicken fights!"

Paige Donnelly continues his law practice and in one highly publicized foray won a $26 million suit against the Federal government.

Fred Macalus now operates a far flung tire replacement empire and still plays roughouse broomball in his sixties.

On the national scene, Spirit of America driver and owner Craig Breedlove is still competing with a prototype of the old machine and just recently took aim at the 700 mph mark. With an engine, of course.

George Foreman became the oldest heavyweight champion at 45 years of age and a multi-millionaire 27 years after leaving St. Paul.

Joan Smith, whose musical talent used to calm the Longshots at the Criterion Restaurant, became the sixth richest lady in the world. Known better as philanthropist Joan Kroc, of the McDonald's hamburger empire, she has contributed over $200 million to charities and good causes, including the devasting Minnesota floods.

Oh yes, St. Patrick's Day boxing headliner, big Jim Beattie, became an accomplished actor and even appeared in the acclaimed film "The Great White Hope" with James Earl Jones. He portrayed boxing champion Jess Willard. He had no speaking lines, but that could happen to anyone.

Index